THE TRANSFORMATION OF
BRITISH NAVAL STRATEGY

The Transformation of British Naval Strategy

SEAPOWER AND SUPPLY
IN NORTHERN EUROPE, 1808–1812

James Davey

THE BOYDELL PRESS

First published 2012

The Boydell Press, Woodbridge

ISBN 978 1 84383 748 0

The Boydell Press is an imprint of Boydell & Brewer Ltd
PO Box 9, Woodbridge, Suffolk IP12 3DF, UK

and of Boydell & Brewer Inc.
668 Mount Hope Ave, Rochester, NY 14620–2731, USA

website: www.boydellandbrewer.com

A catalogue record for this book is available
from the British Library

The publisher has no responsibility for the continued existence or accuracy of URLs for
external or third-party internet websites referred to in this book, and does not guarantee
that any content on such websites is, or will remain, accurate or appropriate.

Papers used by Boydell & Brewer Ltd are natural, recyclable products
made from wood grown in sustainable forests

Typeset in Adobe Caslon by Word and Page, Chester, UK

Printed and bound by
CPI Group (UK) Ltd, Croydon, CR0 4YY

CONTENTS

FIGURES

TABLES

ACKNOWLEDGEMENTS

In writing this book I have built up many debts of gratitude. Much of the research was completed as a doctoral student at the Greenwich Maritime Institute at the University of Greenwich. My thesis was one product of a project investigating the victualling of the Royal Navy during the French Revolutionary and Napoleonic War. I would like to thank the Leverhulme Trust whose grant funded three years of this thesis, and also the National Maritime Museum for their award of a Caird Fellowship. Working at the Greenwich Maritime Institute was an enjoyable experience, made all the more so by the friendly banter of Suzanne Louail, and the advice of Sarah Palmer and Chris Ware. Martin Wilcox proved an expert teammate for three years on the project, and kindly commented on the second and fourth chapters of this book. Having since moved across the road to the National Maritime Museum, I must offer my thanks to all my current colleagues, but particularly Rob Blyth, Quintin Colville and Nigel Rigby for their good-natured camaraderie, and their support in completing this work. John McAleer was an advisor on the Leverhulme Project; he has reprised this role with aplomb. Richard Johns assisted with the cover, while Emma Lefley and Douglas McCarthy were very helpful in sourcing the images.

Researching this book has taken me around Britain and on one occasion across the Atlantic. I would like to thank the staff of the National Archives, the Suffolk Record Office, the Dreadnought Library in Greenwich, the British Library, the New York Public Library, the Bodleian Library and the National Library of Wales for their help and never-ending patience with my requests, while both King's College London and Oxford University allowed a grateful alumnus to make use of their excellent facilities. The archivists and librarians of the Caird Library in particular have provided helpful assistance to me as a student and as a colleague. Joy Moorhead was especially kind when I visited the Mulgrave Archive in Whitby, and I am grateful to the marquess of Normanby for allowing to me to consult and quote from those papers. The National Maritime Museum, the Calouste Gulbenkian Museum and the British Library have all generously provided images. I would also like to acknowledge the *International History Review* and the *Journal of Maritime History* (both can be found at www.tandfonline.com) for permission to reproduce, in shortened form, pieces of work published in those journals.

This book has benefited from the wisdom of many fellow scholars: Bob Sutcliffe has shared his knowledge of the Transport Board, while frequent lunches and conversations with Cori Convertito-Farrar have made visits to various archives more agreeable than perhaps they should have been. Janet Macdonald generously lent me a copy of her completed thesis as I was finishing mine, and has been a source of helpful tips over the years. Roger Morriss kindly provided me with a chapter list for his forthcoming book before publication. Special mention must go to Tim Voelcker, whose scholarship on Sir James Saumarez and the Baltic fleet has proved invaluable. He was also generous enough to lend me his translations of the von Rosen papers from the original Swedish, while his kindness on my frequent visits to Ipswich will not be forgotten. My thanks go to Tim and his wife Sally for their hospitality.

Andrew Lambert has bookended my academic training, teaching me as an undergraduate before returning a few years later to examine my thesis. Since then he has been a constant source of advice and support. John Dunn seconded Andrew in my viva voce examination to good effect, while Mary Clare Martin, Ian McNay and Gavin Rand gave me a thorough upgrade-viva which did much to focus my research and suggest new avenues of inquiry. Other individuals have made comments or suggestions at various points over the past three years. I am grateful to Margrit Schulte Beerbühl, Vicki Carolan, Gareth Cole, Ken Cozzens, Michael Duffy, Doug Hamilton, Richard Harding, Jane Knight, Byrne McCleod, Leos Muller, Des Pawson, Nicholas Rodger, Jakob Seerup, Stig Tenold, Rasmus Voss and Adrian Webb.

Above all, this book owes its existence to my supervisor and mentor Roger Knight. I have been fortunate enough to benefit from his wealth of knowledge and unceasing advice in the course of researching and writing. He has always encouraged (indeed, he has occasionally needed to rein in) and I owe him a great deal. Thanks must also go to Peter Sowden, my editor, who has steered this book into publication with remarkable calmness, and also to Megan Milan and Clive Tolley who patiently saw this book through the production stage. Lastly though, I would like to thank my parents, who not only nurtured my interest in history from an early age, but also undertook the unenviable task of reading my thesis from cover to cover. For this book they have largely been spared the editorial pen, but needless to say, I am more indebted to them than they can possibly imagine. To my parents this book is dedicated.

James Davey, Greenwich, 2012

ABBREVIATIONS

ADM	Admiralty
Commission on Fees	Reports of the Commissioners appointed by an Act 25 Geo. III cap. 19 to enquire into the Fees, Gratuities, Perquisites, and Emoluments which are or have been lately received into the several Public Offices . . . 1786–8
Commission of Naval Revision	Reports of the Commissioners appointed for Revising and Digesting the Civil Affairs of the Navy, 13 reports, 1806 to 1809
MA	Mulgrave Archive
MID	Papers of Charles Middleton (in NMM)
MM	*Mariner's Mirror*
NMM	National Maritime Museum, Caird Library
SRO	Suffolk Record Office
TNA	National Archives, Kew, UK
VB	Victualling Board
WO	War Office records

This book is published with the support of the
Swedish Society for Maritime History (Sjöhistoriska Samfundet)
and the Sune Örtendahl Foundation.

The book is Number 44 in the Forum Navale Book Series

Introduction

Victory at the Battle of Trafalgar in 1805 secured an unprecedented mastery of the seas for Britain but did little to halt the continental hegemony of Napoleon. Under his leadership, the French empire continued to expand, ultimately stretching from Spain to the Danube. By 1808, virtually all of mainland Europe was in a state of enforced hostility to Britain. Political antagonism became economic hostility, as Napoleon set up the Continental System, a continental blockade aimed at removing British economic power from Europe. Unable to defeat Britain at sea, he resorted to economic warfare. The Berlin Decree of 1806 and the Milan Decrees of 1807 prohibited all trade with Britain, banned all British goods and declared that any captured would be 'fair prize' and confiscated.[1] If not a new direction in the war, it represented a change in emphasis. Napoleon envisaged Britain's defeat not as an invasion and a march on London, but in bringing it to its knees by crippling it economically and thus financially. The British responded with a series of Orders in Council, which declared all ports under French control to be under blockade, meaning they could only trade with Britain's acquiescence. The ten years that followed Nelson's greatest victory saw the Royal Navy's role become more subtle, though no less important. Dominant at sea after 1805, it had no need, and little opportunity, to fight decisive battles. Instead, it concentrated on using its naval supremacy to bring the war to a conclusion. Seapower, as ever the nation's major offensive and defensive force, continued to be the keystone of British strategy.

The reality of the Continental System saw a major redeployment of the British fleet away from the old primacy of the Western Squadron in the Bay of Biscay to the North and Baltic Seas and to Portugal and the Mediterranean in the south. Napoleon was in the strongest position to damage Britain's continental trade in northern Europe. This region constituted the most important trading centre for Britain in the eighteenth century, supplying a major source of revenue for British exports to the region, particularly luxury and colonial goods, re-exported to Europe. French

---

[1] Lance E. Davis and Stanley L. Engerman, *Naval Blockades in Peace and War: An Economic History since 1750* (Cambridge, 2006), p. 29.

1

expansion eastwards across Europe threatened this trade altogether. In 1795 the Southern Netherlands, now Belgium, was annexed to France. From 1806, Holland was set up by Napoleon Bonaparte as a puppet kingdom governed by his brother Louis Bonaparte, becoming part of the French empire in 1810. British trade to the northern nations concentrated ever eastwards into the Baltic Sea. This was a long-standing trade, not only as a market for British exports, but also as the source of crucial resources. One was particularly important: the vast majority of naval stores needed to construct and maintain the British mercantile and naval marine came from the Baltic region.

The Baltic Sea, surrounded by the nations of Prussia, Sweden, Denmark and Russia, was an arena in which the most fundamental British interests could be fought for. Between the years 1808 and 1812, a naval fleet under the command of Sir Admiral James Saumarez sailed into the Baltic Sea to protect British trade, organise convoys, while offering the merchants of those nations under Napoleon's orbit the opportunity to continue trading, albeit illicitly, and in the process undermine Napoleon's Continental System. The British Orders in Council deprived Russia of her maritime trade, a major source of her wealth. The presence of a British fleet in the Baltic played an instrumental role in levering Russia away from its French alliance. It was also charged with blockading the Russian fleet in port: after Trafalgar, the Russian fleet was the largest threat to Britain's naval supremacy.

Despite the primacy of the Baltic Sea in British strategic calculations, it is important to consider the seas of northern Europe as one interconnected space. On leaving the Baltic Sea merchant convoys crossed the North Sea, where Dutch and French privateers also threatened.[2] A smaller fleet was stationed in the North Sea to protect merchant shipping. The fleet in the North Sea performed another critical role: containing the new fleet that Napoleon was building at Antwerp. After the crushing defeat at Trafalgar, Napoleon continued to build warships in great numbers: by 1813 the French fleet had been rebuilt, consisting of over eighty ships, with another thirty-five under construction.[3] Much of this building was done at Antwerp, taking advantage of its relative proximity to Baltic shipbuilding materials. While the fleet in the Baltic blockaded the Russian fleet, its counterpart in the North Sea contained the squadron being built by the French, gathering intelligence as to its progress, and, on one occasion in

[2] Patrick Crowhurst, *The French War on Trade: Privateering 1793–1815* (Aldershot, 1989).
[3] Roger Morriss, *The Foundations of British Maritime Ascendency: Resources, Logistics and the State, 1755–1815* (Cambridge, 2011), p. 53.

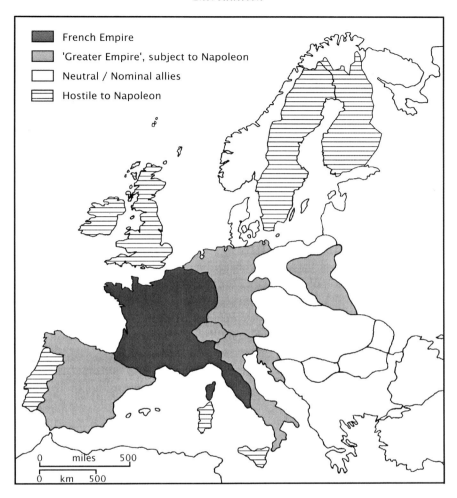

■	French Empire
▨	'Greater Empire', subject to Napoleon
□	Neutral / Nominal allies
▤	Hostile to Napoleon

miles 500

km 500

Figure 1. Europe in 1808

1809, launching a raid to destroy French shipbuilding efforts. Both fleets prompted government concern in Britain; had either fleet escaped, it had the potential to interrupt the flow of trade to and from the Baltic. At the same time, the fleet in the Baltic could cut off the supply of naval stores into France and Antwerp, obstructing French shipbuilding plans less directly. The Baltic was the first line in a defensive war protecting British economic and financial interests; at the same time it was at the forefront of an aggressive war against the Continental System, French shipbuilding efforts and the Russian economy. This book is chiefly concerned with the fleet in the Baltic, though this will be presented in the context of a much broader strategic picture.

Given the importance of these two seas to British interests, it is remarkable that they have been for the most part ignored by historians. In 2004, Jan Glete complained that 'it is unfortunate that there are few modern studies of naval warfare and the political roles of sea power in the Baltic'.[4] The North Sea can be more easily explained, with its smaller force and remit. The Baltic fleet however was the second largest fleet in existence from 1807, until Russia's change of allegiance in 1812. Various historians have downplayed the theatre in calculations of French defeat. Rory Muir comments that 'the war shifted away from the Baltic' after 1808, ignoring five years of conflict and economic warfare.[5] Paul Kennedy in his work on the Royal Navy referred to the Baltic as a 'peripheral' operation.[6] Economic historians have also downplayed the region's commercial worth. M. S. Anderson commented that 'the interruption of trade with Russia' was 'a nuisance rather than a disaster'.[7] D. Kirby and M.-L. Hinkkanen argued in 2000 that attempts to deny British access to the Baltic were crushed by 1807.[8] These scholars fail to account for the significant investment in ships and men made by the Admiralty in the Baltic between 1808 and 1812. Syntheses of naval history and Napoleonic Wars have concentrated on the Atlantic hemisphere; as Glete has noted, 'why there were considerable regional navies in the Baltic and Levant is not discussed and sometimes hardly mentioned'.[9]

Our knowledge of British involvement in the Baltic theatre is largely confined to the work of two men.[10] The first, A. N. Ryan, wrote exten-

---

[4] Jan Glete, 'Navies and Power Struggle in Northern and Eastern Europe, 1721–1814', in Rob Hobson and Tom Kristansen, eds., *Navies in Northern Waters 1721–2000* (London, 2004), pp. 66–7.

[5] Rory Muir, *Britain and the Defeat of Napoleon* (Yale, 1996), p. 26.

[6] Paul Kennedy, *The Rise and Fall of British Naval Mastery* (Macmillan, 1976), p. 133.

[7] M. S. Anderson, 'The Continental System and Russo-British Relations during the Napoleonic Wars', in K. Bourne and D. C. Watt, eds., *Studies in International History: Essays Presented to W. Norton Medlicott, Stevenson Professor of International History in the University of London* (London, 1967), pp. 68–80, at p. 70.

[8] David Kirby and Merja-Liisa Hinkkanen, *The Baltic and the North Seas* (London, 2000), p. 128.

[9] Glete, 'Navies and Power Struggle', p. 66.

[10] There is a growing literature that covers the Danish and Swedish navies: see Ole Felbaek, 'The Anglo-Danish Wars 1801 and 1807–1814', *Revue internationale d'histoire militaire* (Commission internationale d'histoire militaire) 84 (2004), 100–15; Ole Felbaek, *Denmark and the Armed Neutrality 1800–1: Small-Power Policy in a World War* (Copenhagen, 1980); Jan Glete, *Navies and Nations: Warships, Navies and State Building in Europe and America, 1500–1860*, 2 vols. (Stockholm, 1993); Jan Glete, *Swedish Naval Administration, 1521–1721: Resource Flows and Organisational Capabilities* (Leiden, 2010); Glete, 'Navies and Power Struggle'.

sively on Saumarez and his work in the Baltic in defending British trade.[11] The admiral was a canny and skilful commander, both operationally and diplomatically. Recently, this has been updated and taken further by Tim Voelcker, whose work displays the extraordinary lengths Saumarez went to ensure diplomatic harmony with Sweden and the safe passage of British trade to and from the Baltic.[12] The two Copenhagen expeditions, in 1801 and 1807 have received historical scrutiny, but are limited to these specific individual events.[13] References to the five years of Baltic operations between 1808 and 1812 are limited to the work of Ryan and Voelcker on Saumarez and small passages in much broader works.[14] An opportunity exists to build on this historical scholarship.

This book considers the navy and the variety of roles and functions it performed in the waters of northern Europe during the Napoleonic War. It is concerned with British strategy, naval policy and operations but locates this in wider economic and political contexts. It seeks to move the focus away from Saumarez himself and places him as one actor in a broader effort. Naval power rested not only on the commanders and personnel at sea but on a wide range of political and administrative factors. For the fleet sent to the Baltic in 1808, one factor was more important than any other: supply. A ship's time at sea depended on their supplies of food and water. At the height of the Napoleonic War, the navy employed over 140,000 men on its ships, all of whom required the daily ration of a pound of bread, a gallon of beer (or equivalent), a pound of meat on six out of seven days, and supplies of oatmeal, pease, butter and cheese. When multiplied by the many thousands of seamen, supplying these men with food was an immense effort, on a massive, industrial scale.

The widening of operational roles throughout the eighteenth century, to allow ships to spend years on active service without returning to port, often in hostile waters, required increasingly sophisticated logistical systems.

---

[11] A. N. Ryan, 'The Defence of British Trade with the Baltic, 1807–1813', *English Historical Review* 74 (1959), 443–66; A. N. Ryan, 'An Ambassador Afloat: Vice-Admiral Saumarez and the Swedish Court, 1808–1812', in J. Black and P. Woodfine, *The British Navy and the Use of Naval Power in the Eighteenth Century* (Leicester, 1988); A. N. Ryan, *The Saumarez Papers*, Navy Records Society 110 (London, 1968).

[12] Tim Voelcker, *Saumarez vs Napoleon: The Baltic 1807–1812* (Woodbridge, 2008).

[13] Ole Feldbaek, *The Battle of Copenhagen 1801: Nelson and the Danes* (Barnsley, 2002); Thomas Munch-Petersen, *Defying Napoleon: How Britain Bombarded Copenhagen and Seized the Danish Fleet* (Stroud, 2007).

[14] See for example N. A. M. Rodger, *The Command of the Ocean: A Naval History of Britain, 1649–1815* (London, 2005), pp. 557–61; Peter Padfield, *Maritime Supremacy and the Opening of the Western Mind: Naval Campaigns that Shaped the Modern World 1788–1851* (London, 1999).

A fleet's time at sea depended directly on its supplies. As the navy grew in size and was asked to fulfil increasingly challenging strategies, both government and bureaucrats were confronted with many obstacles as they strove to ensure fleets could be supplied at distance from home waters for extended periods. During the eighteenth century, there was a continual process of reform to procedures and systems that enabled the broadening of operational possibilities. It may be said, then, that the eighteenth century witnessed a transformation of naval strategy, with advances in logistical effectiveness firmly at the helm. Strategy, in this sense, means the use of military or naval force in the pursuance of political goals. As a term, strategy did not exist in the eighteenth and early nineteenth centuries.[15] There is no doubt though that the Admiralty, in conjunction with its subordinate boards, considered how naval force would be used to achieve political goals: they did not use the word, but they would have understood its meaning.

The range of strategic possibilities open to policy-makers drastically changed in the second half of the eighteenth century, owing in great part to logistical advances. Whereas in the 1740s a ship's time at sea was directly linked to the amount of food it carried, and no more, by the end of the Napoleonic War a ship could be consistently supplied the year round regardless of its location in the world with logistical structures created and maintained to allow this. This is not to suggest a Whiggish development from chaos through to logistical perfection; on the contrary, developments in naval logistics were met by repeated obstacles and failures. Indeed, the problems posed by the Continental System in 1807, requiring year-long service in hostile regions, provided fresh challenges. Naval administration acted as a constant lever, improving the operational capabilities of the navy, allowing a more and more ambitious strategy to be pursued. This was not an overnight revolution, but a slow transformation. This book considers the last stage of this evolution, in the years following 1807, when logistical advances refined the potential of seapower. In this, it aligns with broader historiographies that have fundamentally changed the way both naval and military history have been studied. Narrow, battle-centric accounts of generals and commanders have been superseded by cross-disciplinary studies that consider the wide range of factors that contributed to naval power. War and military and naval institutions cannot be studied in isolation and must take account of their economic, social and political

---

[15] N. A. M. Rodger, 'The Idea of Naval Strategy in Britain in the Eighteenth and Nineteenth Centuries', in Geoffrey Till, ed., *The Development of British Naval Thinking: Essays in Memory of Bryan Ranft* (Abingdon, 2006), pp. 19–20.

surroundings.[16] Much scholarship, in particular the work of John Brewer and Patrick O'Brien, has attributed Britain's success in the wars against eighteenth-century France to its greater ability to harness the resources of the nation, in particular finance.[17] In early modern Europe, states survived if they possessed sufficient and continuous command over the financial means necessary to defend their territories and citizens against external aggression. To become more powerful required ever increasing amounts of revenue.[18] Certain Western states, Britain in particular, developed a sophisticated system of banking and credit in order to pay for longer and more expensive wars.[19] It is clear that Britain had a huge advantage in the field of finance: such opinions form a rich consensus among historians writing in the late twentieth and twenty-first century. The preoccupation with finance as the mainspring of state power has given rise to studies of financial management in other eighteenth century states, which has shown Britain's methods of raising money to be less exceptional than previously thought. It remains the case though that the scale of British financial capabilities was unmatched.[20] Raising money was one thing, how it was used another: the spending of the British state has been overlooked. How effectively were its resources used?

In particular, and most relevant to this book, the success of the Royal Navy during the Napoleonic wars is increasingly seen to depend on government and administration as much as the fighting capabilities of its fleets or armies.[21] No longer can naval history be studied solely in the form of battles and operations; no longer can it be studied in isolation from its administrative, economic and political moorings. As important as battles

[16] Daniel A. Baugh, *Naval Administration 1715–1750*, Navy Records Society 120 (London, 1977), p. xii; Gerald S. Graham, *The Politics of Naval Supremacy: Studies in British Maritime Ascendancy* (Cambridge, 1965), p. 2.

[17] John Brewer, *The Sinews of Power: War, Money and the English State, 1688–1783* (London, 1989); Patrick Karl O'Brien, *Power with Profit: The State and the Economy 1688–1815* (London, 1991); Patrick O'Brien, 'The Political Economy of British Taxation, 1660–1815', *Economic History Review*, 2nd ser, 41/1 (1988), 1–32.

[18] Patrick K. O'Brien and Philip A, Hunt, 'England, 1485–1815', in Richard Bonney, ed., *The Rise of the Fiscal State in Europe c.1200–1815* (Oxford, 1999), pp. 53–100, p. 53.

[19] Paul Kennedy, *The Rise and Fall of the Great Powers: Economic Change and Military Conflict from 1500 to 2000* (New York, 1987), p. 76; T. C. W. Blanning, *The French Revolutionary Wars* (London, 1996), p. 212. See also Rodger, *Command of the Ocean*, p. 571.

[20] P. K. O'Brien, 'Fiscal Exceptionalism: Great Britain and its European Rivals from Civil War to Triumph at Trafalgar and Waterloo', in D. Winch and P. K. O'Brien, eds., *The Political Economy of British Historical Experience 1688–1914* (Oxford, 2002), pp. 245–65. Morriss, *Foundations of British Maritime Ascendency*, p. 5.

[21] See foreword to Stephen F. Gradish, *The Manning of the British Navy during the Seven Years War* (London, 1980), p. xii.

such as Trafalgar were, there is an increased awareness that administrative efforts in finance and logistics were crucial to Britain's ultimate success.[22] The administrative and technological capacities of the Royal Navy have been examined in studies of shipbuilding, the royal dockyards, the ordnance and gun production, manning levels, overseas yards and the transport service.[23] N. A. M. Rodger's *The Command of the Ocean* is separated into chapters in which 'administration' is placed on an equal footing with 'operations'.[24] There is a consensus now that the first half of the eighteenth century 'marked the epoch in which the navy's institutional arrangements, under the auspices of practical experience, matured'.[25]

Within this historiography the victualling of the navy has received increasing attention. This has focused on the structure of the Victualling Board, the body charged with managing the navy's food supplies, its efficiency and its relationship with the wider British economy.[26] This book focuses on the other side of the coin: it assesses the distribution of foodstuffs and its operational and strategic consequences. During the wars against Revolutionary and Napoleonic France, despite corn shortages, price rises and contractor bankruptcies, the Victualling Board always had adequate stocks of food in its yards.[27] However, failures in the movement of supplies from Britain to fleets on foreign stations did have crippling effects on the movement of victuals out to fleets. Shortages of transports, delays in loading

---

[22] Daniel A. Baugh, *British Naval Administration in the Age of Walpole* (New York, 1965). Baugh, *Naval Administration 1715–1750*. Gradish, *The Manning of the British Navy*, p. 209.

[23] For example see Morriss, *Foundations of British Maritime Ascendency*; Morriss, *The Royal Dockyards during the French Revolutionary and Napoleonic Wars* (Leicester, 1983); Roger Knight, 'The Royal Dockyards in England at the Time of the American War of Independence' (unpublished Ph.D. thesis, University of London, 1972); Glete, *Navies and Nations*, vol. 1, pp. 271–94; Gareth Cole, *The Ordnance Board and the Royal Navy 1790–1815*' (unpublished Ph.D. thesis, University of Exeter, 2008); Mary Ellen Condon, 'The Administration of the Transport Service during the War against Revolutionary France, 1793–1802' (unpublished Ph.D. thesis, University of London, 1968); David Syrett, *Shipping and the American War, 1775–83: A Study of British Transport Organization* (London, 1970). See also the posthumous book by David Syrett, *Shipping and Military Power in the Seven Years War: The Sails of Victory* (Exeter, 2008).

[24] Rodger, *Command of the Ocean*.

[25] Daniel A. Baugh, 'Naval Power: What Gave the British Navy Superiority?', in Leandro Prados de la Escorura, ed., *Exceptionalism and Industrialisation: Britain and its European Rivals, 1688–1815* (Cambridge, 2004), pp. 235–60.

[26] Roger Knight and Martin Wilcox, *Sustaining the Fleet: War, the Navy and the Contractor State 1793–1815* (Woodbridge, 2010); Janet Macdonald, *The British Navy's Victualling Board, 1793–1815: Management Competence and Incompetence* (Woodbridge, 2010). Macdonald is at times highly critical of the victualling commissioners' performance.

[27] Macdonald, *Management Competence and Incompetence*, p. 215.

and organising convoys could all impact on an effective victualling system. It has generally been concluded that 'the Navy's victualling was handled with considerable success'.[28] Detailed analysis is, however, beyond the scope of books on much broader subjects. Michael Steer wrote on victualling operations during the Revolutionary and Napoleonic Wars, but his work is limited to the Channel fleet alone.[29] An article written by Aldridge in 1964 is the only piece of scholarship that covers the supplying of a Baltic fleet, and that in the 1720s. It is tentative in its conclusions, with conspicuous use of the word 'suggests' and phrases emphasising the difficulty in estimating the success of the operation.[30] Although it is agreed that Britain made huge advances in the area of naval victualling, how this was effected in particular operations, especially at a time of total war when the nation's resources were put to its strongest test, has not been studied.[31] This book seeks to link operational, administrative, economic and political history to analyse how operational viability was managed. Only a fleet well supplied would be able to bring British naval power fully to bear.

The victualling service is also a window into the workings of the British state and its reforming instincts during the eighteenth century.[32] The French Revolutionary and Napoleonic Wars were unprecedented in terms of scale, in which the ambitions of states were recast. No longer were conflicts over

---

[28] Christopher D. Hall, *British Strategy in the Napoleonic War 1803–15* (Manchester, 1992), p. 41. For similar opinions see Douglas Hamilton, 'Private Enterprise and Public Service: Naval Contracting in the Caribbean, 1720–50', *The Journal for Maritime Research* 6 (2004), pp. 37–64; Rodger, *Command of the Ocean*, pp. 484–7.

[29] Michael Steer, 'The Blockade of Brest and the Victualling of the Western Squadron 1793–1805', *MM* 76 (1990), pp. 307–16.

[30] David Denis Aldridge, 'The Victualling of the British Naval Expeditions to the Baltic Sea between 1715 and 1727', *Scandinavian Economic History Review* 12/2 (1964), 1–25, pp. 21, 24.

[31] The interaction of administrative and operational naval history has only been examined once, in Christian Buchet, *Marine, économie et société: un exemple d'interaction: l'avitaillement de la Royal Navy durant la guerre de sept ans* (Paris, 1999).

[32] There is a broad literature on the eighteenth century state. See John Brewer, *The Sinews of Power*; P. Harling and P. Mandler, 'From Fiscal-Military State to Laissez-Faire State, 1760–1850', *Journal of British Studies* 32 (1993), 44–70; B. D. Porter, *War and the Rise of the State: The Military Foundations of Modern Politics* (New York, 1974), pp. 36–9, 58–9, 72–121; Philip Harling, *The Waning of 'Old Corruption': The Politics of Economic Reform in Britain, 1779–1846* (Oxford, 1996), pp. 2, 75; Gerald Aylmer, 'From Office-Holding to Civil Service: The Genesis of Modern Bureaucracy', *Transactions of the Royal Historical Society*, 5th series, part 30 (1980), 91–108; Geoffrey Holmes, *Augustan England: Professions, State and Society 1680–1730* (London, 1982); W. R. Ward, 'Some Eighteenth Century Civil Servants: The English Revenue Commissioners 1754–98', *English Historical Review* 70 (1955), 25–54, pp. 41–4.

small slices of land, and far-flung imperial possessions. Napoleon aimed at the overthrowing the British body politic: in name and nature this was the first total war. The state therefore used unprecedented means to achieve victory. This involved changes in traditional ideas about office-holders and prompted new attitudes towards reform. The Victualling and Transport Boards, the two major bodies involved in the production and movement of provisions to fleets, can tell us much about the nature of the British state, at war and under pressure to reform. In wartime, together they made up 13.5 per cent of all state expenditure.[33] By looking at these bodies, as they underwent the stress of war, this book shows that the British state was not the corrupt, inefficient organisation portrayed by contemporary reformers and subsequent historians. The successive administrations of Portland, Perceval and Liverpool increased the effectiveness of the British war machine. Faced with the challenges of a hegemonic Napoleonic empire, the British state required a monumental effort to manage the means to victory. In this respect, the fleet sent to the Baltic is a particularly illuminating case. The Baltic Sea was a new challenge for victualling officials; consequently it is a good opportunity to judge the speed with which naval administrators learnt. Secondly, the Baltic fleet's period of action, 1808–12, came just after the Commission of Naval Revision and thus provides an excellent chance to judge the reforming instincts of the British state, and its success in doing so.

The book begins by asserting the primacy of the Baltic Sea, and northern Europe more broadly, within the British political and public spheres. For policy-makers, merchants and the commercial classes of Britain, there was a deep understanding of the region's importance. Chapter 2 considers the evolution of British logistical systems throughout the eighteenth century, detailing the incremental, though by no means continuous, developments that took place. The chapter ends in late 1807 on the eve of the Baltic fleet's departure. In December 1807, a fleet stationed off Rochefort was forced to return to Britain, having not received the necessary food, allowing a French fleet to leave port, and prompting a parliamentary inquiry. In this context of victualling failure, Chapter 3 considers the specific challenges that faced administrators and commanders in 1807–8 as they planned their Baltic strategy. Chapter 4 considers the administrative system that enabled power projection on a global scale, looking at the naval administration from the Admiralty down through the subordinate Transport and Victualling Boards,

---

[33] Data is from 1797: see 24th Report of the Select Committee on Finance, 1798, Appendix E.1, pp. 49–53. See also NMM, ADM BP/25B, 16 July 1804. Morriss, *Foundations of British Maritime Ascendency*, p. 102.

and considering their respective responsibilities and claims to expertise. It shows how these governmental boards interacted with the private sector, the bedrock of British maritime superiority. The book then takes on a more chronological focus, considering naval operations in northern Europe. This is not a narrow operational history; instead it analyses how operations were shaped by supply and logistics and the administrative, political and economic forces affecting the navy. Chapters 5 and 6 analyse the effectiveness of logistical arrangements, the degree to which they improved over time and how this influenced operations. Chapter 7 looks in detail at a series of reforms made in the winter of 1809–10, as the naval administration responded to the victualling failures of 1809, placing them firmly in the context of the reforming tendencies of the British state. The last chapter considers the consequences of these reforms, before analysing the strategic watershed that came with a logistical supremacy. Ultimately, British naval power was grounded in a flexible and stable administration, run by practitioners who could carry out the logistical effort at sea and on land. The British war effort rested on their shoulders.

My Brother the Eagle, is doing the business by land._
so I'll try a little by water_and in the first place
I'll padlock these little Articles_they look so well in
my part,_besides Johnny Bull has enough
and to spare of these little Articles.__

March, my Companions march.__
Success to Brother Brum

PAULO

This may be pretty amusement to you Gentlemen
But if once I take a leap amongst you
you'll find a little difference.

Pub.ᵈ Janʸ 1.ˢᵗ 1801 by S.W. Fores 50 Piccadilly

Filler of Caricatures lend out for the
Evening

FOREIGN AMUSEMENTS or the BRITISH LION on the WATCH.

Figure 2. *Foreign Amusements or the British Lion on the Watch*
NMM, PAF 3936 (London: S. W. Fores, 1801). © National Maritime Museum.

The Forgotten Theatre:
Britain, Northern Europe and the Baltic Sea

T<small>HE SECOND HALF OF THE EIGHTEENTH CENTURY</small> saw the European state system transformed by the military rise of Russia. Until this point, Western European issues had dominated international relations. By the 1770s, however, Russia was emerging as the leading continental power in mainland Europe. This prompted a mixture of satisfaction and fear in British political circles. For some, Russia's rise was seen in a positive light, not least by Tories, who saw the country as a counter-balance to French power. For others, though, growing fears over Russia's hegemonic ambition prompted anxious insecurity. As early as 1775 Sir Nathaniel Wraxall had written that Russia seemed a power, 'which we regard ever [*sic*] day as more an object of political terror and watchfulness, and from whose arms has ever been taughtto dread another universal monarchy'. Awareness of Catherine II's growing empire became an increasingly prominent theme in the political pamphlets of the era. Sir John Sinclair warned in 1787 that 'all Europe must unite to check the ambition of a sovereign who makes one conquest only a step for the acquisition of another'.[1] Captain David Sutherland, who travelled extensively through the Baltic region, outlined the long-term threat: 'Russia is an evil-disposed, aspiring child; that we now have it in our power to curb her proud spirit; but that if we neglect this opportunity, and allow her to increase in pride and strength, in a few years, perhaps, she may trample on our breast'.[2] Among Whigs and radicals, Russia appeared as a brutal, backward and ultra-conservative nation.

Locked in an all-consuming war with Revolutionary France, successive British governments of the 1790s could only watch as Russia expanded ever eastwards. The partitions of Poland in 1793 and 1795 advanced Russia's

---

[1] M. S. Anderson, *Britain's Discovery of Russia, 1553–1815* (London, 1958), p. 139. Pamphlet attributed to William Eton, *General Observations regarding the Present State of the Russian Empire* (London, 1787).

[2] David Sutherland, *A Tour up the Straits, from Gibraltar to Constantinople* (London, 1790), p. 336.

European frontier over 250 miles westwards, enhancing her ability to intervene in central Europe, while underlining her new political importance.[3] The destruction of Poland fatally undermined the long-standing idea of Russia as a natural ally. 'Poor conquered Poland' came to symbolise, especially to Whigs, the self-evident Russian threat to Europe.[4] Nor were suspicious eastern glances limited to Russia. The growth of Prussia too raised concerns in Britain, not least owing to its proximity to Hanover. Dynastic concerns continued to dominate Anglo-Prussian relations: in 1801 and 1806 Britain moved to protect the king's patrimony in Hanover.[5]

The rise of these eastern powers gained popular prominence, becoming a concern for pamphleteers, authors and politicians alike. In the caricature in Figure 2 from 1801, the Russian bear is shown firmly gripping the combined Baltic navies, with a watchful British lion poised to act. In the background an army of Prussian eagles marches onwards. 'My brother the Eagle is doing the business by land', states the Russian bear, 'so I'll try a little by water.' This was not merely a concern over the 'balance of power' in Europe. Together, the two nations threatened to dominate the Baltic Sea and the nations that surrounded it. Those commentating from the public sphere, and indeed those in government, had a much more sophisticated understanding of power that took in commerce, economics and resource acquisition. In this respect the rise of Russia and the other Baltic nations offered a long-term threat equal to that of France, as it threatened directly Britain's standing as a maritime nation. This had been noticed much earlier than the 1800s. 'Like an immense Whirlpool', wrote the *London Chronicle* in 1791, 'Russia will by degrees swallow up every neighbouring state, till it becomes, what in fact the present Empress aims at rendering it, the sole independent maritime State in Europe.'[6]

In the caricature in Figure 2, the Russian bear is clutching the combined Baltic fleets in his hands: it was the naval threat that so concerned the vigilant British lion. In 1801, 1807 and finally from 1808 to 1812, the British would be forced to send fleets to the Baltic Sea. This suggests a much more complicated picture, in which British maritime interests prompted

---

[3] H. M. Scott, *The Emergence of the Eastern Powers, 1756–1775* (Cambridge, 2001).

[4] Anderson, *Britain's Discovery of Russia*, pp. 194, 198.

[5] Philip G. Dwyer, 'Prussia and the Armed Neutrality: The Invasion of Hanover in 1801', *The International History Review* 15/4 (November 1993), 661–87; Brendan Simms, '"An Odd Question Enough". Charles James Fox, the Crown and British Policy during the Hanoverian Crisis of 1806', *The Historical Journal* 38/3 (September 1995), 567–96; V. R. Ham, 'Strategies of Coalition and Isolation. British War Policy and North-West Europe, 1803–1810' (unpublished Ph.D. thesis, University of Oxford, 1977).

[6] *London Chronicle*, 2–5 April 1791.

ever greater anxieties. The Baltic emerged as a strategically crucial region in which the growth of Russian power in northern Europe could have devastating effects for Britain, and in defence of which Britain was willing to go to war. Britain was worried less about territory than about economics, resources and a burgeoning naval threat.

Commerce and the sinews of seapower

While Russia harboured continental ambitions, the second half of the eighteenth century was also marked by the development of Russian power at sea. The Baltic battle-fleet that had amounted to 54,000 tons in 1770 had nearly trebled to 145,000 tons by 1790. Within twenty years Russia had built the fourth-largest fighting navy in the world. The relative decline of the Dutch fleet during the eighteenth century also moved the naval centre of gravity further eastwards.[7] The Danish navy grew, partly on account of the developing Russian threat. Sweden maintained a constant naval presence. Figure 3 shows the increase in sailing navies throughout the period from 1720 to 1790.

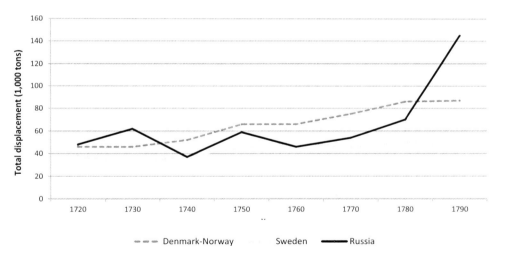

Figure 3. The size of the Baltic sailing navies, 1720–90.
Source: Jan Glete, *Navies and Nations: Warships, Navies and State Building in Europe and America 1500–1860* (Stockholm, 1993), p. 297.

[7] For the Dutch navy see especially Jaap R. Bruijn, *The Dutch Navy of the Seventeenth and Eighteenth Centuries* (Columbia, 1993), pp. 145–214.

The rise of Russia as a major naval power is evident, particularly during the 1780s. Russian seapower was closely connected with modernising ideas and strengthening the country's ties with Western Europe.[8] Britain's one ally in the region, Sweden, was in relative decline as a major power from 1720 and in actual decline from 1780. Danish naval power was largely destroyed by the twin battles of Copenhagen, in 1801 and 1807.

Russian naval might was not universally considered a great threat. In late 1800, as the government prepared to enter the Baltic, Lord Whitworth, the envoy-extraordinary and minister-plenipotentiary at St Petersburg, wrote to the First Lord of the Admiralty Earl Spencer and described the state of the Russian fleet. He had counted forty-five vessels, though he had serious doubts as to their quality:

> Of these one may reckon seven or eight to be tolerable good, having been built during my residence in Russia, although it is to be observed that two out of three which were launched last spring, and which were denominated a part of the Maltese squadron, had their backs completely broken. We may however reckon seven or eight tolerably good as far at least as age goes, twenty-two in the state of the worst of those which were in England, that is to say tolerable good looking, but in want of the most essential repairs, and the remainder good for nothing at all and considered for many years as unserviceable; of these about thirty-two, including the unserviceable ones, are kept at Cronstadt, and the remainder at Reval.[9]

Nevertheless, with Britain unquestionably superior at sea following the Battle of Trafalgar, the Russian fleet remained an obvious threat, one taken very seriously by the British government. In his initial orders of 1808, the new commander in the Baltic, Vice-Admiral Sir James Saumarez, was ordered to watch the Russian fleet and to consider an attack of the Russian arsenal at Kronstadt, 'with a view to acting offensively against them as soon as it may be possible to furnish you with adequate means for doing, without exposing Sweden, in the absence of such Naval Force, to invasion'.[10]

---

[8] Glete, *Navies and Nations*, vol. 1, p. 298.

[9] Lord Whitworth to Lord Spencer, 18 Dec. 1800, George Spencer, *The Private Papers of George, 2nd Earl Spencer*, LIX, ed. H. Richmond, Navy Records Society 4 (London, 1924), p. 275. Other visitors to Russia were critical of the state of the Russian Fleet. See William Coxe, *Travels into Poland, Russia, Sweden, and Denmark, Interspersed with Historical Relations and Political Inquiries* (Dublin, 1794), particularly book VI, pp. 481–4; William Hunter, *A Short View of the Political Situation of the Northern Powers: Founded on Observations Made during a Tour through Russia, Sweden and Denmark in the Last Seven Months of the Year 1800 with Conjectures on the Probable Issue of the Approaching Contest* (London, 1801), pp. 45–7.

[10] SRO, HA 93/6/1/43, Admiralty Orders, 16 April 1808.

The Russian fleet was particularly worrying for British policymakers since it had the potential to command the Baltic Sea. Political concerns over the growth of Russian power, and the other states of northern Europe, were inextricably linked to their economic position. By the end of the eighteenth century northern Europe was the most significant market for British exports. In Table 1, it is noticeable that British exports to northern Europe eclipsed those to any other region.

Table 1. Great Britain exports 1800–6 by region, official values (£000)

Year	Northern Europe	Southern Europe	Asia	United States	British West Indies
1800	14,325	3,404	2,860	7,886	4,087
1801	14,442	3,545	2,946	7,518	4,386
1802	15,015	7,752	2,930	5,329	3,926
1803	11,372	3,968	2,733	5,273	2,380
1804	12,716	3,033	1,766	6,398	4,282
1805	13,026	2,440	1,669	7,147	3,832
1806	10,533	2,678	1,937	8,613	4,734

Source: B. R. Mitchell and Phyllis Deane, *Abstract of British Historical Statistics* (Cambridge University Press, 1962), p. 311. In this table, 'northern Europe' also includes Holland. The Peace of Amiens between 1801 and 1802 explains the rise in northern European trade in these years, as Holland once again became open to British exports. The onset of war in 1803 and the re-closing of the Dutch ports again left only Baltic ports in this 'northern European' category.

From the late 1780s the volume of British exports to that region had been increasing steadily. In 1800, the author P. Colquhoun stated that northern Europe (the nations of Germany, Prussia, Poland, Sweden, Denmark-Norway and Russia) accounted for 49 per cent of all ship voyages leaving from London, and 44 per cent of London's total tonnage.[11] Following in his stead, the economist J. Jepson Oddy wrote a *Treatise on European Commerce* in 1805. In this he asserted that 'the Exportation of Great Britain (till lately), of Colonial and British Produce & Manufactures to the North of Europe was more than double to all Europe put together'. This trade dwarfed that with other areas of the world.[12] In 1800 the British consul

---

[11] This was in direct contrast to a century earlier. In 1686, only 15 per cent of ships cleared London for the north of Europe. P. Colquhoun, 'A General View of the Whole Commerce and Shipping of the River Thames', in *A Treatise on the Commerce and Police of the Metropolis* (London, 1800); Morriss, *Foundations of British Maritime Ascendancy*, pp. 81–2.

[12] See J. Jepson Oddy, *European Commerce: shewing new and secure channels of trade with the continent of Europe : detailing the produce, manufactures, and commerce of Russia, Prussia,*

general to Russia estimated that British imports to St Petersburg alone were over a million pounds sterling.[13] The figures for exports to northern Europe (the Baltic) were double that of its nearest competitor.

It was this export market that Napoleon was attacking with his Continental System.[14] Trade provided capital for war finance. The Baltic was the destination for a significant amount of British goods, and was thus central to Napoleon's plans to ruin British export trade. Baltic trade had increased enormously during the course of the eighteenth century, and convoys which had amounted to no more than twenty or thirty ships early in the century numbered approximately a thousand by 1814.[15] In the years before the Continental System vast convoys passed between Britain and the Baltic. In 1805, 11,537 merchant ships passed through the Sound, over half going to Britain.[16] For those in government, mercantilists or otherwise, and all members of a commercial society, northern Europe was a vital region.

Domestic matters, too, intruded on foreign policy. Britain's grain supply was fragile with annual harvest yields critical, as they determined the scale of imports to meet demand. They could not be relied upon: in 1794–5 and 1799–1800, adverse weather conspired to bring low yields, failed harvest and ever-rising prices. In 1800, Joseph Banks, an internationally famous botanist and expert in the cultivation of many crops, estimated a wheat deficiency of 20 per cent. Agricultural experts too predicted, and indeed contributed, to the crisis. The publication of Arthur Youngs's *The Question of Scarcity Plainly Stated* in March 1800 confirmed the crisis, elevating prices

Sweden, Denmark and Germany . . . with a general view of the trade, navigation, produce and manufactures of the United Kingdom of Great Britain and Ireland (London, 1805), p. 318. An extract from this work can be found in Foreign Office records: 11 March 1811, extract from *Oddy's Treatise on European Commerce*, TNA, Foreign Office Records (FO) 22/63/7–11. For similar arguments concerning Britain's commercial links with Russia, see Anthony Brough, *A View of the Importance of the Trade between Britain and Russia* (London, 1789).

[13] TNA, FO 65/47, Stephen Shairp to George Hammond (undersecretary of State), 20 Oct. 1800.

[14] Davis and Engerman, *Naval Blockades*, p. 31. In evaluating Napoleon's success in terms of reducing Britain's species supply therefore, it should be noted that he was moderately successful in achieving this; bullion at the Bank of England fell from £6.9 million in 1808 to £2.2 million in 1814.

[15] Patrick Crowhurst, *The Defence of British Trade 1689–1815* (London, 1977), pp. 43, 26. The Admiralty's convoy policy in the Baltic centred around the 1798 Convoy Act and close co-operation between the Admiralty and the Secretary of Lloyds, the unchallenged leader in marine insurance. Added to this was the ability of British merchants to continue trading with French controlled territory through neutral agents and forged papers, meant that in spite of heavy losses, the numbers of British owned merchants ships increased from 12,776 in 1792 to 19,585 in 1815. See ibid., p. 71.

[16] Hall, *British Strategy*, p. 89.

still further, threatening domestic riot and unrest. Prices, though largely dependent on ensuring a sufficiency from indigenous stocks, could be supplemented to various degrees by imports. Merchant contractors were commissioned to buy wheat in markets that were politically and practically impossible for the government to participate in. In 1795–6, at a time when Baltic exports were banned, Claude Scott, the great international grain merchant, purchased 50,000 quarters of Prussian wheat. In 1800–1, bounties – minimum prices for the key commodity of wheat – were offered, allowing a successful importation.[17] The vast proportion of this was to come from northern Europe, chiefly from Prussia and in particular Danzig. Between 1800 and 1802, 72.6 per cent of imported wheat came from Prussia, Russia and Germany. The importance of this supply was well known to the British; when questioned by the Corn Committee of 1800 about the probable source of foreign corn, Claude Scott replied 'our principal source . . . may be looked for this year from the Baltic, and chiefly from Poland'.[18] Britain was increasingly dependent on wheat imports, particularly those from the Baltic nations, which saw northern Europe placed at the heart of governmental calculations.

The national reliance on imported wheat was, if anything, overshadowed by the need to secure supplies of shipbuilding materials. British security rested upon a functioning Royal Navy, to protect it from invasion, to protect its maritime trade and to blockade enemy shipping. Moreover, naval stores did not merely have a military function; British trade and economic might rested upon a merchant fleet that carried all of the nation's foreign trade.[19] Naval stores were the most important resource to Britain in the age of the wooden sailing vessel. To construct a ship of the line required as many as 3,000 trees, upwards of twenty miles of rope and a number of sizeable masts. Translated across all the naval fleets, this meant vast quantities of resources were needed. In 1808 there were 636 naval ships in active service.[20] Not all were ships of the line, but each required a significant outlay of naval resources. Repairs and refits, occurring every two to three years, swallowed further

---

[17] Roger Wells, *Wretched Faces: Famine in Wartime England, 1793–1801* (Gloucester, 1988), pp. 36–40, 184–201. Knight and Wilcox, *Sustaining the Fleet*, pp. 10, 75.

[18] Of 3,336,949 quarters of wheat imported between 1800 and 1802, 2,424,718 came from the Baltic. W. Freedman Galpin, *The Grain Supply of England during the Napoleonic War* (New York, 1977), pp. 124–7, 194. For the most recent account of European grain markets, see Victoria N. Bateman, 'The Evolution of Markets in Early Modern Europe, 1350–1800: A Study of Wheat Prices', *Economic History Review* 64/2 (2011), 447–71.

[19] R. J. B. Knight, *Shipbuilding Timber for the British Navy: Parliamentary Papers, 1729–1792* (New York, 1993), p. 13.

[20] TNA, ADM 8/95.

stores. Britain was dependent on these stores to build and maintain fleets and yet could not produce them domestically or at least only in very small proportions. During the eighteenth century Britain's major procurement concern was the supply of naval stores from the Baltic region, the ingredients of British naval, commercial and economic power. The vast majority of these naval stores came from this region: hemp for rope came from Riga and St Petersburg, pitch and tar from Stockholm and oak and deal for planking from Danzig and Pilau.[21] Britain also needed softwoods for masts and spars, particularly pine and fir, which also came overwhelmingly from the Baltic.

Early in the eighteenth century large amounts of timber were imported from New England. However, the supply of North American produce declined through the eighteenth century. Even before the American War cut off supplies from across the Atlantic, the Baltic had become the main source for mast timber.[22] Between 1772 and 1775 Portsmouth dockyard spent £3,788 on masts from America, and £82,575 on timber from the Baltic.[23] By 1801 the Baltic accounted for the vast majority: in the naval yards were 1,186 masts from Riga, compared to a mere 198 from North America.[24] There was plank timber available in Britain but there were concerns over the long-term timber supply, with mounting difficulties of cost and transportation.[25] There was also no domestic supply of hemp. Between 1767 and 1782, 95.9 per cent of Britain's hemp, 82.7 per cent of its flax and 79 per cent of its linen came from Russia.[26] This dependence only increased into the 1790s. Between 1797 and 1806, the proportion of British hemp from the Baltic was even higher.[27] It is no exaggeration to say that Great Britain's importation of Baltic goods was essential to the British way of life, industry and economy.[28]

This was not a question of simple procurement, however. Just as important was the widespread acceptance of the vastly superior quality of Baltic produce for all naval stores. In 1803 the naval architect Sir Robert

[21] Crowhurst, *Defence of British Trade*, p. 74.

[22] R. J. B. Knight, 'New England Forests and British Seapower: Albion Revised', *American Neptune* 46 (1986), 222–3; J. J. Malone, 'England and the Baltic Naval Stores Trade in the Seventeenth and Eighteenth Centuries', *MM* 58/4 (1972), 390.

[23] NMM, ADM BP/2, 29 Sept. 1782.

[24] Morriss, *The Royal Dockyards*, p. 86.

[25] Oliver Rackham, *Ancient Woodland: Its History, Vegetation and Uses in England* (London, 1980), pp. 164–6.

[26] Herbert Kaplan, *Russian Overseas Commerce with Great Britain during the Reign of Catherine II* (Philadelphia, 1995), pp. 67–77.

[27] NMM, CAD/A/10: Appendix to 15th Report of the Commission for Revising the Civil Affairs of the Navy, 1807.

[28] Kaplan, *Russian Overseas Commerce*, p. 63.

Seppings reported on the timber problems facing Britain, outlining that both Canadian oak and masts were inferior to the Baltic equivalents. Two equally long masts were compared; the Riga timber supported 402 quarters about two minutes and then broke; that from Canada piece supported 'only 303 quarters and then gave way'. In 1811, Seppings would speak for everyone when he noted that American oak was 'particularly defective', and inferior to Danzig plank, on top of which it requires longer seasoning and suffered speedier decay.[29] The same was true of hemp. As David Steel's *Elements and Practice of Rigging and Seamanship* stated in 1794, only Baltic hemp was of acceptable quality. The following decade, the Commission of Naval Revision, reporting in 1807, stated that the hemp of America and Canada was vastly inferior to that of the Baltic. Similarly, Richard Russell's *Rope-Makers Guide* of 1804 supported this: 'all Hemps yet produced at our English Markets has proved to be the Russian Hemp . . . the best sort of Riga Hemp has the precedence in the English (and I believe all other) Markets'.[30] Quality was the crucial concern for the Royal Navy, and the Commission stated that no economies must be taken: 'it is of the greatest importance to His Majesty's Service that the Hemp made use of in the Navy should be of the first quality, as the safety of our ships must be at all times depend on the strength of the cables and cordage'.[31]

The British need to secure these resources deeply worried naval administration: Charles Middleton, the comptroller of the Navy Board, wrote in 1786 that 'when the variety of services that are to be provided . . . is considered, and how much the exertion of the fleet depends on punctual and proper supplies of stores, it must be allowed that no branch of the service is of more importance than this to the public'.[32] This concern would go on to impact upon successive British governments' foreign and colonial policy.[33] The British put significant organisational effort into controlling the market for naval stores. With British governmental credit behind them British merchants dominated the market, especially at St Petersburg, where

---

[29] J. J. Packard, 'Sir Robert Seppings and the Timber Problem', *MM* 64/2 (1978), 145–56, p. 148.

[30] David Steel, *Elements and Practice of Rigging and Seamanship*, I (London, 1794), p. 59; NMM, CAD/A/10, no. 129, 'Appendix to the 15th Report of the Commission for Revising the Civil Affairs of the Navy', 1807; Richard Russell, *The Rope-Makers Guide or a Complete Key to the Art of Rope-Making* (London, 1804), p. 2.

[31] NMM, CAD/A/10, no. 129, 'Appendix'.

[32] NMM, Papers of Charles Middleton (hereafter MID) 6/4, Charles Middleton, 'Observations on the Estimates', 21 March 1786.

[33] James Davey, 'Securing the Sinews of Seapower: British Intervention in the Baltic, 1780–1815', *International History Review* 33/2 (June 2011), p. 163.

they achieved political importance. Between 1795 and 1798, 63 per cent of all exports from Russia were carried by British merchants. The British were favoured by being permitted to have their own factory at St Petersburg and to avoid Russian legal and financial restrictions. The export of Russian naval stores became concentrated in the hands of a few merchant houses with headquarters in London. France, Denmark and Sweden used British merchants to buy for them.[34] In a time of war, however, market-based solutions could not be relied upon.

At various points throughout the eighteenth century, British governments also sought to rectify their susceptibility to economic blackmail by encouraging alternative sources of hemp. Spurred by wartime demand, concerned by the recurrent intransigence of the Baltic powers and worried about the steadily increasing prices of naval stores in the Baltic (see Figure 4), from the early 1780s the British did make strenuous efforts to increase their own supplies of timber.

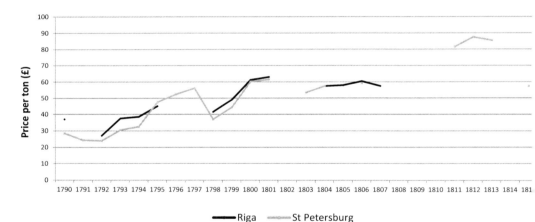

Figure 4. The price of hemp, 1790–1815,
as supplied to Britain from Riga and St Petersburg

Source: House of Commons Parliamentary Papers Online (417) Accounts Relating to Navy and Victualling Contracts, and Pay of Shipwrights, 1790–1823. No data exists for 1802, and 1808–10. Riga prices from 1811–15, where recorded, were the same as those at St Petersburg, though they do not show up on the graph.

[34] Arcadius Kahan, *The Plow, the Hammer and the Knout: An Economic History of Eighteenth Century Russia* (Chicago, 1985), pp. 199, 210, 214; Paul Walden Bamford, *Forests and French Seapower 1660–1789* (Toronto, 1956), pp. 141–2. See also Albion, whose 'Baltic Britons' concentrated the timber trade in their hands to such an extent that it alarmed the French government, Robert Greenhalgh Albion, *Forests and Seapower: The Timber Problem of the Royal Navy, 1662–1852* (London, 1926), pp. 147–8.

The desire to make Britain independent of Russia in the matter of raw materials was central to the Board of Trade's efforts in the last two decades of the eighteenth century. However, in spite of Parliamentary encouragements and pressure from the Board of Trade, Britain repeatedly bought Baltic produce in preference to colonial goods and often did so at higher prices, since it was cheaper to transport and suffered less in shipment.[35] Since the 1780s the British government had sought alternative sources of naval stores. Middleton emphasised the dangerous reliance on Russia for stores. As he argued, 'it is for hemp only we are dependant on Russia . . . but as it is impracticable to carry on a naval war without hemp, it is materially necessary to promote the growth of it in this country and Ireland'.[36] This was a government-wide policy, taking in not just the naval departments, but also the Board of Trade. Quebec, Bengal, Ireland, the Cape, the eastern Mediterranean and the Black Sea were all investigated.[37] None proved workable. Tests carried out by the Navy Board found all to be vastly inferior to Baltic hemp.[38] Putting quality aside, there were also serious doubts as to the quantities available. They found that the quantity of hemp grown in India was 'not more than equal to the consumption of the inhabitants'. Men had been sent to India to cultivate further hemp in 1801, but by January 1807 there had been no reports of success.[39] No ground had been made: the British were still unwilling dependants on Russia.

Britain was not the only nation that required naval stores. French shipbuilding efforts also relied on Baltic stores. British attempts to dominate the Baltic waters – economically as well as militarily – provided the opportunity to deny these crucial resources to her enemies. A British blockade could halt French timber supplies from the Baltic. The Seven Years War

[35] Baugh, *British Naval Administration in the Age of Walpole*, p. 280. See also H. S. K. Kent, *War and Trade in Northern Seas* (Cambridge, 1973), p. ix.

[36] J. K. Laughton, ed. *Letters and Papers of Charles, Lord Barham, 1758–1813*, II, Navy Records Society 38 (London, 1909), p. 223.

[37] Davey, 'Securing the Sinews of Seapower', pp. 167–76. See also NMM, CAD/A/10, no. 129–30, 141, 'Appendix'; NMM, MID 8/7, Charles Middleton, 'Plans & other Papers connected with importation of naval stores, 1804–6'; *Extracts from Publications relating to the Culture and Management of Hemp, Published by the Order of the Trustees of the Linen and Hemp Manufactures of Ireland* (Dublin, 1808). P. Crimmin, 'The Supply of Timber for the Royal Navy, c.1803–c.1830', in Susan Rose, ed., *Naval Miscellany*, VII, Navy Records Society 153 (London, 2008), p. 194; Patricia K. Crimmin, '"A Great Object with Us to Procure This Timber . . .": The Royal Navy's Search for Ship Timber in the Eastern Mediterranean and Southern Russia, 1803–15', *The International Journal of Maritime History* 4/2 (1992), 83–115, pp. 84–5, 90, 94–5, 107.

[38] NMM, ADM B/204, Navy Board to Admiralty, 12 Nov. 1802.

[39] NMM, CAD/A/10, no. 140, 'Appendix', 3 Jan. 1807.

demonstrated that her dockyards could be starved of timber. With supplies already precarious by the depletion of its forests, and facing a northern mast and timber market dominated by British nationals, its supply lines could be throttled by naval blockade. During the early 1760s the port of Brest was left 'destitute of timber'. Unable to defend its maritime lines of supply, France was at a very serious disadvantage. Strategically, over the remaining course of the eighteenth century, France become insular, and extremely vulnerable to a naval rival commanding the sea.[40] Preventing stores falling into the hands of the enemy was as important as securing them. Britain had a unique position, able to enforce a prohibition of trade using a very broad definition of 'contraband', including both naval stores and food.[41] During the War of American Independence, Britain was again successful in cutting off supplies to its enemies and British shipping dominated the Baltic trade. A few French and Dutch ships under the Russian flag entered American ports, bringing valuable supplies to the hard-pressed colonies. In the main though, as Sir James Harris, British ambassador to Russia, confirmed:

> Nothing can be greater than the Distress of the French, Spanish and Dutch Merchants here how to get home their several Commissions for Hemp, Iron and naval stores they have contracted for by order of their respective Admiralties. Of about Seven Hundred ships, arrived at Cronstadt four hundred and thirty are English and of the rest none, except a very few Swedish and still fewer Prussian, will return to take these Articles: only sixteen Russian ships have yet sailed, and these in so bad a condition that it is very doubtful whether they will reach the place of Destination.[42]

During the Revolutionary and Napoleonic wars this would continue; preventing naval stores reaching France severely undermined its efforts to reconstruct her navy.

It was vital then that Britain continued to access the markets and resources of northern Europe through the Baltic. Predominantly, this was a defensive policy, protecting her economy and access to naval stores. It proved impossible to guarantee these ambitions through peaceful market-based solutions. On three occasions – in 1801, 1807 and 1808–12 – Britain was forced to send a fleet to the region to enforce her interests. On the last of these occasions, naval power took on a more offensive mantle, as the Baltic became a crucial theatre for economic warfare. Britain replied to the Continental System with Orders in Council in 1807 and blockaded

---

[40] Bamford, *Forests and French Seapower*, pp. 40, 65–6, 210–11.
[41] Frank Spencer, 'Lord Sandwich, Russian Masts, and American Independence', *MM* 44/2 (May 1958), p. 117.
[42] Ibid.

any port refusing to trade with their merchants. Sir Stephen Sharp, British consul-general in St Petersburg, hoped that economic difficulties would persuade the tsar to abandon his participation in the Continental System. As he wrote in December 1809, 'Let her be one year without exporting and she will really appreciate the value of our connexion'.[43] Various observers saw the economic pressure that could be brought to bear on Russia. The pamphleteer William Hunter wrote in 1801 that Russia was

> chiefly indebted for its actual situation, to its uninterrupted connection and intercourse with Great Britain and its dependencies; and that, from the moment those relations cease, the most solid and beneficial part of its resources will be annihilated, and its commerce dwindle to decay . . . even the internal commerce of the country is carried on, chiefly, with British capital.

He noted that three-quarters of Russia's commerce was carried by British merchants, and that the balance of payments favoured Russia by upwards of 9 million roubles. The continuation of the trade was 'interwoven with the political existence of Russia . . . the regular income of the treasury would cease; and, in the course of a few years, the country would be involved in one general scene of confusion and distress'.[44] This would not be a direct attack on the tsar, or his military forces. Instead it was an attack on the merchant class and the Russian economy. Late in 1807, this was demonstrated clearly in a British caricature that showed the Russian bear about to be attacked by savage dogs, representing a specific type of naval store: hemp, fir, tar and iron. The dogs are temporarily restrained by Russian merchants, who worry about their future livelihoods. One merchant states, 'We may as well die fighting for our bread as have our Merchandise shut up in our warehouses and not suffered to export them. . .'; another states 'you'll stop our trade by selling hemp will you & so starve us to death'.[45] The effect of a continental blockade, and indeed British naval presence in the Baltic, would have significant consequences for the Russian economy.

British intervention in the Baltic

Britain considered the Baltic as an increasingly important region, politically, strategically and economically. Ten times in the fourteen years between

---

[43] TNA, FO 65/71, Dec. 1809.

[44] Hunter, *A Short View of the Political Situation of the Northern Powers*, pp. 35–41.

[45] British Museum, AN624287001, 'The New Method of bear baiting' (London, 1807).

1714 and 1727 a British fleet was sent to the Baltic. British concern centred on Hanoverian ambition: the British monarch George I was also the elector of Hanover, and hoped to advance his claims to the duchies of Bremen and Verdun. Additionally, though, the 'want of naval store', as the Tory Secretary of State for the North, William Bromley, put it, was never far from the mind of government.[46] During the Seven Years War, Britain refused to send a fleet to the Baltic in support of its ally Prussia, so as not to risk its supply of naval stores.[47] By the end of the 1770s, there was a widespread acknowledgement, not just of the importance of naval stores, but of Britain's reliance on the Baltic region, and the potential consequences. *The Morning Intelligencer* wrote in 1780:

> A Correspondent well acquainted with the present state of the British Navy asserts . . . as we have lost America, all our hemp for cordage, iron for building and repairing our ships, tar, pitch, deals for ships decks, timber for masts, yards, bowsprits, &c &c, all come from the Baltic.

Noting the opportunity this provided for a foreign fleet to 'annihilate our Baltic trade, and of course our Navy', the article urged the sending of a fleet to the Baltic, 'or we must inevitably become a province of France, and Ireland of Spain'.[48]

During the War of American Independence the Royal Navy began to seize Dutch, Danish, Swedish, Prussian and latterly Russian ships carrying naval stores to the American colonies and France, and bought their cargoes.[49] Between November 1778 and May 1780 ninety-six freights of neutral ships were sold to the Navy Board.[50] This had the effect of angering the neutral countries: Catherine II, however, had always viewed with unease the dependence of the Russian export trade on British ships. As Sir James Harris claimed, 'The Empress is envious of our opulence, jealous of our power'.[51] In 1778, 5.6 million roubles worth of goods exported from St Petersburg left on British ships, compared to 5.4 million roubles on the ships of all other nations. In March 1780 Russia issued a Declaration of Armed Neutrality that became the basic doctrine of maritime law regarding neutral rights at sea during war. It defined the rights of neutral

---

[46] Albion, *Forests and Seapower*, p. 178. David Denis Aldridge, *Admiral Sir John Norris and the British Naval Expeditions to the Baltic Sea 1715–1727* (Lund, 2009), pp. 65, 67.

[47] Rodger, *Command of the Ocean*, p. 269.

[48] *General Advertiser and Morning Intelligencer*, 8 Jan. 1780.

[49] Isabel de Madariaga, *Britain, Russia and the Armed Neutrality of 1780: Sir James Harris' Mission to St Petersburg during the American Revolution* (London, 1961), 57–67.

[50] Madariaga, *Armed Neutrality*, p. 384.

[51] Sir James Harris to Stormont, 3/14 Sept. 1781, TNA, FO 65/4, no. 127.

vessels, contraband (goods directly supportive of a military programme) and the conditions and restrictions of an embargo. In the event, the British managed to agree a diplomatic deal with the Danes: Denmark conceded the British definition of naval stores as contraband, in return for the right to carry foodstuffs, in the process sacrificing Russia's exports heading to France and Spain.[52] The Royal Navy remained able to stop and search the majority of neutral ships if they believed they were for America or France, while removing the need to protect British merchant shipping in the Baltic. The League of Armed Neutrality did nothing to stop the flow of naval stores into Britain. British procurement of these resources, though, was always tenuous and based on the co-operation of the Baltic states. Diplomatic manoeuvres got around this problem, but Britain had been warned for the future.[53]

British relations with the Baltic throughout the 1790s were stable, largely because of Russia's enmity towards republican France. Commercial treaties were signed to enhance trading links between the two nations.[54] And yet, long-term concerns over Russia's maritime rise remained at the forefront of the public mind. In 1798, the erratic and unpredictable Tsar Paul I issued an *ukaz* – a tsarist declaration of law – forbidding timber exports, to conserve Russian stocks. The Foreign Secretary, Lord Grenville, instructed Charles Whitworth to appeal against a policy 'of so serious and embarrassing a nature', and Russia finally agreed to release supplies. However, as the Foreign Secretary's brother, Thomas Grenville, noted privately, a powerful instrument of coercion was being placed in Russian hands.[55] In November 1800, Tsar Paul formed a second League of Armed Neutrality, and ordered an embargo on British vessels in Russian ports. Formally designed to defend neutrality principles, in reality the League was a co-ordinated alliance of the Baltic powers, led by Tsar Paul, designed to uphold Russia's long-standing interests in Europe.[56] The commercial and strategic consequences of the embargo were outlined succinctly by the *Albion and Evening Advertiser*. A rupture with Russia would be disastrous:

[52] Rodger, *Command*, 346.
[53] Davey, 'Securing the Sinews of Seapower', p. 167. 30 Sept. 1781, NMM, MID 8/5. 28 Jan. 1782, NMM, ADM BP/3.
[54] See for example the *Treaty of Navigation and Commerce between His Britannick Majesty and the Emperor of Russia* (London: Edward Johnston, 1797).
[55] Davey, 'Securing the Sinews of Seapower', pp. 169–70.
[56] Ole Feldbaek, 'Denmark and the Baltic 1720–1864', in Göran Rystad, Klaus R. Bohme and Wilhelm M. Carlgren, eds., *In Quest of Trade and Security: The Baltic in Power Politics, 1500–1990*, I: *1500–1890* (Lund, 1994), pp. 257–95, at p. 272.

Its consequences must prove prejudicial not only to our trade but also to our national security . . . What we take from Russia in exchange [for colonial goods] consists principally in naval merchandize and stores, such as timber for ship-building, masts, iron work, hemp, tar . . . the advantages accruing to England from our trade in all these important articles are incalculable; but the most prominent and essential advantages we derive from it is our possessing in Russia under our unobstructed management and controul [*sic*], an inexhaustible source of everything that contribute to the creation to the reproduction, and the augmentation of a marine both military and commercial.[57]

By 16 December 1800, the northern powers had declared the Baltic a closed sea, prompting Britain to intervene in the region for the first time since 1727. Spencer, the First Lord of the Admiralty, wrote to Admiral St Vincent, commanding the Channel fleet, outlining the effects the League would have on Britain, and immediately called for serious economies in the expenditure of stores; 'it is not improbable that we may have a more extended naval war on our hands than we have ever yet had'. Whitworth, the minister in St Petersburg, had bought naval timber 'to the limit' when he saw the trend of the affairs.[58] In a letter the following month that detailed 'giving to Great Britain everything she contends for', the British ambassador to Russia, Lord Carysfort, listed three things; the right to search and gain access to naval stores, as well as the ending of privateering.[59] All meant the same thing: Britain's ability to remove naval stores from the Baltic, without risk of capture, while stopping France from doing the same. The prime minister, William Pitt, outlined the economic rationale of British policy in a speech given to Parliament, asking:

Shall we allow entire freedom to the trade of France? Shall we suffer that country to send out her twelve million of exports and receive her imports in exchange to enlarge private capital and increase the public stock? Shall we allow her to receive naval stores undisturbed and to rebuild and refit that Navy which the valour of our seamen has destroyed?[60]

Britain re-invigorated attempts to find alternative sources. The higher echelons of British government began to form a naval stores policy, in particular for hemp. On 18 December 1800, at the Council Chamber,

---

[57] *Albion and Evening Advertiser*, 9 Aug. 1800.

[58] Spencer to St Vincent, 28 Nov. 1800, Sir Charles Whitworth to Lord Grenville, 19 May 1800, in Spencer, *Private Papers*, vol. IV, pp. 273–4; TNA, FO 13/1. Pitt to Shairp, 9 Aug. 1800; TNA, FO 65/47.

[59] Carysfort to Lord Grenville, 17 Jan. 1801, *Report on the Manuscripts of J. B. Fortescue, Esq., Preserved at Dropmore*, VI (London, 1908), p. 450.

[60] William Pitt, quoted in Spencer, *Private Papers*, vol. IV, p. 264.

Whitehall, a secret committee met for the first time, with further meetings taking place over the next three months, seeking to establish 'a system, on which this Government may in future act, in order to Restrain, at Least in some Degree, the Evil Consequences of the monopoly of that necessary Article which the Russian Government at Present Possesses'.[61] With a direct order from the king, the committee was to consider all measures for encouraging the importation of hemp 'from Dominions other than those of the Emperor of Russia'. Their reasoning was clear: 'in a political view it cannot but be highly important that this kingdom should not any longer be dependent, in so great a degree as it is at present on the produce of one foreign state for almost all the Hemp that is used either in our military or mercantile marine'. Moreover, they insisted that no time be lost.[62] These meetings continued through the winter of 1800–1 as the military intervention to the Baltic was planned and executed. In the meetings various regions of the world were discussed, with experts on each called in to discuss their suitability for cultivation. It was not a success; each in turn poured cold water on the schemes.[63] The committee had attempted to find a long-term solution to the problems and failed. Thomas Grenville, also a member of Parliament, wrote to his brother, hoping that peace between Britain and France would have been secured by then, 'enough to allow us to look this Northern comet in the face as we ought'.[64]

A fleet was prepared numbering twelve ships of the line, and gathered at Great Yarmouth. This fleet would serve two purposes: to maintain British supplies and halt French ones. The clearest exponent of a Baltic strategy was Henry Dundas, the secretary for war from 1794 to 1801. In a letter of January 1801, that undermines the idea that politicians at the turn of the nineteenth century had no thought for strategy, he wrote to the first secretary to the Admiralty, Evan Nepean, fully outlining the importance of the Baltic to Britain. 'We must all agree that we have now the greatest stake to contend for that ever called forth the exertions of this country', he wrote.

> But that as to all Baltick operations the game is lost, which alone can make success certain, if we are not able to have a powerful fleet there the moment it is accessible, with the possessive object of annihilating the confederacy of the north by the capture of the Danish fleet.

[61] Alan Frost, *Botany Bay Mirages: Illusions of Australia's Convict Beginnings* (Melbourne, 1994), p. 70.

[62] NMM, MID 8/7, 'Minutes at the Council Chamber', Whitehall, 18 Dec. 1800.

[63] Ibid., pp. 18–19, Dec. 1800, 14 Jan. 1801, 21 March 1801.

[64] Thomas Grenville to Lord Grenville, 28 Nov. 1800, *Manuscripts of J. B. Fortescue*, pp. 375–402.

With this objective in mind – the destruction of the Armed Neutrality – the capture of a fleet was a means to an end, rather than an end itself. He finished by specifying the importance of the Baltic: 'in the Baltick we must act with vigour in the offensive, for it is on such an exertion that the whole contest turns . . . that the force for the Baltick should be of the first importance, and be of a nature to commanding as to cause no room for Doubts of success'.[65] Nelson's crushing victory at Copenhagen removed any such doubts and instantly opened the entrance to the Baltic. Only Paul I of Russia maintained the embargo. Grenville despaired of dealing with such an irrational leader. At his most honest, and perhaps having heard whispers of the plots against Paul, he wrote, 'the thing [the League] must be drawing to its crisis. I cannot conceive how so manifest a madman can be permitted to go on even so long as he has'.[66] Paul I was indeed murdered on the 1 March, bringing to an end the second League of Armed Neutrality. For the first, but not the last, time in the 1800s, Britain had been forced into military intervention in the Baltic to keep it free for trade in naval stores.

The Copenhagen campaign of 1801 had done little to solve British problems in procuring resources in the long-term. In 1807 Britain was confronted with a new and concerning political settlement. The new tsar, Alexander I, had initially set about reshaping Russian policy, denouncing the League and determining to fight Napoleonic France, forming an instrumental part of the third and fourth coalitions against Napoleonic France from 1803. The collapse of Russian resistance to France in 1807 aroused great bitterness in Britain. The ensuing treaty of Tilsit, signed on 7 July 1807, that allied Russia to France and brought her into the Continental System, saw the respect enjoyed in Britain by the Russians and their ruler sink to the lowest in living memory. The *Anti-Jacobin Review*, which in 1806 had been full of praise for the tsar, denounced him in 1808 as 'the weak, the thoughtless, the unprincipled Alexander', and as the 'acknowledged self-recorded tool of Europe's tyrant and oppressor, the promoter of his views, and the instrument of his ambition, and the pander of his power'. The *European Magazine* was by 1808 pained to see Alexander 'so far degrade himself'.[67] Russia, and Prussia, were brought into the Continental System. The Danes, it was assumed, would soon join them, thrusting Denmark to the forefront of British political calculations for the second time.

---

[65] TNA, ADM 1/4168, Dundas to Even Nepean, 9 Jan. 1801.

[66] Lord Grenville to Carysfort, 16 Dec. 1800, *Manuscripts of J. B. Fortescue*, p. 409.

[67] Ole Feldbaek, *Denmark and the Armed Neutrality 1800–1: Small Power Policy in a World War* (Copenhagen, 1980), pp. 44–5, 70–9; Anderson, *Britain's Discovery of Russia*, p. 210.

Once again, Britain was faced with the threat of the removal of its source of naval stores, and once again, military intervention would be necessary; the Navy Board had no plans for alternative sources. A note written by Lord Canning, Foreign Secretary between 1807 and 1809, reporting intelligence from Tilsit detailing the proposed creation by France and Russia of an anti-maritime league, was written on 22 July 1807. However, preparations for drastic action against Denmark were already under way.[68] Lord Castlereagh wrote to the Admiralty on the 18 July, outlining the nation's interests: 'First to co-operate with this Majesty's ally the King of Sweden for the Security of his dominions, Secondly to protect any reinforcements which it may be necessary to send to Pomerania'; these were military requirements. Thirdly, the commander was 'to secure against all annoyance the large mass of British property which is now afloat in the Baltic, and to preserve to this country an uninterrupted intercourse and supply of Naval Stores from the Baltic.[69] Later that day, further details were sent, not to the Admiralty, but direct to the commander, Admiral Lord Gambier, referring to the ability of Denmark to deprive Britain 'of the means of Naval Equipment'.[70] On 3 August, Castlereagh again wrote to Gambier, confirming his main fear. 'The case of Prussia is quite clear', he stated. 'By her treaty with France all Prussian ports are absolutely shut against us including the *Free City* of Danzig.'[71]

The Danish refusal to surrender their ships to British protection led to war and the now infamous bombardment of Copenhagen in early September 1807. Admiral Gambier, commanding the expedition, used his naval force to surround and isolate the island of Zealand, cutting off the greater part of the Danish army from the defence of Copenhagen. A British force of 27,000 troops was landed to face a Danish army of 13,000, taking the Danes unawares. Only a bombardment, that blurred lines between civilians and combatants, would force a Danish surrender. Lord Erskine condemned it by saying 'if hell did not exist before, Providence would create it now to punish ministers for that damnable measure'.[72] Denmark surrendered its fleet, which was towed back to Britain on 21 October. There were other material dividends: Castlereagh congratulated Gambier for 'carrying His

[68] A. N. Ryan, 'Documents relating to the Copenhagen Operation, 1807', in *The Naval Miscellany*, V, Navy Records Society 125 (London, 1984), pp. 297–8.
[69] TNA, WO /6/14, Castlereagh to the Lords Commissioners of the Admiralty, 18 July 1808.
[70] Ibid.
[71] TNA, WO 6/14, Castlereagh to Gambier, 3 Aug. 1807.
[72] Anthony N. Ryan, 'The Navy at Copenhagen in 1807', *MM* 39 (1953), 201–10. For the most recent account see Munch-Petersen, *Defying Napoleon*.

Majesty's Orders and Execution for Preventing the Danish fleet and Naval Resources being placed in the hands of our enemies'.[73] Naval stores worth £305,665 7s 1d were confiscated.[74] The Baltic now briefly re-opened; the Admiralty took advantage, calling for over 10,000 tons of Petersburg and Riga hemp 'and as many Masts as will probably amount to twenty five or thirty cargoes which we have every reason to expect from those ports'. The Admiralty immediately offered convoy protection for 'these valuable and important items'.[75] A few months later, Canning privately summed up the operation, describing 'our operations off Copenhagen, by which a Northern Confederacy, an invasion of Ireland, and the shutting of the Russian ports have been prevented'.[76] He was to speak prematurely.

The situation in 1808

By late 1807 British policy-makers had great concerns over their trade with the Baltic nations. The pre-emptive attack on Copenhagen had virtually guaranteed Denmark's hostility. The agreement at Tilsit had seen Russia enter into the Continental System, cordoning off many vital ports, centres for British trade, along the Baltic coastline. Prussia, a demoralised French client-state after its humbling at Jena in 1806, also continued to pay allegiance to France, and thus the Continental System. In 1808, only Sweden in the Baltic region remained neutral and that country too would become an ally of Napoleon in November 1810. Despite the successful expedition to Copenhagen towards the end of 1807, the Baltic continued to be closed to British trade, preying on British government sensitivity to the Baltic region. The break with the Baltic powers had been foreseen and efforts had been made to obtain large supplies of iron and naval stores, in Anderson's words 'before the blow fell'. Seventy British merchantmen arrived at Kronstadt for this purpose as late as October 1807, of which only four were in port (and were therefore sequestered) when war was declared on 7 November 1807.[77] Nevertheless these supplies did not last and by April 1808 the Victualling Board, who needed hemp for bisket bags, was referring to 'the present scarcity of hemp'.[78] Only though illicit means could small supplies be procured. In a letter marked 'secret', it was revealed that 'Two ships in the margin are expected every day to arrive at

---

[73] TNA, WO 6/14, Castlereagh to Gambier, 19 Sept. 1807.
[74] NMM, ADM B/234, 5 Nov. 1808.
[75] NMM, ADM B/228, 31 Oct. 1807.
[76] Hall, *British Strategy*, 160.
[77] Anderson, 'The Continental System', p. 71.
[78] TNA, ADM 111/187, Victualling Board Minutes, 12 April 1808.

the Nore laden with Hemp in account of a secret Contract with the Navy Board'.[79] The Navy Board again urged economy.[80] Neither economy, nor the small quantities arriving, would suffice. A Navy Board letter at the end of 1808 mentioned 'the present critical situation of this country' in regards to hemp.[81] To ensure naval supplies, a fleet would have to be sent.

Between the years 1808 and 1812, Admiral Saumarez commanded a fleet in the Baltic, charged with the protection of this British maritime trade. Barring the ice-bound winter months, there was a constant British naval presence. It was essential that the trade continued, despite the war with France. The remarkable amount of trade passing through the Baltic was a source of much complaint to those charged with directing it. Charles Fenwick, the British consul general in Denmark, wrote that 'the immense British Trade and Navigation thro' the Sound, have been truly arduous. Forty to fifty, and latterly nearly double that number of British Convoys, with 4,000 Sail of our Merchant ships, arriving annually in the Sound; have engaged more than half of my time'.[82] And continue it did: merchants would bring colonial goods into the Baltic, and return with naval stores.[83]

In their instructions to Saumarez, the Admiralty decided that the protection of trade was his foremost responsibility. 'Their lordships consider the security of the trade from capture or annoyance as of the first importance', they wrote.[84] Ships under neutral colours were furnished with licenses to avoid capture.[85] Crucially, despite the Continental Blockade, Sweden remained open and Gothenburg became a vital centre for British exports, which continued their journey into the Baltic under the guise of neutral goods on neutral ships, especially as the economic incentive to sabotage French prohibitions on traffic with Britain steadily increased.[86] As early as 1808, the widespread hostility to French policies was evident across northern Europe, as was the urge to trade with Britain. One of Saumarez's captains, Peter Paget, was tasked with collecting intelligence on the north German coast. He wrote that 'the people in general appeared dissatisfied

---

[79] NMM, ADM BP/28, Navy Board to Lord Mulgrave, 29 Sept. 1808.

[80] NMM, ADM B/229, Navy Board to Admiralty, 7 Dec. 1807.

[81] NMM, ADM BP/28, Navy Board to Admiralty, 22 Nov. 1808.

[82] TNA, FO 22/58/20–1, Charles Fenwick to George Canning, 8 Jan. 1808.

[83] This was a long-standing economic pattern, using colonial commodities to help with the British balance of payments to the Baltic region. See Klas Rönnbäck, 'Balancing the Baltic trade: Colonial Commodities in the Trade on the Baltic, 1773–1856', *Scandinavian Economic History Review* 58/3 (Nov. 2010), 188–202.

[84] Admiralty to Saumarez, 27 June 1808, Ryan, ed., *Saumarez Papers*, p. 27.

[85] SRO, HA 93/6/1/43, Admiralty Orders, 16 April 1808.

[86] Ian R. Christie, *Wars and Revolutions: Britain 1760–1815* (London, 1982), p. 307.

with the French, whom the Masters said took everything, and paid for nothing . . . they everywhere speak of the English in terms of praise, and peace is the universal cry'.[87] Napoleon's attempt to control and prevent the British export trade through the Continental System was ultimately to fail: corrupt customs officials in the Baltic ports and the widespread use of 'neutral' (often disguised British) ships and papers created loopholes in the Continental System.[88] Added to this should be the genuine desire of Baltic citizens and merchants to trade with Britain, and the work of the Royal Navy in protecting and convoying British merchant fleets through the hostile region. As Saumarez commented to the Admiralty in 1808:

> The State of the war with subject to Russia, and Prussia, is maintained in a manner heretofore unprecedented. An immense trade is carried on by British merchants under his Majesty's license with the different Ports of those countries: both Nations are known to be amicably disposed towards Great Britain, and openly avowed their earnest desire to be on terms of peace, and amity, with England, as well as of their alliance with France.[89]

Through such means, British trade in northern Europe was maintained, overcoming inconveniences such as declarations of war.

The Baltic fleet under Sir James Saumarez had objectives that were crucial to British interests. The importance of the Baltic to British officials was reflected in the size of the fleet sent to deal with the Russians, Danes and later the Swedes in that sea. By July 1810 there were twenty ships of the line and almost 16,000 men in the Baltic theatre, more than any other theatre barring the Mediterranean.[90] Organising a fleet to be sent to the Baltic was a formality. Supplying it, once there, was a more daunting challenge.

---

[87] TNA, ADM 1/6/352, Captain Peter Paget to Saumarez, 26 June 1808.
[88] Silvia Marzagelli, 'Napoleon's Continental Blockade: An Effective Substitute to Naval Weakness?', in Bruce A. Elleman and S. C. M. Paine, eds., *Naval Blockades and Seapower: Strategies and Counter-Strategies 1805–2005* (London, 2006), p. 29; Crowhurst, *Defence of British Trade*, p. 26.
[89] TNA, ADM 1/7/396–7, Saumarez to Admiralty, 21 Nov. 1808.
[90] TNA, ADM 8/95–100, Admiralty: List Books 1808–12.

2

'To keep a fleet above a fortnight': The Evolution of Naval Logistics during the Eighteenth Century

The want of timely supplies . . . at several times . . . greatly obstructed those Designs, which otherwise might have been carried on with greater Advantage to the Publick.[1]

Josiah Burchett, 1703

A NAVAL FLEET relied on its supplies; navies, like armies, moved in accordance with their stomachs. A naval ship could expect to carry four months of provisions in its hold; its ability to maintain operational effectiveness depended on its receiving further supplies. In other words, the quantity of food and water on board a ship directly dictated its ability to remain at sea: while it was adequately supplied, it was able to pursue its objectives. Without adequate food and water though, ships were forced to return to port, abandoning their operations. In 1703 the secretary of the Admiralty, Josiah Burchett, made a clear connection between victualling success and his government's strategic designs. Victualling delays and shortages severely impacted on the navy's ability to project power. Over the ensuing century, this was a recurring problem. As the navy increased in size, and its commitments became increasingly far-flung, the relationship between supply and seapower was repeatedly tested. As the British Empire grew and its global commitments increased, so did the pressure on the victualling service. Responsibility fell into the hands of the British naval administration, tasked with improving the logistical arrangements that shaped naval power. As these administrative systems improved, so did the operational possibilities available to the Royal Navy.

---

[1] Burchett participated in the naval administration of William III. Baugh, *British Naval Administration in the Age of Walpole*, p. 373. As Baugh notes, Burchett's comments were highly accurate estimations of victualling occurrences.

Supplying a ship at sea was not an issue of domestic food shortages. Throughout the eighteenth century the navy's victualling storehouses were rarely short of food. The British state developed strong relationships with merchant contractors. Lacking the infrastructure to produce the vast quantities of victuals needed for the Royal Navy, the state benefited from the resources of the private sector. This was not always an easy relationship, but it was one founded on mutual reliance. Merchant contractors provided knowledge, experience and expertise outside the remit of the eighteenth-century state. Conversely, the state provided reliable payment and a guaranteed income not provided by the market economy. This has been termed the 'contractor state', in which the majority of state spending was directed towards the private sector.[2] This mutual supportive relationship became increasingly prominent through the century: as the navy grew in size, so did the victualling demands of the state, and quantities of foodstuffs contracted for. As Stephen Conway has noted, the ability to use contractors on terms set by the state was a strength in which there was growing confidence, a product of repeated wars, growing expenditure, experience and efficiency.[3]

The naval administration's reliance on the private sector influenced the way they dealt with the expanding operational range. It was impractical, and too expensive, for the navy to maintain a victualling yard in every part of the world. The solution was to turn victualling over to a contractor, a local merchant who undertook to provide the full range of sea provisions at a given place. These contracts allowed foodstuffs to be provided without the trouble and expense of setting up a state-run establishment. It could also be dismantled quickly at the end of hostilities. By the 1740s all sea-provisions contracts were made by competitive tender, ensuring the state paid the best price for the foodstuffs. At the same time, the costs, responsibility, administration and liability for victualling the fleet were passed to the contractor. In an age of slow communications which were easily disrupted by weather and enemy action, decentralised systems proved the most flexible. It was important to ensure that provisions could be procured locally, where achievable. Among the largest foreign sea-provision contactors were those on Jamaica and the Leeward Islands, who between them covered an area as far north as Virginia. Canada and the East Indies were also supplied by local merchants through such sea-provisions contracts. These contractors were vulnerable to corruption, though this occurred much less

[2] See Knight and Wilcox, *Sustaining the Fleet*, particularly pp. 1–18.
[3] Stephen Conway, *War, State and Society in Mid-Eighteenth Century Britain and Ireland* (Oxford, 2006), pp. 31–55.

frequently than commentators and pamphleteers believed. Victualling in the remoter places in the world was a particular problem, with distance from the accounting offices in London providing an occasional screen to mismanagement. In the case of the East Indies, it took until the 1790s for a properly effective victualling system to be devised, under the management of Basil Cochrane. Even this ended in an acrimonious dispute between the contractor and the Victualling Board over his accounts.[4]

However, the victualling system worked because it provided a variety of ways of procuring provisions, giving it the flexibility to work in a number of situations. The navy operated around the world in many climactic, economic and diplomatic contexts, and sourcing local supplies was not always an option. Local agriculture and climate might not supply the necessary foods or quantities, while naval fleets could operate in foreign environments surrounded by hostile leaders who might refuse to sanction contracts with the Royal Navy. The vast majority of Royal Navy fleets were in fact supplied through the British victualling yards at Deptford, Portsmouth, Plymouth, Chatham and Dover. In 1804 for instance, the value of provisions supplied directly to ships by contractors amounted to only 18 per cent of the Victualling Board's spending: the majority were supplied through the domestic yards. Ships would depart from these ports for foreign stations, completed with four of five months of provisions. Subsequently, as ships remained in foreign stations, supplementary supplies would also originate from the British victualling yards. The challenge was if, and then how, a system of remote supply could be managed.[5]

Throughout the eighteenth century, the victualling service's ability to provision its fleets and squadrons around the globe rested on its *distribution* of foodstuffs. Early in the century, ships were often tied to home waters, constrained by victualling limitations. Advances in naval logistics meant ships could remain on station for longer periods, reducing and eventually removing the need to return to port and revictual. The dynamic between supply and seapower, referred to by Burchett in 1703 in the quotation that began this chapter, remained. If the provisioning system excelled, a fleet or squadron was able to pursue its objectives. If the system failed and a fleet was forced to leave its station British naval strategy and seapower was undermined. In other words, the evolution of the victualling service – the service that existed to move foodstuffs to where they were needed quickly

---

[4] Knight and Wilcox, *Sustaining the Fleet*, pp. 132, 136–7. For a detailed analysis of Cochrane's management of the East Indies contract, see pp. 155–76.

[5] Ibid., pp. 36–7, 132.

and effectively – corresponded directly with the increasing effectiveness of British seapower. It is the evolution of this logistical structure that is the focus of this chapter.

The ability of the naval administration of Great Britain to provision fleets in foreign waters improved incrementally during the eighteenth century, culminating in the efficient and timely service provided in the last years of the Napoleonic War. This improvement was not reliant on technology. In terms of food preservation, the ships, transports and preservation materials available to the various governmental departments in the 1800s were for all intents and purposes the same as those used in the 1690s; this wouldn't change until the invention of canning in the nineteenth century. The evolution of the victualling service, and consequently the effectiveness of seapower, was the consequence of systemic and administrative change.

The early eighteenth century, 1683–1755

The Victualling Board was first established as a distinct department of the Admiralty in 1683. The business of the Victualling Board was 'to provide, either by contract or otherwise, all the Provisions, and also certain Stores, required for Your Majesty's Navy; arranging and distributing the whole to several ports and places at home and abroad'.[6] Throughout the first half of the eighteenth century, and indeed for long periods afterwards, it would grapple with the problems of supplying men on foreign stations. Problems of food preservation at sea were impossible to solve, given the state of technology at the time. Early in the eighteenth century there was a high rate of wastage. William Jenkins, the chief dairy-product supplier to the Royal Navy during the 1740s, provided over 200,000 lbs of butter and over 400,000 lbs of cheese: 23,000 lbs of butter and 48,000 lbs of cheese were condemned by a fleet in the Baltic.[7] Stores, however, were never the main problem; the distribution of victuals was the greater issue. Once a fleet was on station, there was no certainty that, assuming ships were initially victualled for between four and six months, revictualling could be carried out. After this period there was no administrative infrastructure to keep ships at sea supplied. A ship's time at sea could be measured by the food taken along. After this had been consumed, the vessels returned to port, often limiting, or in the worst cases severely harming, a fleet's operational viability. On one occasion

---

[6] Commission of Naval Revision, Tenth Report, p. 4.
[7] Aldridge, 'Victualling of the British Naval Expeditions to the Baltic Sea', p. 25.

in August 1717, for instance, all but ten ships were sent back from the Baltic to enable the remaining ships to maintain a 'whole allowance' of victuals.[8]

As Britain entered the Wars of Jenkins' Ear and of the Austrian Succession (1739–48), the naval administration was confronted by a further problem: administrative inefficiency. Logistical distribution was a systemic problem and the movement of supplies and stores across the globe was a challenging and occasionally impossible task. Problems of management made matters worse: even assuming resources could be distributed there was no guarantee that what was sent would be a well-judged or accurate amount. Clerks worked from reports that were out of date; consequently calculations of spoilage and supply were inaccurate and unreliable. As a result, administrators learnt to provide more than enough and to accept waste as an unavoidable consequence of preparedness.[9] Wastage of provisions, administrative inefficiencies and faults in the provisioning system connived against naval operations.

Daniel Baugh has outlined the improvements the victualling services made during the war of 1740–8. The Victualling Board took great initiative in anticipating the needs of various squadrons. The government office did remarkably well in answering sudden demands, helped by a dynamic London food market and Irish beef and butter, and stood ready to fill gaps in the army's victualling arrangements.[10] Facilities at Portsmouth and Plymouth were expanded, which made them the two most important out-ports after Deptford. Not only would this enable the Royal Navy to distribute higher volumes of provisions, but also the location of both south-coast ports enabled them to play a significant role in supplying fleets blockading French northern and western ports. The proximity of closer victualling out-ports meant reprovisioning could be completed much more quickly. Baugh comments that 'it is striking how seldom, during the war of 1739–48, they altered plans or postponed their moves because of inadequate victuals'.[11]

Supply problems were magnified when distributing victuals to squadrons and bases further overseas. Fleets cruising in foreign waters were victualled through local contracts. This was limited by politics and geography. As the war escalated, the increasing number of ships in service added to victualling difficulties. At the same time, with the

---

[8] Ibid.

[9] Baugh, *British Naval Administration in the Age of Walpole*, pp. 444, 449.

[10] Baugh, *Naval Administration 1715–1750*, p. 406.

[11] Ibid., p. 374.

expansion of overseas operations the challenges of distance and climate grew more formidable.[12] Moreover, the problems of securing transport tonnage were profound. At times there was a dearth of shipping available for government hire, without which supplies could not be transported. Victualling commissioners complained that shipping was hard to procure. This was not because shipping was not available: on the contrary, the government was slow in adjusting its rates and terms of hire to meet wartime market conditions.[13] This would not be a problem limited to the 1740s. Despite limited improvements in the victualling service, the naval administration could not yet guarantee timely arrivals of foodstuffs at ships, and admirals and captains continued to complain of bad provisions and to worry about future supplies. Ships or fleets could not act independently of their supplies.

The Seven Years War

During the Seven Years War victualling standards continued to rise, as the naval administration of Britain grappled with the problems of distributing provisions. Victualling efficiency was improved, and the proportion of victuals condemned shrank drastically: for bread only one pound in every 294, and for beef only one pound in every 1,691 was condemned.[14] Calculations of supply became more exact. Ships were given four months of rations: enough to sustain a fleet for that period but not so much that provisions would go off and thus be wasted. It followed that in 1756, Admiral Boscawen could write that:

> This ship has now been at sea twelve weeks, which is longer than I ever knew any first-rate ever at sea . . . at the beginning of the Spanish War our cruisers would not keep the sea above a fortnight, till one or two of them were broken for it, now three months is but a common cruise.[15]

The Seven Years War also saw a key development in naval logistics. The centrepiece of British naval strategy was the maintenance of a strong battle fleet off the French Atlantic coast for as long as possible. The 'Western Squadron' could cover the English Channel and Atlantic ports: the naval ports of Brest and Rochefort in particular, but also the commercial ports

---

[12] Ibid., p. 406.

[13] Baugh, *British Naval Administration in the Age of Walpole*, pp. 441–2.

[14] Gradish, *The Manning of the British Navy*, pp. 144–6.

[15] Peter Kemp, 'Boscawen's Letters to his Wife, 1755–56', in Christopher Lloyd, ed., *The Naval Miscellany*, IV, Navy Records Society 92 (London, 1952), p. 248.

of Le Havre, St Malo, Nantes and Bordeaux.[16] This blockade required constant naval vigilance, to imprison the French fleet and attack French mercantile commerce; it had to be continuous to be effective. The length of cruise was determined by its supplies, and particularly the onset of disease.[17] For the fleet to remain on station required provisions greater than the four months' worth of provisions they left port with, to enable them to remain of the coast of France the year round. Early in the war, the navy had yet to organise a system whereby fleets outside victualling ports could be regularly supplied without simply returning to port. As a result a force of at least one and a half times that of the squadron at sea was required so piecemeal detachments could be made for repairs and refreshment.[18] This meant that a significant proportion of ships of war available would be engaged in revictualling at any given time, rather than serving operational or strategic functions. It was an inefficient use of naval force, and a precarious foundation for naval blockade.

During the Seven Years War, occasions when fleets were forced to abandon operations as a result of poor logistics were common. Two of Admiral Hawke's cruises in 1755–6 lasted barely two months.[19] Admiral Anson, although aware of the strategic risk involved in raising the blockade, was forced to leave his station in 1758. Given the perilous shortage of provisions for his fleet he had to grasp any expedient to preserve the health of the crew. He sent a large minority of his fleet back to port because of scurvy, with the intention of allowing them to restore their strength, otherwise, they 'will be destroyed and the ships in the end will become useless'. They were not home long enough: in August the fleet had almost one thousand sick on board, half of these ill with scurvy and fever, and the worst-affected ships had to be sent home again, reducing the strength of his squadron by three vessels.[20] Operations continued to be seriously affected by victualling shortfalls, with the result that the blockade was periodically broken.

---

[16] Rodger, *Command of the Ocean*, p. 264. Michael Duffy, 'The Establishment of the Western Squadron as the Linchpin of British Naval Strategy', in Michael Duffy, ed., *The Parameters of British Naval Power, 1650–1850* (Exeter, 1992), pp. 66–81.

[17] Michael Duffy, 'Devon and the Naval Strategy of the French Wars 1689–1815', in Michael Duffy, Stephen Fisher, Basil Greenhill, David J. Starkey, Joyce Youngs, *The New Maritime History of Devon: Volume 1 From Early Times to the Late Eighteenth Century* (London, 1992), pp. 182–91, at p. 188.

[18] Baugh, 'Naval Power', p. 250.

[19] Duffy, 'Devon and the Naval Strategy of the French Wars 1689–1815', p. 188.

[20] Anson to Shelburne, 16 July 1758, William L. Clements Library, Shelburne MSS, vol. CXXXVII, p. 91, cited in Gradish, *The Manning of the British Navy*, pp. 137–8.

The link between the distribution of foodstuffs and naval strategy had been perceived, however: from 1759, the victualling service improved. There were developments in packing and processing of victuals, with production of naval victuals centralised in the major ports in Portsmouth, Plymouth and Deptford.[21] That year, the decision was taken to transport fresh victuals such as beef and vegetables to seamen on board the Western Squadron, without which the squadron could not have maintained such a constant and effective blockade of the French Atlantic ports. As Hawke wrote in 1759, 'the relief of the squadron depends more on the refreshment of the ships companies than the cleaning of ships'.[22] From May 1759 the Admiralty instructed the Victualling Board to have supplies of fresh beef available at Torbay for revictualling. By July there were two transports carrying live cattle and sheep to the blockading fleet.[23] On 2 August 1759, the Admiralty ordered four transports to carry live cattle out to Hawke's fleet.[24] Ships were sent from Portsmouth and Plymouth to revictual and refresh their crews, including a steady flow of fresh victuals.[25] The strategic consequences of this were significant. For the first time ships could remain on station regardless of the state of their provisions: no longer would they need to return to port every few months. Dr James Lind, a leading advocate of the use of citrus fruit for the prevention of scurvy, described a fleet during the Seven Years War:

> Of about twenty ships of the line, and ten or more frigates, in which were embarked about fourteen thousand men. On the day of action, many of those ships and men had been above six months from Spithead; notwithstanding which, there was . . . twenty sick in all . . . It was hardly ever known before that ships could cruise in the Bay of Biscay much above three or four months at a time, without having their men afflicted with scurvy. An exemption from which was entirely owing to this fleet having been well supplied with fresh meat and greens.[26]

---

[21] Christian Buchet, 'The Development of Victualling Board Bases in London, Portsmouth, Plymouth, Chatham and Dover, 1701–1763', *Transactions of the Navy Dockyards Society* 4 (2008), 53–68.

[22] Hawke to Cleveland, 4 Aug. 1759, cited in Richard Middleton, *The Bells of Victory: The Pitt-Newcastle Ministry and the Conduct of the Seven Years War, 1757–1762* (Cambridge, 1985), p. 124.

[23] TNA, ADM 2/525/546, 19 July 1759.

[24] Admiralty to Victualling Commissioners, 2 Aug. 1759, John B. Hattendorf, R. J. B. Knight, A. W. H. Pearsall, N. A. M. Rodger, Geoffrey Till, eds., *British Naval Documents 1204–1960*, Navy Records Society 131 (London, 1993), p. 442.

[25] TNA, ADM 111/19/426–7, May 1759.

[26] Gradish, *The Manning of the British Navy*, pp. 167–8; Baugh, 'Naval Power', pp. 235–6.

In a similar vein, he wrote again, 'it is an observation, I think, worthy of record – that fourteen thousand persons, pent up in ships, should continue, for six or seven months, to enjoy a better state of health upon the watery element, than it can well be imagined so great a number of people would enjoy, on the most healthful spot of ground in the world'.[27] Logistical breakthroughs brought strategic dividends. The Victualling Board's 'greatest achievement' during the Seven Years War, in the words of David Syrett, was the resupplying ships of the Royal Navy in the Bay of Biscay, enabling Hawke to fight the battle of Quiberon Bay, and to closely blockade Brest for six months, an unprecedented strategy, and one not repeated until the French Revolutionary Wars.[28]

Nonetheless, it is important to put these developments in context; these were still very primitive moves. There were still significant problems in shipping and distributing the victuals, particularly in navigating the conflicting interests of state and ship-owner. All transports were hired merchant vessels, contracted for a set period: arrangements that did not always result in constructive relationships. A victualling commissioner reported that the master's inability to navigate, a want of manning and damages sustained loading and unloading (threatening the master's profits) meant that 'almost all the masters of the victualling vessels . . . had come to him in a body and requested their discharge'.[29] Proximity to the ports of Plymouth and Portsmouth meant provisions could be sent to the Channel fleet, but to stations further away this became a much more imposing challenge. In the mid-eighteenth century, transporting victuals was limited to fleets in home waters, and also to the summer months. Bad weather and insufficient shipping forced seamen to rely on a standard diet during the winter months.[30] In the Americas and West Indies, supply remained the sum of what could be carried on board ship, and what could be bought locally. Here the Victualling Board continued to organise local merchants to supply provisions to ships stationed overseas.

The Victualling Board's actions during the Seven Years War were an important ingredient in the establishment of British seapower during the latter half of the war. During the war, operations were carried out that could

[27] James Lind, *An Essay on the Most Effectual Means of Preserving the Health of Seamen* (3rd edn. 1779), in Christopher Lloyd, ed., *The Health of Seamen*, Navy Records Society 107 (London, 1965), p. 121.

[28] David Syrett, *Shipping and Military Power in the Seven Years War: The Sails of Victory* (Exeter, 2008), p. 55.

[29] Admiralty to Victualling Commissioners, 2 Aug. 1759, Hattendorf *et al.*, *British Naval Documents 1204–1960*, p. 442.

[30] Gradish, *The Manning of the British Navy*, pp. 167–9.

not have been executed twenty years earlier.[31] Indeed, the British system was markedly superior to their enemies'; the British navy never experienced the desperate food shortages of the kind that so often forced French squadrons to return home.[32] The French monarchy faced vast financial problems, meaning naval administration was often in arrears, and payments to suppliers were often delayed. France suffered from shortages of merchant shipping, compounded by governmental failings.[33] Without the administration or the finance to support such operations, French operational effectiveness was consistently undermined. In 1746 the French launched an expedition to North America that was beset with victualling disasters. The commander, D'Enville, was forced to take out all the supplies he needed with him, including sufficient victuals for the return voyage. On arriving in Santa Maria, on the other side of the Atlantic, provisions on several vessels were already starting to diminish. Remarkable amounts of victuals were condemned, while 40 per cent of the fleets' naval strength failed to reach Chibouctou. Much of this was down to victualling failure: on *Le Mars* half the crew perished from bad food, while on board *Le Northumberland* more than fifty men were dying daily at one point. Storeships were not organised for the 380,400 supplementary rations being prepared at Rochefort.[34] Delays and undelivered cargoes did not stem from the appearance of enemy ships on the French coast, but from the financial collapse of the government: not even the navy's largest contractor was immune to the financial disasters that befell the service in 1759.[35]

Even when these problems were surpassed, France did not have the logistical infrastructure to support fleets at sea. In 1761 Martinique was captured by a British force under Admiral Rodney. A relief force had been sent from France under Rear Admiral le comte de Blénac-Cordon, but he reached Martinique the day after it fell, and spent the next six months at Cap François, immobilised by sickly crews.[36] The Royal Navy and British naval administration had financial and logistical systems far in advance of its major rivals. However, the security fostered by this knowledge brought an ambivalent approach to further development. As Baugh has put it, 'until the disasters of the war for American Independence, few Englishmen

---

[31] Ibid., p. 171; Baugh, 'Naval Power', p. 235.

[32] Baugh, 'Naval Power', p. 247.

[33] Jonathan R. Dull, *The French Navy and Seven Years War* (London, 2005), pp. 113–14.

[34] James Pritchard, *Anatomy of a Naval Disaster: The 1746 French Naval Expedition to North America* (Montreal, 1995), pp. 61–2, 111, 117.

[35] James Pritchard, *Louis XV's Navy, 1748–1762: A Study in Organization and Administration* (Montreal, 1987), p. 183.

[36] Rodger, *Command of the Ocean*, p. 284.

saw the need, and fewer still felt the inclination, to reform a navy which, for all its faults, was the acknowledged mistress of the seas'.[37] Success in the Seven Years War covered up the deficiencies that remained with the victualling service. It took the prospect of defeat against the Americans to shake Britain and her naval administrators into action.

The War of American Independence

British strategic problems in the War of American Independence were complicated by the unprecedented administrative and logistical problems arising from the necessity of supporting a naval force and a great army in the western hemisphere.[38] The twin aspirations of timeliness and efficiency would be much sought after. For example, the Victualling Board was still struggling with wastage. The agent victuallers Marsh and Cherry, in Cork and Rotherhithe respectively, rejected and condemned large quantities of provisions delivered by contractors as being unfit for human consumption. On one occasion in 1780, Cherry reported that one contractor had failed to deliver 54,920 lbs of beef and 229,767 lbs of butter for the last convoy of the year.[39] By and large, though, the production of foodstuffs was never an issue operationally.[40] The main challenge, again, was in distributing provisions around the globe. Shortcomings in the victualling service were not due to failure to purchase or contract for sufficient provisions, but to delays in getting transports.[41]

Failure to provide adequate transport tonnage undermined the best efforts of administrators to create an efficient supply service. A system of calculating cumulative supplements had long been evolving, but was honed to a fine art during the War of American Independence. Then estimates took into account shipments on passage as well as deliveries by contractors, and saw bureaucrats in London attempt to arrange specific supplies for specific forces. Reports of provisions on an individual station were compiled and compared to the known numbers of seamen at that location. Estimates were drawn up, with specific quantities of provisions

[37] Baugh, *British Naval Administration in the Age of Walpole*, p. 505.

[38] David Syrett, *Shipping and the American War: A Study of British Transport Organisation* (London, 1970), p. vii.

[39] Ibid., p. 150.

[40] The contracting side of victualling during the War of American Independence is covered in Norman Baker, *Government and Contractors: British Treasury and War Supplies, 1775–83* (London, 1971).

[41] M. J. Williams, 'The Naval Administration of the Fourth Earl of Sandwich 1771–82' (unpublished Ph.D. thesis, University of Oxford, 1962), pp. 533–6.

arranged to feed a calculated number of men. For example, on 9 February 1775, it was calculated that there were eighty-four days of provisions left on the North American station. That day a supply was sent out calculated to last 4,275 men for four months. If reinforced, it would last 6,000 men for 79⅔ days.[42]

These administrative developments would mean very little without an adequate transport system. Where transports were available, or where inadequacies could be offset by local provisioning, fleets were supplied and operations maintained. However, the regularity of complaints demonstrates that victualling from a discrete, centralised location had yet to be mastered. Transport procurement was a slow and laborious task. As Syrett put it: 'ordinary business concerning the transport service moved through the hierarchy of British government in a sluggish and inefficient manner . . . weeks and in some cases months might be required to resolve simple problems relating to the transport service'.[43] Delays in transport and victuals were frequent. In 1779 a convoy requested by the Navy Board on the 5 June was only loaded and ready by 4 September. The speed with which a convoy was secured was even slower. That same example of 1779 did not receive its convoy until 24 December, despite reminders being sent. Similarly, in 1780 another attempt to secure an escort resulted in months of delays.[44] The problem was not one of technology, or indeed of a more widespread global shortage of mercantile tonnage, but of management: as the Navy Board observed in 1782, 'if all the shipping in Europe was employed in the service of the Army they would not prove sufficient, under this kind of management'.[45] By 1782, the Navy Board did not have the tonnage to meet the logistical needs of 1783.[46] Further evidence of the Navy Board's struggle to complete its primary duties comes with its reluctance to take on the army provisioning. In 1778 it wrote:

we find that the great increase of the navy, and equipment of the fleet, which there is in appearance will be further extended, together with the having the heavy load of the transport service upon this office, there now being now near 78,000 tons of shipping under our directions, renders it impossible to undertake the management of a business if such variety and uncertainty in addition to it, without prejudice to His Majesty's affairs, and subjecting them to disappointments and inconveniences more especially

[42] NMM, ADM DP/107, 28 Sept. 1775, Morriss, *Foundations of British Maritime Ascendency*, pp. 295–9.
[43] Syrett, *Shipping and the American War*, pp. 12–15.
[44] Ibid., p. 156.
[45] Ibid., p. 180.
[46] Ibid., p. 162.

in our department as commissioners of the navy which no consideration can lead us to hazard.[47]

It was, nevertheless, given the responsibility for the army the following year. That it was given to the Victualling Board early in the Napoleonic War is a relevant judgement on the board's perceived capability.

Throughout the American War there were also consistent failures to provide warships promptly to escort outward bound convoys. On several occasions during the years 1779–80, the Navy Board saw months of preparation wasted by the failure of the naval vessels required to escort the convoy to appear at the appointed time and place.[48] As a result operations were greatly affected by failures of naval administration. In 1779 there were victualling problems with the Channel fleet, particularly with water. Portsmouth, the nearest watering port, could not meet Admiral Hardy's demands. The most serious problems involved the victualling of the West Indies squadron, with many complaints levelled at Blackburn, the West Indies contractor. He himself complained that his victuallers had been delayed for nearly six months at Spithead, awaiting order. By February 1780, Admiral Hyde Parker was complaining of shortages of provisions.[49] Naval administration had failed to learn from Hawke's experience in 1759, whereby regular shipments of provisions to a blockading force could keep it at sea without the need to return to port. As a result, the continuous or 'close' blockade was removed as a strategic option. Lord Howe commented that 'stationing a large fleet off the coast of France was a very improper and harzardous measure', as crews became sickly, and ships battered by the elements. 'A station off Brest', he concluded, 'was a dangerous station, and should not be taken but upon great emergencies.'[50] A close blockade would not be adopted until scurvy had been conquered, in the 1800s. Hawke himself, having pioneered the close blockade and logistical system to support it, found this frustrating. As he wrote to Geary, 'six weeks is long enough in all conscience . . . I wish the Admiralty would see what was done in former times'.[51]

Despite the preference for 'open blockade' the Channel fleet continued to suffer from lack of provisions, with sometimes detrimental effects on naval capabilities. Geary, in command of the Channel fleet, left for sea

---

[47] NMM, ADM/B/195, 16 Jan. 1778, quoted in Syrett, *Shipping and the American War*, p. 133.

[48] Ibid., p. 154.

[49] Williams, 'Sandwich', pp. 553–4.

[50] Piers Mackesy, *The War for America, 1775–1783* (London, 1964), p. 193.

[51] Lloyd, Christopher and Coulter, Jack L. S., *Medicine and the Royal Navy 1200–1900: Volume III, 1714–1815* (London, 1961), p. 126.

on 8 June 1780. By the end of August 2,000 seamen were suffering from scurvy.[52] He was compelled to return to Spithead. The First Lord of the Admiralty, Sandwich, feared for strategic ramifications: the loss of another convoy 'would occasion such distress to this country that no-one can tell the consequences it might have'. Scurvy broke out again in the Channel in the summer of 1781, with Admiral Darby forced to sail to Spithead. He made sure two convoys from Charleston and the Leeward Islands arrived safely home first, as well as a fleet of East Indiamen, ensuring that British interest did not suffer.[53] Still, it was a further example of administrative failings, unable to ensure the supplies of a fleet operating in the English Channel, let alone further afield. The following year, 1781, there were complaints from Sir Edward Hughes of scurvy in the East Indies. Rodney on the Leeward Islands, however, had the benefit of local contractors; Blackburn, supplying 50 per cent of provisions in the West Indies in 1780, wrote that 'no Fleets were better supplied with good and wholesome provisions' during 1780–1'.[54] However, 'there was an uncomfortable gap in the provisioning of the American squadron between July and October'. Admiral Graves complained his agent victualler was 'slenderly provided with provisions' owing to the scarcity of transports of any kind at home in 1781.[55] The tardy delivery of provisions would plague the navy until the end of the war.[56]

The victualling system had failed to learn from earlier conflicts. During the Seven Years War a force one and a half times a squadron's strength was required so that piecemeal parts of it could return home for victualling. Such inefficiencies of naval strength were repeated between 1776 and 1783. Middleton was of the opinion that blockading 'squadrons should consist of such a number of ships as would admit that a fourth or third part of each of them should be able to go into the nearest port to refit, to victual or to store; and the remaining three-fourths or two-thirds should be of such force as still to have a decided superiority over the enemy'.[57] The principle of regular and timely delivery of foodstuffs by transports to blockading fleets had yet to be instituted.

[52] 'Admiral Francis Geary', *Oxford Dictionary of National Biography*, XXI, ed. H. C. Matthew and Brian Harrison (Oxford, 2004), p. 687.

[53] Mackesy, *The War for America*, pp. 357, 397.

[54] Williams, 'Sandwich', p. 557.

[55] Ibid., p. 562.

[56] Syrett, *Shipping and the American War*, p. 150.

[57] Middleton to Philip Patton, 2 June 1794, *Letters of Lord Barham*, II, p. 386.

The French Revolutionary and Napoleonic Wars

This would change as Britain once again entered a war with France with the recreation of the Transport Board in 1794 (an earlier reincarnation had been disbanded 70 years earlier). Its central task was the procurement of transports for the use of the other government departments, both army and navy. Britain's disparate empire had always required transport services: before 1794 each naval department had secured its own tonnage. The British state continued to harness the assets of the mercantile private sector, contracting with merchants for the hire of vessels, though now this was managed exclusively by the Transport Board. With its re-institution many of the abuses revealed by the Commission on Fees were eliminated, the most important being the competition among the different boards for tonnage. The Commission had complained in 1788 that:

> The professional knowledge of the members at that Board would prevent purchase or hire of improper vessels; and the competition being removed, the tonnage wanted would be obtained at a fair and reasonable rate, by several Boards bidding against each other, the price will be raised, and vessels unfit for the service frequently engaged.[58]

Following the problems of securing tonnage during the American war, and with the arrival of a new conflict in 1792, the Transport Board was brought back into existence, largely at the prompting of Charles Middleton, at the time comptroller of the navy.[59] Not having a Transport Board 'operated so much on the mind [of Middleton] that it induced him to submit to Mr Pitt, the absolute necessity there was for its existence'; and Pitt 'was so convinced of it as immediately to put it into execution', wrote the war secretary, Henry Dundas.[60] Instead, the Victualling, Ordnance and Navy Board would apply to the Transport Board, whose sole duty was the hiring of transports from the merchant community.[61] It was intended not only to remove competition between the other boards, but also to rationalise the whole system of procuring transports. In a further consolidation, the Victualling Board took on the duty of supplying the army. As the Admiralty explained, 'it was considered that the service would be 'performed with greater advantage to

---

[58] Commission on Fees, Fifth Report, VII, p. 190.

[59] M. E. Condon, 'The Establishment of the Transport Board – A Subdivision of the Admiralty – 4 July 1794', *MM*, 58 (1972), 69–84, p. 73.

[60] Melville MSS 1044, f. 107, National Library of Scotland, quoted in Condon, 'The Establishment of the Transport Board', p. 79.

[61] In 1806, with the demise of the Sick and Hurt Board, the Transport Board would be given responsibility for prisoners of war and naval hospitals. Condon, 'The Establishment of the Transport Board', p. 82.

the public . . . than in any other war'.[62] It promised new economies since the victualling commissioners could engage for army supplies with contractors who supplied the navy.[63] From this point on the provisioning of military forces abroad would be the responsibility of the Victualling Board.

During the French Wars, the worldwide distribution of foodstuffs was attempted on an unprecedented scale. Centralised, remote supply was not a universal policy: fleets in the East Indies and West Indies would continue to be supplied using local contractors.[64] However, the majority of fleets would be supplied from British out-ports. Remote supply removed the dependence on local politics and climates that could not be guaranteed, and allowed victualling decision-making to be centralised in London. As we have seen, remote supply was nothing new: during the Seven Years War, the Channel fleet had been supplied by this method. In the 1750s, it was beyond the administrative and managerial capacity of naval administration to continue this remote system of provisioning at larger distances from British out-ports. By 1795, fleets in the North Sea, the Channel, the Mediterranean, the Cape, the Brazils, North America and periodically in the Baltic (in 1801, 1807 and 1808–12) were provisioned in this manner, with fleets of transports travelling from Deptford, Portsmouth and Plymouth. Fleets would not be reliant on local provisioning, not always possible in politically unstable or geographically unsuited regions. Fleets would no longer need to return to port.

Torbay took on an important role in the provisioning of the Channel fleet, with vessels completing there on their way to blockading stations. In 1805 plans were announced that Falmouth would become the base for ships coming from Ushant to complete (it was closer to Brest). As in 1755 when Hawke's squadron had received convoys of victuallers, once again fleets of transports were arranged from Plymouth to sustain the blockading squadron.[65] From 1805 and the institution of the 'close blockade' ships were only to come into port when the weather forced them to. The 'close blockade' differed from the previous form, placing warships within sight of the respective coast or port to ensure the immediate interception of any ship

---

[62] TNA, ADM 109/102, 24.

[63] Roger Morriss, 'Colonization, Conquest, and the Supply of Food and Transport: The Reorganization of Logistics Management, 1780–1795', *War in History* 13/3 (2007), 310–24, p. 321.

[64] There were economic as well as logistical reasons for this. With an abundance of local supplies it made both economic and operational sense to cut out the delays that accompanied victual distribution and obtain supplies locally. An abundance of local supplies could not always be guaranteed though.

[65] Steer, 'Blockade of Brest', pp. 309–14.

entering or leaving. It was both the most effective and the most difficult form of blockade to implement. Difficulties arose because the blockading ships needed to remain continuously at sea, exposed to storms and hardship. No longer would ships be forced back to port to revictual. Significantly, this meant that a third of a fleet's strength would be absent from their station as they picked up provisions. This advance was instrumental in allowing the 'close blockade' to be executed.

The success or failure of victualling operations would therefore depend on the success with which these convoys of victuallers could be organised. This would not be a given during the following years. There continued to be instances where victualling delays did obstruct strategic designs, such as at the Cape in 1796. The Royal Naval administration did not immediately comprehend or deal with the challenges posed by the unprecedented scale or extremity of the French Revolutionary and Napoleonic Wars. During the Peace of Amiens provisions failed to reach Malta and scurvy and debility resulted in seamen's deaths.[66] Delays in provisioning and water contributed to the disastrous Walcheren expedition of 1809.[67] Despite use of victuallers, the ships blockading Brest between 1800 and 1805 suffered regular shortages.[68] In 1804, the Channel fleet was forced into Torbay to resupply.[69] The battle of Trafalgar was prompted when Nelson was forced to send six ships of his squadron away for provisions and water, leaving him an inferior number of ships, and inadvertently drew out the combined French and Spanish fleet.[70] Fortunately for Nelson, this gave him the opportunity to fight a decisive battle; victualling shortfalls rarely had such positive results.

The Victualling Board's system of calculating cumulative supplements had been carefully refined by the 1800s. For instance, the close correlation between foodstuffs needed and distributed was evident throughout the French Revolutionary and Napoleonic Wars. Two deliveries in 1801 were designed to provision the Mediterranean fleet for eight months. The first, on 10 February, was calculated to support 15,000 men for four months. The second, on 9 June, was the allowance for 20,000 men for a further four months.[71] Between May and December 1801 there were between

---

[66] R. J. B. Knight, *The Pursuit of Victory: The Life and Achievement of Horatio Nelson* (London, 2005), p. 443.

[67] Gordon C. Bond, *The Grand Expedition: The British Invasion of Holland in 1809* (Athens, GA, 1979), pp. 145–6.

[68] Steer, 'Blockade of Brest', pp. 314–15.

[69] Duffy, 'Devon and the Naval Strategy of the French Wars 1689–1815', p. 188.

[70] Rodger, *Command of the Ocean*, p. 537.

[71] TNA, ADM 111/159, 15 July 1801.

15,500 and 21,700 men in the Mediterranean.[72] The Admiralty lists show that 4,300,199 lbs of bread were needed to sustain the fleet for this period, while the Victualling Board minutes indicate that 3,920,000 lbs were actually sent out.[73] In addition there were 360,000 lbs of flour sent with the 10 February delivery, and 480,000 lbs with the shipment on 9 June, which would have more than made up for the slight deficit. Flour was not sent exclusively since baking it required a lengthier cooking process, with consequent demands for wood or coal. On the other hand it was less bulky than sending ready-made bread. Thus, the Victualling Board settled on a compromise whereby mostly bisket bread would be sent, with additional flour to make up the rest.

Further rationalisations of the victualling service were enacted in 1808. From this year, the Victualling Board prepared periodic global statements 'of the quantities of provision remaining in the several stores at home and abroad shewing the number of days the same will serve the men at the respective stations'.[74] These would prove invaluable in keeping control of stocks, accounts and the precise provisions on station. They also prompted structural change within naval administration. Whereas the Admiralty was in contact with commanders' needs and requirements, the Victualling Board dealt with the merchant contractors who provided foodstuffs. Since the beginning of the eighteenth century, as befitting its senior status, all orders and correspondence from the Admiralty to the Victualling Board passed through the Navy Board. The Navy Board and Victualling Board communicated with each other directly and, as the newer department, 'the Victualling Board was part of the naval establishment and considered to be inferior in rank to the Navy Board'.[75] The onset of war in 1793, however, witnessed an increase in the scale and responsibilities of other naval departments. There was a pressing wartime need to speed up inter-departmental communication. The lessons taught by the early years of the Napoleonic War had brought this to the attention of the naval administration. The Navy Board's role in the provisioning process was seen to serve only to slow down victualling arrangements. In July 1808, three months after Saumarez had sailed for the Baltic, the Admiralty ended this labourious practice, advising that from this point on, direct correspondence between the two was necessary. 'Whereas', they wrote to the Victualling Board,

---

[72] TNA, ADM 8/81–2.
[73] TNA, ADM 111/159–60.
[74] See NMM, ADM DP 29, 2 Jan, 1 Feb. 1809.
[75] Syrett, *Shipping and the American War*, p. 9.

we have had under our consideration the practise hitherto adhered to, by this Board, of causing the orders and directions, issued for Victualling His Majesty's Ships and Vessels, when Commissioned, and Fitted and refitted, and completed for Foreign, or Channel service, to be conveyed to you through the medium of the Navy Board. And it being our intention for the purpose of giving celerity to the Victualling of Ships and Vessels under the circumstances above stated, that in future our orders for the supply of their provisions, shall in all cases be addressed immediately to your Board; and you are . . . to cause the utmost dispatch to be used, in carrying the same into effect.[76]

In the last months of 1807, the Admiralty had had it brought home to them how important the victualling service was. In the most politically damaging example of victualling arrangements influencing operations, Sir Richard Strachan was forced off his blockading station off Rochefort because of a lack of victuals. Such was the fall-out from this that the incident was presented to Parliament. Initial concern for the fleet arose on 11 December as Admiral Lord Gardner warned that 'at this time the Line-of-Battle Ships have not more than Eight Weeks Provisions on board'. Sir Richard Strachan wrote on the 1 December that 'we failed with the hope of falling in with the Victuallers, which I concluded would have sometime past left Plymouth'. The *Superb*, *Spencer* and *Cumberland* were sent to Rochefort to replace the ships forced off station as a relief force, but it arrived too late to prevent the French fleet escaping from port. The 'State and Condition' of the squadron of 21 December noted that the *Impeteux* and *Donegal* had only fifteen and nineteen days' bread left, while the *Emerald* and *Raleigh* had only nineteen, and twenty-two tons of water remaining. The *Colossus* and *Mediator* were delayed in setting off from Deptford, as reported on the 31 December, not to sail until the 6 January. The supplies would not arrive until the 16 January, by which time it was too late.[77] The fleet was forced to leave its station to find the *Mediator*, and allowed the French fleet to escape. A mere two months after this incident was presented to Parliament, and amidst widespread anxieties over victualling performance, Saumarez's fleet set sail for the Baltic.

[76] TNA, ADM 2/154/448–9, Admiralty to Victualling Board, 12 July 1808.

[77] House of Commons Parliamentary Papers Online, 1808 (103) *Papers Presented to the House of Commons Relating to the State and Condition of the Squadron Employed off Rochefort under the command of Sir Richard J. Strachan, printed 15 March 1808*, nos. 9–59, 16, 18, 35, 28, 44, 46, 56, 59. http://parlipapers.chadwyck.co.uk/fulltext/fulltext.do?area=hcpp&id=1808-001747&pagenum=1&resultNum=1&entries=1&queryId=../session/1340961753_17394&backto=FULLREC. Accessed January 2012.

There is a clear correlation between advances in the victualling system and increasing operational and strategic capabilities. As the logistical support for fleets improved, they were able to remain at sea for longer periods, at distances further from Britain than had been attempted before. An evolution of the means available transformed the strategic ends that could be pursued.[78] The improvement of the victualling service was incremental. Advances, particularly with the Channel fleet during the Seven Years War, were not implemented across all squadrons, while fleets operating during the War of American Independence suffered from an inability to learn from previous mistakes. Strachan's logistical difficulties demonstrated that even by the Napoleonic Wars, naval fleets were not guaranteed a timely or effective service, and this explains why commanders continued to worry about their supplies. Delays and inefficiencies would continue to affect operations. This would not suffice in the wars against Napoleon, where the necessity of a full-scale international war raised the bar of administrative competence higher than ever before. As naval administrators turned their attention to supply in early 1808 they would discover further challenges. There would be good reasons to doubt the viability of provisioning a Baltic fleet.

[78] Baugh, *Naval Administration 1715–1750*, pp. 406, 402.

3

The Challenges of the Baltic Sea

This station affords much greater anxiety than the Channel Islands and I may add than any other station I have hitherto been upon and its being so perfectly novel in all respects makes it the more interesting.

Vice-Admiral Sir James Saumarez, 8 July 1808[1]

THE BALTIC SEA provided formidable obstacles to both naval commanders and administrators. Although closer to Britain's home ports than further flung stations, the Baltic Sea provided challenges that exacerbated the existing problem of moving large amounts of provisions to ships on station. In 1801 and 1807, fleets had briefly been sent to the Copenhagen, in the former case involving a brief voyage across to the Gulf of Finland. These short expeditions aside, there had not been a sustained British fleet in the Baltic since 1727 and Saumarez was faced with a considerable challenge to ensure the provisioning of his fleet – with inadequate charts, in unknown waters, all the while surrounded by hostile states and with a supply line open to attack from Danish gunboats.

Agriculture, economics and administration

There were serious concerns for the Baltic fleet's ability to provision itself. One anonymous officer, calling himself 'Observator', wrote to Mulgrave, the First Lord of the Admiralty, at the outset of the Baltic operation to express his fears for the fleet. Having served the Victualling Board earlier in his life he was a man with some knowledge of provisioning and trenchant opinions, who expected his views to be taken seriously. As he stated:

No man can be more attached to His Majesty's Service with more respect than myself…I now very respectfully address your Lordship, and as I profess to have some knowledge of the Victualling of Ships from having spent many years in that service I trust I may be allowed to presume on that point.[2]

---

[1] SRO, SA 3/1/2/1, Saumarez to Martha Saumarez, 8 July 1808. See Voelcker, *Saumarez vs. Napoleon*, p. 44.

[2] MA 20/30, 'Observator' (anonymous writer) to Lord Mulgrave, 13 July 1808.

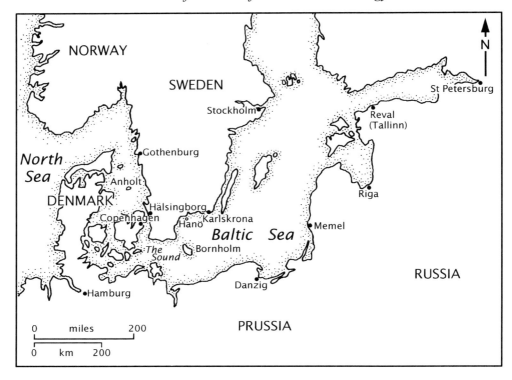

Figure 5. The Baltic, 1808

The author made particular mention of the logistical problems suffered by Sir Richard Strachan's squadron when off Rochefort, a logistical failure that had come before Parliament the previous winter. The author noted that 'from a source of information I cannot make known', the fleet 'was much in want of Provisions and Water' since supplies 'did not arrive until too late'. This made him especially worried for the Baltic fleet: 'from these circumstances I cannot suppress my anxiety when I look to the Ships in the Baltic, and employed on such detached services from each other, blockading the coasts of Holstein, Jutland, the Island of Zealand and the different Islands near it, the indispensable necessity of timely supplies being sent from here to that quarter'.[3] He was right to be concerned. The dispersal of the Baltic fleet was indeed a serious obstacle. In 1808, for example, there were ships stationed at Gothenburg, in the Sound, in the Belt, at the entrance of the Great Belt, off the Skaw, off Christiansand and in the Gulf of Finland, with other ships sent in convoys across the Baltic Sea.[4]

---

[3] Ibid.
[4] SRO, HA 93/6/1/115, Fleet disposition, 24 May 1808. See also SRO, HA 93/6/1/697,

Indeed, even the ships in the Sound and Belt were dispersed over large distances, often on separate duties. Nor was the anonymous writer alone in fearing for the fleet. After one year's service in the Baltic, the physician to the fleet warned measures would need to be taken 'to prevent from their suffering by Scurvy, which the quality of the water, and the humidity of the atmosphere, in that climate so much encourage'.[5] Saumarez himself anticipated problems as the fleet moved to the peripheries of the Baltic Sea, particularly in 1809. 'Apprehension of the great difficulties that will exist, in keeping up the supplies of the Squadron when in the upper parts of the Baltic', he wrote; 'I cannot too early draw the attention of the Lords Commissioners of the Admiralty to that important object.'[6]

The Observator left Mulgrave in no doubt as to the potential consequences, operationally and politically. 'I am aware the large ships are fitted out for 5 months' he wrote,

> but when it is considered the small Vessels are numerous and provisioned for much less time, they will sooner cry out for relief, and if they should unluckily not happen to be on the station, to be supplied from the large ships, their wants will be magnified in a London newspaper and afford a good subject for an Editor to throw his invectives, besides when the *large ships* are reduced to the necessity of affording supplies the *general want* will become rapid, therefore precaution is very early to be purchased, and as there are many months yet to look forward to in the Baltic supplies *eventually must be sent.*[7]

The Observator's fears for the Baltic fleet did not end there. Sweden could supply water but not bread, spirits or wine, while the fleet's sheer size would consume prodigious quantities, which it was not certain could be procured in Scandinavia.

> Sweden is unable to afford the necessary supplies our Ships are accustomed to have, & of the same quantity, Bread especially being of an extreme coarse quality, Spirits exported from this country chiefly Prize Brandy, and very dear, Wine from the Mediterranean hardly any to be got, these my Lord are material Articles, and in Victualling of the most consequence; the other parts are material and entitled to due consideration which I must respectfully entreat may be considered in time; Water can be supplied from Gothenburg river, or other parts of Sweden that need not be considered.[8]

Plan for the protection of trade, Keats to Hood, 6 May 1809.
  [5] TNA, ADM 1/8/265–6, Dr Jamison to Saumarez, 23 April 1809.
  [6] TNA, ADM 1/8/310, Saumarez to Admiralty, 10 May 1809.
  [7] MA 20/30, 'Observator' to Lord Mulgrave, 13 July 1808.
  [8] Ibid.

Saumarez's provisioning efforts would face significant political obstacles, with Denmark hostile, and Prussia and Russia members of the Continental System. It was common practice for naval fleets to procure supplies locally when on distant stations. With Russia, Prussia and Denmark all hostile to Britain, securing sea-provisions contracts for all varieties of foodstuffs would be impossible. As the anonymous writer observed, only Sweden remained on friendly terms, a country not known for its vast quantities of arable land. Nor did it have the agricultural infrastructure to cope with the demands of a Royal Navy fleet numbering thousands of men.[9] Throughout the conflict in the Baltic, a Royal Naval squadron arriving would double the population of nearly all Swedish ports: Gothenburg for example had a population of only 12,000.[10] The Swedish historian Ingvar Anderson noted that three-quarters of Sweden's population was directly employed in agriculture at the beginning of the nineteenth century, yet this was farming still based largely on 'medieval methods'. This had become even more problematic when Sweden lost its grain-producing provinces on the southern Baltic shore at the Peace of Nystad in 1721.[11]

Sweden was therefore dependent on imported supplies from northern Germany for subsistence. The Royal Navy would be charged with ensuring that food shipments crossed the Baltic in safety to feed Swedish mouths, rather than benefiting from it themselves. Mr Christopher Fay, agent for victualling from Norway at Gothenburg, wrote in 1809 'representing the distressed situation of his Country for want of Provisions'; it was ordered that 'all British Cruizers [were] to suffer all Vessels laden with Provisions destined for Norway, to proceed free and unmolested'.[12] In November

---

[9] Indeed, Sweden did not have enough grain to supply its own population. Sweden, dependent on grain from north Germany, was deeply worried that this supply could be cut off by the British blockade in the Baltic. George Foy, a British businessman and agent in Stockholm, wrote to Saumarez in 1811, reporting Sweden's intense happiness that Saumarez had allowed the grain trade to continue under special licence, that he had 'occasion to see Baron D'Engestrom very often now, and in a conversation with him to day, he desired me to say that His Government is most gratefully sensible of the value of Your Excellency's humane motive in granting the licenses in question to allow the trade with Pomerania . . . This year's Crop of Grain has almost entirely failed in Sweden, at least in the greater part of the country, and consequently these indulgencies, whilst the season admits of getting grain into the Country from the Baltic Ports, are of the greatest importance.' SRO, HA 93/6/1/1874, Foy to Saumarez, 5 Sept. 1811.

[10] Stockholm was the one exception, with a population of 70,000. Ships from the Baltic fleet did not visit Stockholm, however.

[11] Ingvar Andersson, *A History of Sweden*, trans. Carolyn Hannay (London, 1955), pp. 297–9.

[12] TNA, FO 22/60/9, Barrow to Bagot, 26 Sept. 1809.

1809 the British would grant forty licences for importing cargoes of grain into Norway.[13] The Baltic region was a sparsely populated area unsuitable for large-scale military operations on land. Large armies could not be maintained through local resources and had to be supplied from outside.[14] Moreover, in other theatres, commanding naval officers had the benefit of merchant contacts built up around repeated British naval involvement in the region; there were no such advantages in the Baltic. On arrival in the Mediterranean in 1800, Keith's agent victualler could write to him that 'it has been the prevailing practise before . . . for the ships to take live bullocks aboard which they slaughtered themselves'. Commanders and administrators stationed in the eastern Mediterranean could draw upon decades of seafaring and provisioning knowledge of the area. In May the agent victualler in Port Mahon, James Yeo, wrote to Keith that, 'it has always been a practice to put three or four Galleons [*sic*] of Brandy into the Syracuse Wine to make it keep in summer, whereas the Marsala wine will keep in any climate and any length of time'.[15]

Knowledge of local conditions, merchants and victualling practices were invaluable in the Mediterranean; they were absent in the Baltic. As Nelson himself found in his brief voyage through the Baltic in 1801, the last British fleet to enter the Baltic had been in 1727, since when ships of the line had become larger, with greater draught of water, and had more numerous crews. Nelson's voyage was fraught with victualling problems. When Admiral Totty arrived to reinforce Nelson, he found vessels 'in want of fuel and cannot purchase any, as their bills are non-negotiable', whilst the governor of Bornholm refused to supply the British ships moored off the coast with vegetables. Cattle were eventually supplied from Danzig, though there were difficulties and delays. Nelson, an astute organiser as well as a celebrated tactician, kept a firm financial hand on victualling matters; 'it must be noted that the lowest price & best provisions must both combine', he urged when in the Baltic. Aware of the problems he had encountered, and in a letter that can be read as a warning for the Baltic fleet that would arrive seven years later, he commented on Baltic provisioning, 'such iniquity, I fear, has been going on in Denmark that the victualling must look out before they pay the horrid bills'.[16] The inclusion of an agent victualler with the fleet in

[13] TNA, FO 22/60/21, Office of Committee of Privy Council for Trade, to William Hamilton, 30 Nov. 1809.

[14] Glete, *Navies and Nations*, vol. 1, p. 295.

[15] NMM, KEI/L/2/68–9, James Yeo to Keith, 10 May 1800.

[16] Knight, *Pursuit of Victory*, pp. 395–6.

1808 suggests that the Victualling Board had paid attention to Nelson's experiences.

The limited provisions procured locally in 1801 proved to be of inferior quality. 'It was afterwards found', it was reported

> that the Hides and Tallow from being too long kept on board (notwith-standing all possible means were adopted and ordered by the Commander in Chief and Rear Admiral Totty) were generally, when returned to Mr Booth, stinking, full of maggots and so very offensive as to be complained of as a nuisance, by the orders of the Stores contiguous to that in which they were lodged, which obliged him to dispose of them, for one third of what they would have fetched, had they been returned in good condition; and that the Cattle, from unforeseen and unavoidable causes, owing to the weather, and their having, with a scarcity of hay, been kept on board ship longer than was at first imagined, naturally experienced a diminution in their Weight.[17]

As Saumarez's fleet entered the Baltic there were severe problems procuring good-quality provisions. Charles Fenwick had been a consul in Denmark: at the outset of war with the Danes in 1807 he had crossed the Sound and taken up residence at Hälsingborg, where he stayed on in a private capacity. In April 1808 he wrote to the Foreign Secretary of the lack of agricultural resources available: 'provisions do not appear plenty in the last mentioned Provinces [Holstein, Schleswig, Jutland, Funen]. I even think I remarked a scarcity of Bread.' On the subject of beef he complained that 'the Danish Government had collected much, and forbid the exportation'.[18] Four years later, in 1812, he would still be writing of food shortages: 'the poor can scarcely obtain food and the daily application at the bakers shops are not only very tumultuous but the purchasers are obliged to fight their way to procure bread'.[19] Procuring supplies locally would be difficult, and for the majority of foodstuffs, Saumarez's fleet would have to rely on supplies from Britain.[20]

---

[17] NMM, ADM DP/21, 20 Oct. 1801.

[18] TNA, FO 22/58/98–9, Charles Fenwick to George Canning, 28 April 1808.

[19] Voelcker, *Saumarez vs. Napoleon*, p. 177.

[20] Sea-provisions contracts could not be brokered; however Saumarez did manage to secure the supply of some individual species from Sweden, namely fresh meat. Local procurement, even if on a limited level, helped supplement the deliveries from Deptford. This supply was constrained by diplomatic and political factors, particularly after Sweden joined the war against Britain. Indeed, the supply continued even after Sweden had declared war on Britain after 1810. For a full analysis of the procurement of local supplies, see James Davey, 'Supplied by the Enemy: The Royal Navy and the British Consular Service in the Baltic, 1808–1812', *Historical Research* 85/228 (2012), 265–83.

The Observator reminded Mulgrave of the victualling problems that existed in 1807, noting that the fleet had been forced to go onto two-thirds allowance owing to 'unforeseen circumstances'. This was proof that foodstuffs 'should be sent early to guard against every necessity and the stigmas of opposition'. He urged Mulgrave to arrange for supplies to be sent out immediately, especially given the huge number of men to be fed: 'from the enquiries I have made and information received', he wrote, 'the number of Men employed in the Baltic on board ships amount to at least 11 thousand, this is an alarming number to take care of, and on whom a careful eye should be directed.' He even went so far as to recommend the quantities of provisions that would be needed. Mulgrave's response simply stated that 'I hope this is already taken care of'.[21] As war with Russia became a certainty, the Admiralty was confident in its abilities to permanently provision a fleet in the Baltic. Mulgrave was bombarded with information concerning the fleet, so much so that at one point he was forced to reply that 'with respect to the Baltick Service I consider every consideration relating to it as closed'.[22]

For all the external concerns, and despite the lack of local knowledge, the Admiralty had reasons to be confident. Similarly scaled operations had been executed before, albeit in different locations. Periodically, throughout the French Revolutionary and Napoleonic Wars, a fleet of up to 20,000 seamen had been provisioned in the Mediterranean Sea. The Mediterranean was similar to the Baltic in many ways; both were insular seas, in which British naval forces found themselves surrounded by hostile shores. In both, the provisioning of British seamen would not only be an administrative challenge but also a task involving diplomatic skill and economic awareness. British naval activity across Europe was concerned primarily with the protection of British trade, which was of paramount importance. In both theatres, the naval war would cease to be defensive: it was in Portugal, through the Mediterranean, and in the Baltic especially that the Continental System would first be attacked and ultimately defeated. The Mediterranean fleet commanded by Lord Keith between 1800 and 1802 faced Britain's sternest challenge to naval superiority during the Napoleonic Wars, and was beset with challenges of isolation and insecure supply lines. Keith and his squadron were responsible for maintaining the blockade, transporting and supplying amphibious operations under

[21] MA 20/30, 'Observator' to Lord Mulgrave, 13 July 1808.

[22] MA 20/318, Lord Mulgrave to Rear Admiral Essington, 4 May 1808. For letters concerning the Baltic situation, see also MA 20/211, John Coulsen to Lord Mulgrave, 20 March 1808.

General Abercromby in the Levant and also co-operating with the Austrian army under General Melas in northern Italy. Keith's ability to victual his forces, as well as the Austrian army for much of the campaign, was of vital importance to its success.[23] The Mediterranean was therefore a useful precedent for those planning the provisioning of the Baltic fleet. As in the Baltic a small proportion of supplies would be sourced locally; flour and wheat from Egypt, fresh beef from Naples and Leghorn (now Livorno), and water from the *beys* (governors) of northern Africa. Three victuallers, with a combined tonnage of 1,196 tons, were employed conveying cattle from Leghorn to Minorca. A slaughterhouse was set up in Lisbon for the purpose of victualling the navy in the Mediterranean.[24]

The majority of supplies needed in the Mediterranean came from Britain. The system for the remote supply of provisions was in essence very simple and was similar in all European theatres. The commander in chief, in this case Lord Keith, would tell the Admiralty of his forthcoming needs. The Admiralty would then inform the Victualling Board of the fleet's requirements, who would then organise the manufacture of the said amount, whilst ordering the Transport Board to secure the necessary tonnage. This supply system, which was in place in the Mediterranean throughout the French Revolutionary and Napoleonic Wars, would be repeated in the Baltic from 1808 through to 1812 and characterised the logistical base for all major British naval operations in stations close enough to Britain to be supplied from the victualling bases there. In the Mediterranean, for example, between February 1801 and January 1802 there were three huge shipments, each containing over 3,000 tons of provisions, sent from Portsmouth to Gibraltar.[25] From here, permanent victuallers with a combined tonnage of over 10,000 relayed these provisions across the Mediterranean, in particular to the focal point of victualling operations, Minorca.[26] Secure in the knowledge that similar numbers of seamen to those that would be stationed in the Baltic had been adequately provisioned, the victualling officials were confident of their ability to provision a fleet in the Baltic.

[23] James Davey, 'Within Hostile Shores: Victualling the Royal Navy in European Waters during the Napoleonic Wars', *The International Journal of Maritime History* 21/2 (Dec. 2009).

[24] NMM, KEI/L/23/1, Keith to Hibil Sarlasty, 22 July 1799. NMM, KEI/L/1/143–5, Transport Board to Keith, 8 March 1800. NMM, KEI/L/23, Keith to James Yeo, 8 Jan. 1800. James Davey, 'Within Hostile Shores'.

[25] TNA, ADM 111/159, 160, Victualling Board Minutes. There was one Victualling 'delivery' of this size on 10 Feb, 9 June 1801 and Sept. 1801 (there was a subsequent delivery on 14 April 1802); see TNA, ADM 111/163.

[26] NMM, KEI/L/1/143–5, Transport Board to Keith, 8 March.

Figure 6. Entrances to the Baltic

Climate, geography and hydrography

Yet there were clear grounds for thinking that victualling the Baltic fleet would prove a much tougher task than in the Mediterranean. Firstly, there were the issues concerning the supply routes to the region. There was a long-standing idea of the Baltic as 'a narrow, shallow, dangerous navigation'. One pamphlet, written in 1791, asked: 'What misfortunes, then, are a fleet of thirty or forty ships of the line liable to, conducted by foreign pilots, in those dreadful straights, in a tempestuous night, and when all the buoys and beacons are taken up – the lights put out!'[27]

---

[27] *An Address to the People of England, upon the Subject of the Intended War with Russia* (London, 1791), pp. 33–5. See also *Observations and Reflections on a War with Russia* (London, 1791), p. 42.

Crossing the North Sea was a common voyage: entering the Baltic Sea was a different proposition altogether. There were two entrances from the North Sea to the Baltic, through the Sound and through the Belt.[28] The Sound was the traditional maritime route, being a shorter and quicker passage than the Belt. However, the narrow waters, the likelihood of calms and its proximity to Danish ports made the passage particularly vulnerable to attacks of enemy gunboats. The Danes were in a position to wreak havoc on the Baltic fleet's supply lines; indeed the Danish threat to British shipping in the Baltic was one of the key reasons for the Baltic fleet's existence. Between the years 1808 to 1812 British shipping, victuallers and transports struggled to pass through the Sound. The fear of privateers abounded across ships; it seems evident that the Baltic was not the first choice for most serving naval personnel. A naval seaman, Whitworth, wrote of his fears on learning he was heading to the Baltic:

> I am well in health but truly miserable and wretched. I expect we sail on Friday for the Baltic but for how long I can't tell . . . I am not the only unhappy mortal here no Indeed I am not. The Baltic at present swarms with Privateers there for its likely we may have something to do before we return to England.[29]

Gunboats based at Copenhagen constantly harassed passing shipping. Even ships of the line were vulnerable in calms. Captain John Harvey Boteler recounted how the naval vessel *Africa*, got a terrible mauling at the hands of the Danish gunboats, who caught her in a calm:

> There was a whole fleet of boats, she unable to get shot at them . . . and in this condition the fleet was fired at for two or three hours, the ensign shot away more than once; in fact it was down so long the Danes declared she had stuck, and claimed her as a prize. The breeze fortunately sprung up, and the ship got her anchor up, and the fight soon ended, and the Danes rowed away well satisfied with their work.[30]

---

[28] For the British 'the Baltic' began east of the Skaw, at the top point of Denmark. In Scandinavian eyes, both the Skagerak and the Kattegat are separate regions, the Baltic beginning south and west of the Danish archipelago. See Mark Brackenbury, *Baltic SouthWest Pilot* (London, 1983), p. 9. For commanders and administrators during the Napoleonic Wars, the Baltic station conformed to the earlier definition, certainly including Gothenburg and its maritime surrounds.

[29] NMM, Whitworth Papers, WHW 1/6, Whitworth to his wife, 3 June 1812, off North Yarmouth.

[30] Captain John Harvey Boteler, *Recollections of My Sea Life; From 1808 to 1830*, ed. David Bonner-Smith, Navy Records Society 65 (London, 1942), pp. 13–14.

Saumarez's supply lines were thus at worst precarious, at best unreliable. This was a frustration for Saumarez, 'particularly when the Intricacy of the passages of the Belts and Sound are considered and the various obstacles thrown in the way by the numerous Flotillas of the enemy'.[31] Strongly supported convoys could make the passage through the Sound, especially once the threat of Danish gun boats and privateers had been brought under control, though Saumarez allowed the convoy commander to decide whether 'the state of the wind and weather may render it most advisable'.[32]

Ships sailing into or from the Baltic therefore passed through the Great Belt instead. This passage did not preclude the threat of privateers. There were a number of small harbours on both sides of the Belt where both gunboats and privateers lurked, though the passage did remove the necessity of passing Copenhagen. The Belt also raised additional challenges. Shallow, rocky and largely uncharted, the Belt was an unknown passage for most of the fleet's captains. In 1795 the Hydrographical Office had been created to collate nautical charts for the use of the Royal Navy, with one of its greatest challenges being to provide reliable charts for fleets sent to the Baltic Sea: operational viability rested upon this. In the years immediately after 1795 charts of the Baltic were inaccurate and unreliable. In 1790 the surveyor of the navy had minuted that if a Baltic fleet was needed, it would constitute a service that was 'entirely new, at least to anyone now living'.[33] Five years later, this had not improved. The hydrographer to the navy, Alexander Dalrymple, summed up the Admiralty's hydrographical knowledge of the seas of northern Europe. He explained that there existed charts of Elsinore, the Norwegian coast, the Kattegat and the Sound and Belt, including 'part of the Baltic as far as Bornholm, made in 1777'. Dalrymple himself drily noted that the charts mentioned were 'to be hereafter improved', stating that 'when any New Editions are published they ought to be commissioned'.[34]

Only when the Baltic became a strategically sensitive region would the Hydrographical Office turn its sights to that region. Repeated incursions into the Baltic during the following twenty years provided an opportunity to gather hydrographical information. British understanding of the Baltic Sea improved dramatically, opening the region to the potency of British naval power. During the 1801 and 1807 expeditions attempts were made by the Admiralty to improve their knowledge of the Baltic waters. In 1801, with only inadequate charts to guide them, the navy used pilots

---

[31] TNA, ADM 1/7/398–405, Saumarez to Admiralty, 21 Nov. 1808.
[32] TNA, ADM 1/8/431, Saumarez to Admiralty, 31 May 1809 (italics added).
[33] Aldridge, *Admiral Sir John Norris*, p. 29.
[34] TNA, ADM 1/3522, no date.

and soundings to navigate the waters surrounding Copenhagen. As the fleet returned home, it chose to leave the Baltic via the Great Belt rather than the Sound, in a deliberate attempt to scout and sound what was becoming a strategically vital region.[35] The soundings and courses taken were transmitted to Nepean at the Admiralty, and then Dalrymple at the Hydrographical Office. By 1807 a series of charts and directions covered the many of the most important parts of the Baltic: the Kattegat, the Gulf of Finland and the main entrance to the Baltic, the Sound. Crucially, a chart of the Great Belt was engraved in the Hydrographical Office before Admiral Gambier's expedition to Copenhagen. Fifty-nine copies of a chart of the Great Belt and the same number of 'directions to the Great Belt' were sent to the Baltic, one for each ship.[36]

In 1808 Saumarez and his rear admirals, Samuel Hood and Sir Richard Goodwin Keats, were sent three sets of charts for the Baltic, identical to those sent to Gambier the year before.[37] They concentrated on only a few specific areas: the Baltic generally, the Kattegat, the entrances to the Baltic (especially the Sound) and also a chart of Bornholm.[38] A small chart of the Gulf of Finland was also included. This was not an exhaustive list, but significant quantities were sent out. In January 1809, the new hydrographer to the navy, Hurd, counted 113 boxes of charts issued to ships employed on various stations since June 1808. Thirty-three (by far the most) had gone to the Baltic and North Sea; the next best was fifteen to the Leeward Islands, and to America.[39] In 1808, however, more complicated operations were planned than in the previous year: it was intended that a fleet should remain stationed in the Great Belt the whole year round, leading through large convoys – numbering as many as two hundred – to and from the Baltic. This required charts of great detail. Every rock, shoal and bank

[35] For a full analysis of the Hydrographic Office's attempts to chart the Baltic Sea in this period, see James Davey, 'The Advancement of Nautical Knowledge: The Hydrographical Office, the Royal Navy and the Charting of the Baltic Sea, 1795–1815', *The Journal for Maritime Research* 13 (2011), 81–103. TNA, ADM 1/4, Nelson to Nepean, 12 June 1801; British Library, Add. 34,934, f. 119, Nepean to Nelson, 26 June 1801; NMM, CRK/10, Pole to Nelson, 30 July 1801; TNA, ADM 1/4, Pole to Nepean, 26 June 1801; TNA, ADM 1/4, Pole to Nepean, 9 Aug. 1801.

[36] Davey, 'Nautical Knowledge', p. 94. TNA, ADM 1/3522, Dalrymple to W. W. Pole, 22 Feb. 1808. Hydrographical Office, 7 Dec. 1807, 'A List of Charts Sent to Lord Gambier & not returned'.

[37] TNA, ADM 1/3523, Hurd to Admiralty, 20 April 1808.

[38] TNA, ADM 1/3523, 'A List of Charts (selected by the Committee appointed for that purpose) for the Atlantic Ocean, and the Seas branching out of it: With an Estimate of the Expense', 26 May 1808.

[39] TNA, ADM 1/3523, Hurd to Pole, 17 Jan. 1809.

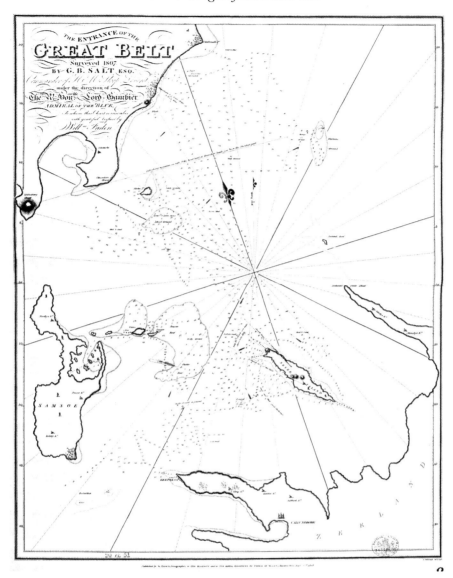

Figure 7. The entrance of the Great Belt, surveyed 1807 by G. B. Salt

British Library, Maps 34465.(14) The Entrance of the Great Belt, Surveyed 1807 by G. B. Salt, Esq. Commander of H. M. Sloop *Leveret*, under the direction of the Rt. Hon. Lord Gambier, to whom this chart is inscribed with grateful respect (London: William Faden, 22 September 1808). © British Library

needed to be recorded. In particular, the Great Belt still posed problems for the Royal Navy. Captain Graves of the *Goliath* wrote to Hood in 1808 speaking of the difficulty in passing through the Belt. 'I cannot help expressing the great degree of embarrassment I feel', he wrote, 'in the responsibility that will attach itself to me, in going through the difficult navigation of the Belt without Pilots.'[40] By 1808, a further chart had been published (Figure 7), taking into account a survey ordered by Gambier the previous year. This was not reliable, nor extensive enough for the lengthy and intricate operations planned in 1808. Rear Admiral Keats, a veteran of the 1807 campaign and a man chosen because of his experience of the region, pressed for continuous surveying to be done, as ships passed through the Great Belt. He wrote in a memo to his subordinates:

> As it is deemed of national Importance to obtain the most correct knowl-edge of the Navigation of the Great Belt, the Several Captains and Com-manders are desired to combine that object as much as circumstances will permit with the important one of their instructions, and neglect no opportunity of Sounding and laying down the different rocks and shoals as well by land marks . . . noting leading marks for the fair channel where they can be laid down, the rise, strength and set of tides, influence of the wind . . . and it is believed a more correct chart than any hitherto in use, may be made from the survey and remarks.[41]

As late as September 1808, improvements were still being made to the chart. Soundings and directions were passed around the fleet; the charting of the Great Belt had opened up the Baltic to the Royal Navy. Over the next few years, the naval fleet would work tirelessly to improve its knowledge of the Baltic waters. George Hope, captain of the fleet, organised soundings to be taken wherever possible in the Baltic.[42] Officers on station dedicated time to hydrographical pursuits, circulating the data to their peers and to the Hydrographical Office. The existence of a centralised hydrographi-cal institution meant that such information was retained, compiled and used to make increasingly accurate charts, which in turn assisted the next generation of naval operations. This was British seapower, the conjunction of administrative and operational expertise, at its most effective.[43]

Crowhurst estimates that 'it was not unusual for ships to take up to six weeks to pass through the Belt'.[44] Provisions, convoyed carefully by Royal Naval ships, moved much faster. One typical convoy of victuallers sailed

[40] NMM, MKH/110, Captain Puget to Hood, 17 May 1808.
[41] TNA, ADM 80/145, Keats, Memorandum, 16 Sept. 1808.
[42] See for example NMM, G.217:2/1, 'Chart of the Gulf of Bothnia and Tilsern rocks, on scale communicated by Rear Admiral George Hope', August 1811. The chart shows the traverses and soundings taken by the Royal Navy finding their way into newly published charts.
[43] Davey, 'Nautical Knowledge', p. 97.
[44] Crowhurst, *Defence of British Trade*, p. 74.

from the Nore on 13 June 1809, arrived in the Belt on 1 July and then reached Saumarez in the eastern Baltic (Nargen Island) on the 21 July.[45] However the threat to British supply lines was a consistent problem. The threat of Danish privateers spread to the Belt as well as the Sound; large numbers of gunboats were placed at Nyborg and other Danish ports. Captain Graves, of the *Brunswick*, wrote to Saumarez in August 1808, after only a few months of action in the Baltic, that 'the increasing force of the enemy's Gunboats render it absolutely necessary that convoys should be very strongly protected'.[46] Captain John Harvey Boteler would later observe the difficulty of convoying large numbers of vessels through the Belt: 'we were mostly employed conveying large bodies of merchant vessels through the Great Belt, and arduous service; the passage was swarming with privateers and row-boats'.[47] Rear Admiral Keats warned his captains that, 'it is my direction that the Ships and Vessels under my orders in the Belt are kept in readiness for action at the Shortest notice, that the most vigilant look-out be established, and in calms and light winds that guard be showed especially in those directions that is may be more particularly requisite to guard against surprise from'.[48] Even through the Belt then, the Baltic fleet's supply lines were far from secure.

Adverse currents also hampered ships passing through the Sound and the Belt, sometimes delaying communications and individual voyages for weeks. In July 1808, Saumarez wrote to his wife, reporting that he was 'proceeding thro' the Great Belt, but such is the contrariety of Currents that with a fresh breeze and favourable, we scarcely make any progress'. A year later he would again write

> A favourable breeze brought us to the Entrance of the Baltic but here I fear we are likely to be detained by the adverse currents which are so strong that even with a fresh breeze we can make no way against them, and we have been obliged to anchor at different times – it is very trying to our Patience, anxious as I have [been] for some time to join the ships in the Baltic; a large Convoy is following us under the same predicament, and I wish only a few of the wealthy Merchants were on board to witness the causes of the delay to their Trade – without so unreasonably ascribing it to the negligence of Officers.[49]

---

[45] See convoy of *Curlew*, TNA, ADM 7/791/118.
[46] TNA, ADM 1/6/401–2, Captain Gates to Saumarez, 3 Aug. 1808.
[47] Boteler, *Recollections*, p. 10.
[48] TNA, ADM 80/145, Keats, Memorandum, 15 Sept. 1808.
[49] Saumarez to Martha Saumarez, 8 July 1808, 24 May 1809, Voelcker, *Saumarez vs. Napoleon*, p. 46.

Even beyond the Sound and Belt there were further dangers. A number of French corsairs operated continuously during the period from bases on the south coast of the Baltic.[50]

Geographical factors played a huge role in determining eighteenth-century naval operations, most notably the extreme difficulty in making progress against the wind.[51] Prevailing westerly winds during the summer made entering the Baltic easier than leaving it. And indeed, ships travelling in either direction could spend days waiting for suitable winds. This could delay victuallers and put at risk the whole fleet. Saumarez wrote in 1808 that 'the contrary Winds have prevented these last five weeks the arrival of the Victuallers I expected from England with the Provisions for the Squadron under my command. It was not until four days since that they have been enabled to join Rear Admiral Sir Samuel Hood off Moen Island, and I waited here for those supplies in order to proceed off Hango Udd and join the Squadron of His Swedish Majesty'.[52] In late 1809, Saumarez contemplated the relative merits of sending merchant ships under only a light convoy, to ensure their earlier arrival in Britain. In a letter to the Admiralty, he wondered

> whether under the present circumstances of the Season I am of opinion His Majesty's Ships may with safety be sent upon this service . . . I do not consider it in the safety of His Majesty's Ships appointed for the protection of the Trade and those stationed in the Belt to defend them against the Attack of the Danish Gun Boats, that they should be ordered to remain in the Baltic to a later Period, particularly after the disastrous events that occurred last season, when so many of His Majesty's Ships were lost, and others exposed to imminent *Danger*, besides the number of valuable Vessels which were wrecked and fell into the hands of the enemy.[53]

It was always to be a difficult choice between the threat of the enemy and the threat from the climate. While much of the trading season suffered from calms, after October the weather could deteriorate rapidly. The passage home from the Baltic Sea made victims of many ships. In 1808, a convoy was lost in the Sound when trying to force its way through the ice. In 1810, the *Minotaur* was wrecked returning from the Baltic. In 1811 the last convoy to leave the Baltic was hit by a storm, with the loss of *St George*, *Defence* and *Hero*. This 'melancholy fate', as A. N. Ryan termed

---

[50] Ryan, 'Defence of British Trade', p. 449.
[51] N. A. M. Rodger, 'Weather, Geography and Naval Power in the Age of Sail', *Journal of Strategic Studies* 22/2 (1999), 178–200, p. 178.
[52] SRO, HA 93/6/1/237, Saumarez to Baron de Rajalin, 5 Aug. 1808.
[53] TNA, ADM 1/9/306–7, Saumarez to Admiralty, 7 Dec. 1809.

it, shocked the nation: 'the deaths of 2,000 men of the Baltic fleet were a loss heavier by far than those suffered in any of the great sea-battles of the Revolutionary or Napoleonic Wars'.[54]

Depending on the weather, the last convoys would leave the eastern Baltic by late November to avoid winter storms and the sea freezing over. Every winter the Baltic would freeze over for up to four months, bringing further problems, as the majority of the fleet sailed back to English ports, leaving a number of smaller ships to be victualled at anchorage in the Baltic. 'The proportion must be calculated for the time it will be neces- sary for the large Ships to remain in the Country', wrote George Hope, anticipating the winter months ahead in the Baltic, 'and for the number of smaller vessels that may be kept out during the winter months.'[55] It left a considerable challenge of timing to the commander in chief. Should he return early, ensuring his fleet's safety from storms and ice, or should he risk the latter, in the hope of ensuring every last merchant ship could be convoyed home before the ice advanced? Such decisions weighed heavily with Saumarez.

Dealing with the ice during those winter months led to further victual- ling problems. Keats spoke of 'the impediments arising from the Season', in particular 'the difficulties I experience in providing the Ships with Provisions and water especially'.[56] Talking of a convoy, Captain Bathurst reported that HMS *Magnet* had run aground, and that he was 'sorry to say that the whole got so entangled in the ice as not to be able to get through'.[57] The process of removing a ship from the ice is recounted in some detail by Boteler:

> It was getting rather late in the year when we returned to Wingoe Sound, and I well remember thrashing through the ice, occasionally brought up by it, and our having capstan bars over the bows to save the copper: all the fore part of the ship was covered with ice, the ropes so frozen as with difficulty to run through the blocks. However, we got into Wingoe, in perfect smooth water, and one morning there was a sort of film over it, and by the evening thick ice had formed, and next morning the ship was hard and fast in ice five or six inches thick . . . I don't know how long we were frozen up, but I recollect the fun of clearing a transport of provisions with our boats on skids. In the end we were relieved by ice-saws, sent I believe from England. We set to work, and by cutting out squares of ice,

---

[54] A. N. Ryan, 'The Melancholy Fate of the Baltic Ships in 1811', *MM* 50/2 (May 1964), 123–34, p. 131.
[55] TNA, ADM 1/6/382, Captain George Hope, Memorandum, 1 Aug. 1808.
[56] SRO, HA 93/6/1/458, Keats to Saumarez, 28 Dec. 1808.
[57] SRO, HA 93/6/1/477, Captain Walter Bathurst to Bertie, 7 Jan. 1809.

which with the capstan bars, handspikes, and hooks we shoved under ice on either side, till we made a canal, and warped the ship to open water outside.[58]

Victuallers too would be vulnerable, such as when the *President* victualler was lost in December 1809.[59] The following year, Captain Honeyman of the *Ardent* reported 'the loss of the *Jean* Transport', and asked for another to replace it 'without delay, in order that the Island of Anholt may not suffer from this accident . . . we have to request you will forthwith provide us with another Vessel, capable of conveying to Anholt a supply of Provisions to the extent of about 180 tons'.[60] These supply problems were compounded by the fact that there was no naval base in the Baltic. The Mediterranean benefited from a number of British bases, in particular Gibraltar on its western edge, and Port Mahon in Minorca, where victualling operations were centred. Alongside their lack of precedents to guide them, Saumarez's Baltic fleet did not have the luxury of British naval ports. Moreover, the Victualling Board had been able to transport fleets of victuallers through the Bay of Biscay to Lisbon, but had never attempted passages as dangerous as the Great Belt. As Ryan argued, 'the want of a base in the Baltic was not as serious as had been the want of a base within the Mediterranean; but it had its inconveniences and perils'.[61]

The various climactic, geographical and hydrographical challenges provided by the Baltic Sea also influenced commercial ship-owners. The following chapter shows how the victualling system was dependent on hiring merchant tonnage to transport provisions. James Thornton, the agent in South Shields for Henley and Sons, ship-owners who regularly chartered their ships out to the British government, wrote of the difficulty he had had in securing tonnage to go to the Baltic in September, particularly places away from the main commerce routes: 'I have used every Endeavour to get [a] Vessel at our Port and the Neighbouring Ports without effect, Money will not tempt them to go to the Anholt to discharge Cargo this day of the year.' The climate and the likelihood of being taken by Danish gunboats were huge disincentives for ship-owners deciding whether to allow their vessels to travel to the Baltic. Thornton went on to say that a

---

[58] Boteler, *Recollections*, pp. 39–40.

[59] The wreck of the *President* transport ship may have provided the inspiration for the painting on the cover of this book, J.M.W. Turner's 'Wreck of a Transport Ship'. Painted in 1810, it depicts a transport vessel battling a violent sea, with a Norwegian coastline in the background.

[60] TNA, ADM 110/62/390, Victualling Board to the Transport Board, 24 Sept. 1810.

[61] Ryan, 'Melancholy Fate', p. 131.

friend of his 'did write for vessels there and offered 50/- ton to load scotch coals . . . I hope we shall have answer tomorrow or Sunday, I still flatter my self that money will tempt some of them in Scotland'.[62] Indeed, two days later the agent believed he had found a vessel to go, but was informed that the owners had 'refused to let her go to the Anholt'. He was doubtful that he would find a vessel to carry coal to Anholt, though he promised to use all of his powers to secure one.[63] Two weeks later, after considerable delay, the *Ann* came forward to supply the necessary tonnage but even then on the condition that it would go to Gothenburg first. The owners of the *Ann* had secured a steep price, no doubt sensing the desperation of the agent. 'I am to be paid the sum of one hundred Pounds per keel in full on the safe delivery of the Cargo', recorded the ship's owner.[64] Mobilising the assets of the British economy for war always faced the conflicting demands of national need and cost. Providing transport tonnage for Baltic operations would require careful management between 1808 and 1812.

The challenge for the Victualling Board in supplying the Baltic fleet was considerable. Mulgrave may have underestimated the challenge when he hoped provisioning arrangements were in order in July 1808 but the Victualling Board was sure of its ability to transport large quantities of victuals to a foreign fleet. Previous precedents suggested that logistical issues could be overcome. Yet as this chapter has demonstrated, and as Chapters 6 and 7 will also show, problems deriving from the geography, weather and climate would continue to influence Baltic provisioning throughout the 1808–12 period. The challenges facing the Baltic fleet in 1808 in ensuring regular and good-quality provisions must not be underestimated nor forgotten in any analysis of its success. The task would be taken up by the British naval administration.

[62] NMM, HNL 13/17, f. 7, 22 Sept. 1809.
[63] NMM, HNL 13/17, f. 10, 29 Sept. 1809.
[64] NMM, HNL 13/17, f. 11, 9 Oct. 1809.

4

The Administration of Power Projection

THE CONCEPTION OF BRITISH STRATEGY, and its ultimate execution, required the involvement of personnel from across government, from cabinet ministers to the lowliest departmental clerk. At the head of government was the Cabinet, the executive branch comprised of members of the legislature, the House of Commons and House of Lords. It was here that government policy was determined. In 1808 it was a Cabinet decision to send a fleet to the Baltic. This marked a much broader movement to ratchet up the British war effort. In March 1807, following the collapse of the misleadingly named 'Ministry of All the Talents', the supporters of Pitt once again returned to power, headed by the duke of Portland, and brought fresh direction to the war against Napoleon. Very little of this was down to Portland himself; the historian Peter Dixon has noted that 'he did not regard personal parliamentary activity as one of his obligations'.[1] An increasingly ill man, Portland was an acceptable figurehead for a group of ambitious ministers who took on more responsibility, bringing increased organisation and drive to British war-planning. In particular, the Foreign Secretary, George Canning, and Lord Castlereagh at the War Office took control of the war against France. Both understood that Britain was fighting in a conflict for national survival. Canning embarked on an assertive foreign policy that saw Britain's place in the world in almost Hobbesian terms. He ordered the attack on Copenhagen in 1807 that pushed the boundaries between realpolitik and international law. In its aftermath he laid out his world view, and his plans for victory:

> With a northern confederacy formed against us, we should have had to contend with fears at home as well as with the enmity of all Europe (for we must not disguise the fact from ourselves – we *are* hated throughout Europe and that hate must be cured by fear); not to mention America who will probably now listen to reason. We have now, what we had once before and once only, a maritime war in our power unfettered by any considerations of whom we may annoy or whom we may offend. And we

---

[1] Peter Dixon, *Canning: Politician and Statesmen* (London, 1976), p. 107.

have (what to God poor Pitt had ever resolved to have) determination to carry it through.[2]

His colleague Castlereagh well understood the demands of a war unprecedented in scale. The war, he noted in 1807, was 'no longer a struggle for territory or for point of honour, but whether the existence of Great Britain as a naval power is compatible with that of France'.[3] Castlereagh brought new vision to the War Office. On finding only 12,000 troops available as he took office, he began to increase the size of the army. From the militia 30,000 men were taken and trained as first-rank troops. The system of transports was improved, so that what force existed could be made available for rapid service wherever it might be needed.[4] Portland's government determined to follow up the attack on Copenhagen by landing an expeditionary force in Europe. Canning briefly considered opening up an offensive front in Denmark, but became less enthusiastic following Sir John Moore's failure in Sweden.[5] It eventually went to Spain, beginning Britain's involvement in the Peninsular War.

A government determined to wage war at a new level depended on the success of its departmental administrative system. Secretaries of state executed the Cabinet's plans and kept government administration working: they alone had the power to coordinate the actions of various departments.[6] The Cabinet determined strategy, while it fell to the Foreign Office, the War Office, the Board of Ordnance and the Admiralty to execute it. The Admiralty oversaw subordinate boards with differing responsibilities: the Victualling Board, the Transport Board and the Navy Board. It required sophisticated planning between the fiercely independent Cabinet institutions to ensure that operations were kept secret, and executed.[7] That this was sometimes lacking should not be surprising; delays and deficiencies in equipment frequently occurred, though the state did become increasingly adept at planning, assembling and dispatching foreign expeditions relatively quickly, especially while Castlereagh was in office.[8] Indeed, the

---

[2] TNA, PRO 30/29/8/4/324.

[3] Boyd Hilton, *A Mad, Bad and Dangerous People? England 1783–1846* (Oxford, 2006), p. 212.

[4] J. Steven Watson, *The Oxford History of England: The Reign of George III, 1760–1820* (Oxford, 1960), p. 454.

[5] Sir John Moore, sent with his army to Sweden to assist their war against Russia, managed to offend the Swedish king so much he was arrested, and forced to return to Britain. Watson, *Reign of George III*, p. 457.

[6] Syrett, *Shipping and the American War*, p. 5.

[7] Hilton, *England 1783–1846*, pp. 85–6.

[8] C. J. Bartlett, *Castlereagh* (London, 1966), p. 53.

duke of Portland's government was defined by its departmentalism. As his chancellor, Spencer Perceval wrote 'it is not because the Duke of Portland is at our head that the Government is a Government of Departments, but it is because the Government is and must be essentially a Government of Departments that the Duke of Portland is at our head'.[9] Once a strategic decision had been made that concerned the navy its implementation fell upon naval administration to execute it.

The Admiralty and the naval administration

The Admiralty was the centre of naval administration. Headed by the First Lord of the Admiralty, and made up of seven commissioners, it was the political arm of the navy, and the sole representative of the navy in Cabinet. If the navy had a role in forming national strategy it was in this capacity. Aside from its influence in shaping Cabinet decisions, the Admiralty governed the naval branch of government, issuing orders on operational and tactical matters: assigning ships and captains in line with the orders of Cabinet, issuing orders for ship movements, assigning convoys, recruiting (and impressing) and confirming appointments. It had further minor administrative roles: paying off ships, purchasing prizes, dispensing with accounts, organising courts martial. The naval officer's point of contact with home, with the government and with the civil branch of the navy was always through the Admiralty. It was through the Admiralty they received their orders and instructions, and sent their dispatches.[10] Grievances concerning the administration of the navy were sent to the Admiralty. Complaints about the victualling system would therefore land at the Admiralty office. The First Lord in 1808, Viscount Mulgrave, would be a major recipient of comments, suggestions and criticisms. In 1810 he annotated a letter outlining abuses in the contracting for staves. He ordered the letter to be kept, and noted 'his charges of abuse in the Conduct of the Victualling Board should be addressed to the Admiralty Board collectively.[11] The Admiralty was the body that connected commanders at sea with the Victualling Board. The decision to arrange a victualling shipment to a fleet was the Admiralty's. The day-to-day running of the board fell on its secretaries and clerks; accordingly a sudden change in the membership of the Board did not disturb the navy's business. It therefore employed men of long professional service, while its correspondence and proceedings were formally recorded.

---

[9] Watson, *Reign of George III*, p. 444.
[10] Wilkinson, *The British Navy and the State*, p. 20.
[11] MA 22/9, W. Budge to Lord Mulgrave, 13 Jan. 1810.

Departmentalism in the naval administration meant that different boards had discrete responsibilities unaffected by political changes in the Admiralty. The main departments subsidiary to the Admiralty were the Navy Board, the Victualling Board, the Sick and Hurt Board and the Transport Board, the latter also reporting to the War Office. The Admiralty had seniority over the subordinate boards, appointing commissioners for each, though the relative longevity of each department influenced its status. For example, the newest, the Transport Board, which had been re-established in 1794 after a seventy-year absence, lacked the standing of its neighbours. The oldest, the Navy Board, was largely left to its own devices. Although the senior body, the Admiralty's control over the Navy Board was 'often meaningless', since the Navy Board was left to its own expertise: 'to avoid a situation where the amateurs of the Admiralty were directing the experts in the Navy Board'.[12] The Navy Board administered the dockyards, contracted for and administered all naval stores and equipment (except for ordnance), food and medicines and, before 1794, transport. It was also responsible for ship design, compiling the estimates that the Admiralty would submit, the payment of wages and appointing dockyard personnel. The Navy Board was made up of professional men, frequently naval officers or shipwrights.[13]

The administration of the provisioning system was in the hands of the Victualling Board and Transport Board. Both of these departments relied on the strength of the British economy to function, particularly a large merchant marine, and a vast and varied agricultural market that made contracting on a large-scale possible. The state lacked the means and infrastructure to produce the vast quantities of foodstuffs needed for the navy, or indeed to build and maintain the substantial amounts of transport tonnage needed to ship resources around the world. In this regard, naval strength was directly tied to the broader economic context. Neither France nor Spain could count on the same level of private-sector resources, or the procedures and mechanisms for mobilising them. Both the British Victualling and Transport Boards forged a complex and mutually reliant relationship with the private sector.

The Victualling Board was responsible for the production of foodstuffs, either through its victualling yards or by securing contracts with merchants to supply the necessary amounts of provisions. Foodstuffs were purchased centrally by contract or on commission, locally by agents at the yards, or by

---

[12] Wilkinson, *The British Navy and the State*, p. 23.
[13] Syrett, *Shipping and the American* War, p. 20.

officials of the forces overseas.[14] All stocks were monitored meticulously in London, from where orders for new deliveries were made. By end of eighteenth century the Victualling Board had shaken off its reputation for inefficiency. In 1788 the commissioners on fees noticed that the department had 'for some time past' been the focus of public attention, but acknowledged 'the zeal and integrity' which had motivated its 'many able servants of the Crown' and observed 'the ability, practical knowledge and character' of those in post. By the 1790s, the board possessed an unrivalled knowledge of the food supply.[15] They obtained estimates for the provisioning requirements for up to a year at a time and were responsible for producing and contracting for these amounts. In August 1808 the Victualling Board requested the Admiralty to estimate the number of men 'intended to be provided for' the following year, so that they could have sufficient warning to direct such supplies of beef and pork to be procured.[16] On receiving an order from the Admiralty to provide provisions for a fleet in foreign waters, it was the Victualling Board's responsibility to work out the amount needed to provide for a fleet for a given period of time.

The Victualling Board officials could be very deferential to the Admiralty, even when they had better access to victualling information than their overseers. A letter from Rear Admiral Dixon in 1809, indicating that the squadron under his command had only three months' provisions remaining and requesting that a further supply of two months' provisions of all species be sent out soon, prompted diffidence rather than an assured response. The Victualling Board wrote to the Admiralty and requested 'such directions thereon as to their Lordships may appear expedient, noting that two months' worth of provisions had recently been sent out, unbeknownst to Rear Admiral Dixon'.[17] Again, it was felt necessary to gain Admiralty authorisation when sending out deliveries. Since Victualling Board commissioners were appointed by the Admiralty, deference on the part of Victualling Board officials is unsurprising. Certainly the Victualling Board was an obedient servant to the Admiralty: in 1811, speaking of an Admiralty order, they stated that 'we cannot presume to deviate from it, nor is it for us to question its

[14] For an authoritative analysis of the make-up, tasks and economic functions of the Victualling Board during the wars against revolutionary and Napoleonic France see Knight and Wilcox, *Sustaining the Fleet*.

[15] See the Eighth Report of the Commissioners on Fees, p. 15. Morriss, *Foundations of British Maritime Ascendency*, pp. 271, 281.

[16] TNA, ADM 1/154/506, Admiralty to Victualling Board, 4 Aug. 1808.

[17] TNA, ADM 111/192, 13 Oct. 1809. The Admiralty's reply arrived three days later, stating that no further supply was needed, see TNA, ADM 111/192, 16 Oct. 1809.

propriety'.[18] Authorisation aside, for the most part the Admiralty was happy to leave the Victualling Board to its expertise in the area of provisioning. Its orders appear less dictatorial, delegating authority to officials who knew their business. The absence of virtually any Victualling Board correspondence in the Admiralty 'in-letters' after 1810 is testament to this. In 1809, a request by Saumarez for four weeks' provisions for his fleet was given a simple 'refer to Vict. Bd.' notation.[19] Writing directly to the Victualling Board saved time, and enabled the Victualling Board to demonstrate its specialist knowledge and expertise with minimal Admiralty interference or friction.

There were two ways in which provisions could be ordered to a distant station. Initially, in 1808 and 1809, the Admiralty would receive a request from a commander in chief for provisions.[20] The Admiralty then informed the Victualling Board of a fleet's needs, and directed the Victualling Board to comply accordingly.[21] Secondly, and increasingly, the Victualling Board oversaw provisioning demands, and took on greater responsibility for ordering and managing shipments of foodstuffs. By 1810, it was the Victualling Board, who by paying attention to the state of provisions in the Baltic, were deciding and organising victualling shipments themselves. Either way, orders for the provisioning of a fleet always came from the Admiralty. While this order to the Victualling Board could be done by letter, it was sometimes done verbally, for example on one occasion in 1809, 'the Chairman having represented that he has been verbally directed by the Lords Commissioners of the Admiralty, to cause a further supply of Provisions to be forthwith sent out for the use of His Majesty's Ships in the Baltic'.[22] Occasionally, when discussing specific supplies of individual foodstuffs, some commanders would write directly to the Victualling Board, leaving it to that board to gain Admiralty acquiescence.[23]

It was crucial to have either Admiralty or Treasury authorisation to arrange a shipment of provisions. On one occasion in August 1809, the Transport Board wrote to the Victualling Board, and requested provisions for 20,000 men. The Victualling Board was adamant that Admiralty authorisation must be secured first. They replied that 'there is not any

---

[18] TNA, ADM 111/199, 13 June 1811.

[19] TNA, ADM 1/9/215–16, Saumarez to Admiralty, 7 Nov. 1809.

[20] See for example, TNA, ADM 111/192, 11 Sept. 1809, an order from Sir James Saumarez for provisions for 12,000 men for two months.

[21] See for example TNA, ADM 2/156/185–6, Admiralty to Victualling Board, 19 May 1809.

[22] TNA, ADM 111/192, 16 Aug. 1809.

[23] See for example TNA, ADM 2/156/441–2, Admiralty to Victualling Board, 19 Aug. 1809.

instance of Provisions being furnished by this Department, and sent out of the Kingdom without the immediate directions of the Lord Commissioners of His Majesty's Treasury, His Majesty's Secretaries of State or the Lords Commissioners of the Admiralty'. The Victualling Board were not simply sticklers for procedure. They did propose a compromise, 'in order that no time may be lost in the execution of the service mentioned in their letter'; they informed the Transport Board that 'the Tonnage required for the Provisions in question will be equal to 1,200 Tons, and that the necessary orders will be given to our officers to have the Provisions in readiness to be shipped on board the vessels that may be appropriated to receive them, the moment we receive the requisite authority for supplying the same'.[24] The hierarchy of naval administration was clear. The Treasury order for the same came through on 31 August.

There were two things the board looked at when calculating the amount to send out. Firstly, they considered the number of men on the station, with supplies sent out to feed them for specific periods.[25] Secondly, the board also consulted the reports of the state of provisions in each fleet, which could override all other calculations if it appeared that a fleet was in desperate want. In September 1809, the chairman of the board having seen 'the last state of the Provisions on Board the Baltic Fleet', he ordered a further supply of flour, raisins and suet. The board was continually assessing the state of provisions in their distant fleets and covering any potential oversights. In this case, it was ordered that the quantities of those articles mentioned were to be forwarded to the Baltic: 72,000 lbs of flour, 12,000 lbs of raisins and 6,000 lbs of suet, each calculated with regard to the fleet's needs.[26] As it was left to the Victualling Board to work out the specific amounts needed by the fleet, decisions over supply were, for the most part, centralised in London: there was an assumption that the Victualling Board had better access to information and could judge the wider picture better than commanders at sea. In one case in 1808, the board wrote to Saumarez, advising him of the precise quantities of provisions shipped, designed to last until 'the middle of December next'.[27] The Victualling Board made careful calculations as to what was needed, aware of the perils that could come from either over-supply or under-supply. The former was considered wastage, and to a naval administration obsessed with avoiding

---

[24] TNA, ADM 111/192, 26 Aug. 1809.
[25] There were quarterly lists made up by the Admiralty, detailing the number of ships and men on each station around the world, now TNA, ADM 8.
[26] TNA, ADM 111/192, 11 Sept. 1809.
[27] TNA, ADM 111/188, 22 Aug. 1808.

unwanted surpluses was very much frowned upon. Conversely, a shortage would result in the starvation of a fleet, with consequent ramifications for operational (and therefore strategic) viability. Judging this estimate was a crucial part of the board's duties.

Once an order to provision a foreign fleet was received, the Victualling Board would then request the necessary tonnage for its delivery from the Transport Board. The Transport Board was located in Dorset Square in Westminster.[28] As such, it was a thirty-minute walk from the Victualling Board offices in Somerset House on the Strand; close enough to ensure letters could be exchanged daily, but far enough to preclude verbal communication and decision-making. All Victualling Board correspondence with the Transport Board was therefore written. This ensured official business could be substantiated and minuted in case a board's activities came into question. The Transport Board's domain was the delivery of all stores worldwide, not just food provisions. It hired and appropriated ships and vessels for the conveyance of troops and baggage, victualling, ordnance and naval and military stores of all kinds, including convicts to New South Wales, with many other smaller services.[29] This took place on hired vessels or 'freight', which were paid relative to their tonnage to transport victuals to the fleet. Just like their colleagues in the Victualling Board, the Transport Board relied on mobilising resources from the private sector to organise the vast amounts of transport shipping needed to fulfil the British state's needs. By 1801 the board had contracts with over 300 owners. As a result, it was more able to pick and choose its ships and contractors. Registration of shipping having begun in 1787, the process of hire was simplified by the decision to take the registered tonnage of ships to indicate their size instead of measuring their tonnage. This reduced the cost of surveying – the cumulated saving was estimated at £1,222,000 in 1815. By end of the War of 1812, the board had nearly a thousand ships under hire, which was 5 per cent of the ships and 11 per cent of the tonnage of the entire British merchant fleet.[30]

Since the Transport Board possessed an authority that was independent of the existing naval boards, it tried to maintain a spirit of fierce

---

[28] This is now Cockspur Street, running into eastern Pall Mall, and is not to be confused with the Dorset Square near Paddington. See John Tallis, *London Street Views 1838–40* (London, 2002), p. 85.

[29] Commission of Naval Revision, Ninth Report, p. 9.

[30] Simon P. Ville, *English Shipowning during the Industrial Revolution: Michael Henley and Son, London Shipowners, 1770–1830* (Manchester, 1987), p. 96. Morriss, *Foundations of British Maritime Ascendency*, pp. 23, 341.

independence from the Admiralty and its subordinate departments.[31] In 1811, it wrote to the Admiralty, stating that only over naval concerns were they to be considered to be in the naval hierarchy: 'the services relating to the Transport Department are placed, by Patent, under the authority of the Lords Commissioners of the Treasury, and those which have reference to sick and wounded seamen and Prisoners of War, under the Lords Commissioners of the Admiralty'.[32] The distinction was important, for the Transport Board always emphasised its connection with the Treasury rather than with the Admiralty. When asked by the Admiralty if there were any reforms that could be implemented 'with advantage to the public service', the board's retort questioned why the Navy Board should be involved in passing their accounts:

> The Navy Board only are authorised to pass the Accounts of the Victualling Board with the treasurer of the Navy. The accounts of this office with the treasurer of the Navy have hitherto been passed in the same manner, by order of the Lords of the Treasury, but as there seems an Impropriety in the Commissioners of the Navy passing accounts of an office with which they have in fact nothing to do.[33]

While it certainly attempted to distance itself from the Admiralty, helped by the direct link to the Treasury and its other duties hiring for the Ordnance Board and the army, when it came to the organisation of victualling shipments to the navy, the Transport Board was very much one of the subordinate boards to the Admiralty. The Admiralty issued the formal orders for victualling the fleet, the other boards complied. The Victualling Board, having requested the necessary tonnage from the Transport Board, was free to complain to the Admiralty if it showed any negligence in the duty of procuring tonnage. Indeed, the Victualling Board appears to have relished the task, given the frequency of their complaints. A letter to the Admiralty in September 1808 was one of the many letters of complaint about their peers in the Transport Board:

> for the information of their Lordships, that upon the receipt on the 6th inst. of their Lordships abovementioned directions, we, on that day, applied to the Transport Board requesting they would cause us to be furnished with all possible expedition, with proper Vessels for the conveyance of the Provisions we were directed to send out for the aforesaid service; to which application not any reply has hitherto been given to us by the Transport Board.[34]

[31] Morriss, 'Colonization, Conquest', p. 317.
[32] TNA, ADM 1/3763/515–37, 7 Feb. 1811.
[33] Ibid.
[34] TNA, ADM 110/58/239/41, Victualling Board to Admiralty, 16 Sept. 1808.

The Admiralty would again be involved when transports were ready to sail; on being told by the Victualling Board that the 'delivery' was ready, it was the Admiralty's responsibility to organise a convoy. Victualling transports were generally added to trade convoys heading to the Baltic. Important deliveries could, however, be assigned their own convoy.

The Transport Board: contracting for tonnage

As shown in Chapter 2, the victualling system was rarely troubled by shortages in the victualling yards. Conversely, shortages of shipping were a recurring and significant problem. A delay in securing tonnage would have huge consequences for the victualling system; power projection relied on those administering the transport service. Fleets in foreign waters, such as in the Baltic, depended on the Transport Board's ability to secure a constant supply of transports on which the essential provisions could be shipped. As in the 1780s, the majority of ships contracted to the navy entered under charters which ran for an indefinite period of time. The success of the British war effort depended to a considerable degree on the ability of naval administration to charter sufficient shipping on a long-term basis.[35] It is not the purpose of this chapter to consider the full challenges that faced the Transport Board, only to consider their part in the provisioning system. As with their colleagues in the Victualling Board, the success of the British war machine would depend on the success with which the Transport Board could harness the resources of the private sector.

There were two forms of transport freight. Firstly there was short-term transport procurement for particular services. Secondly long-term shipping was hired for specific periods. The latter, the longer-term transports, were the backbone of the transport service. They were termed 'transports on tonnage', that is vessels hired at a certain rate per ton each month,[36] However, short-term, specific hires could make up for temporary shortages in transport tonnage. These were of particular importance to the board since they were a means of increasing the amount of tonnage available at short notice. During times of high transport demand, these were common means by which transport tonnage could be raised. The board's ability to secure short-term tonnage gave it huge flexibility, and could also be beneficial to the merchant. With the transport only being hired for the outward journey, it would free up vessels to return with a valuable cargo on board. Alternatively, they could be organised to bring back supplies

[35] Syrett, *Shipping and the American War*, p. 77.
[36] Commission of Naval Revision, Ninth Report, p. 9.

for the navy. They could also return with victualling stores for general use in the victualling yards.[37]

The process by which transports were procured was similar, whether for short-term or long-term hire. The Ninth Report of the Commission of Naval Revision, reporting in 1809, stated that when transports were wanted, the demand was usually signified by sending notice to Lloyds Coffee House, 'where Ship Owners and Brokers continually resort'. Current rates of hire were already established.[38] The board then awaited tenders. An unsent tender lies in the Henley records and provides an example of how this was organised:

> We beg leave to offer to your Honble Board our ship *Anna* 226 Tons, Register Measurement, lying at Union Stairs Wapping for a Regular Coppered Transport at six months certain at the rate of Twenty Five Shillings per ton per Kalendar Month and to be subject to all the rules and conditions of the usual printed Charterparty. We beg leave to observe that this vessel is adapted for the service of your Honble. Board, having Heights in her Hold and 'tween decks, and also that she is in complete readiness for any voyage she may be ordered upon (saving the extra stores requisite in the Transport Service).[39]

Both the Victualling Board and Transport Board had links with the merchant community. On 9 September 1809, for example, the Transport Board wrote to James Henley, requesting his attendance at the board 'on Monday morning at 11 o'Clock'.[40] The following day, after the meeting, the Henleys submitted a tender to supply the island of Anholt in the Baltic with coal. No doubt the board had hinted at a price that was likely to be found acceptable. The Henleys tendered at £6 10s per chaldron (a chaldron was the equivalent of 28 hundredweight, or 3,136 pounds, or 1,422kg) which was accepted by the Transport Board.[41] The Henleys were well known to the Transport Board and had a long history of supplying the board with shipping. It was logical for the board to patronise merchants it knew to be reliable and had a proven history of delivering what was needed. As such, its courting of the Henleys amounts to intelligent organisation of the mercantile sector, and maritime resources. Many ship-owners were powerful

---

[37] See for example TNA, ADM 111/191, Victualling Board to Transport Board, 24 April 1811, which arranged for vessels to be loaded with rice on their return journey from Rio de Janeiro.

[38] Commission of Naval Revision, Ninth Report, p. 10.

[39] NMM, HNL 14/5, f. 10 (no date).

[40] NMM, HNL 13/17, f. 3, 9 Sept. 1809.

[41] NMM, HNL 13/17, f. 4, 12 Sept. 1809.

men, with contacts in government. On one occasion, several of Isaac Solly's ships were detained in Swedish ports, prompting much fury in London. It testifies to Solly's influence, and to Britain's need for hemp, that Canning instructed his consul in Sweden to make representations to the Swedish government, and 'every exertion' in their power to procure their release.[42] He reiterated in a subsequent letter for Merry to 'do everything in your power to protect the whole of them from any molestation'.[43] Ship-owners, particularly those carrying vital resources, were worth looking after.

Once tenders had been received and accepted the ship in question was examined and underwent a survey by the inspecting and surveying officers as to fitness for service. If it passed, this was reported to the board, and a charter party was prepared and executed by the owner, or his agent.[44] The survey was an important part of the procurement process: the Transport Board strove to ensure only high-quality shipping was used. It was written into the contract that the ship-owner did

> promise and agree, that the said Ship or Vessel be strong, firm tight, staunch, and substantial, both above water and beneath, and shall and will sail forthwith as may be directed (Wind and Weather permitting), equipped, fitted, furnished and provided with Masts, Sails, Sail-Yards, Anchors, Ropes, Cords, Tackle, Apparel . . . and shall not have less than tow Bower Anchors and Cables, and One Stream Anchor and Cable, all in good Condition, and shall have all proper Sails, and a complete Set of smaller Sails.[45]

Hall argues that transports were sometimes not ideal for service: for instance, General Sir John Moore grumbled about the unwieldy nature of the convoy taking his troops to Sweden in 1808.[46] However, the Transport Board took this issue very seriously, rejecting those ships that did not meet their standards. On one occasion in 1813, after insisting on a specific quality of ship, Henley was forced to withdraw one of his ships. As he explained, 'the repairs required by your Surveyor to be done to my ships Economy being made to a much greater extent than I could possibly be aware of, I must beg to decline engaging her in the transport service'.[47]

A ship would have to be manned to designated levels, with five men and a boy for every hundred tons, four carriage guns, with twenty rounds per

[42] TNA, FO 73/50, Canning to Merry, 10 Nov. 1810.
[43] TNA, FO 73/50, Canning to Merry, 11 Nov. 1810.
[44] TNA, ADM 1/3763/515–37, 7 Feb. 1811.
[45] NMM, HNL 13/20, f. 8, 4 Sept. 1810.
[46] Hall, *British Strategy*, p. 43.
[47] NMM, HNL 14/5, f. 8, 27 Aug. 1813.

gun, and a secure magazine. No risks were to be taken over the health of the transport seamen, and victuals, furnaces, pumps and cooking utensils were to be placed on board for the crew.[48] Again, this was taken very seriously, particularly by the masters and agents for transports. The order book of one remains, and reveals the lengths ship masters would go to ensure the well-being of their crews. Lieutenant Philip Lamb, principal agent for transports in the Mediterranean in 1799, insisted that no stores or provisions were to be delivered from the transports 'without my knowledge'. 'The Transports Sea Stock of water' was 'to be kept constantly complete and the ships in every other respect perfectly Ready to Proceed to sea on the shortest Notice, there crews and Stores to be kept constantly complete.'[49] Such efforts were not in vain: in December 1801 it was ordered that 'every Transport in this port is to put ready for sea with all possible dispatch & the masters are to report to me immediately they do so'. There was a clear threat if this was not done. 'Those refitting are to use every exertion', he wrote, 'as, if they are not fit to proceed when ordered they will be discharged from service.'[50]

The Henley papers provide an example of a long-term contract, which bears much similarity to the Navy Board's 'standing contract' for hiring transports from 1776.[51] In September 1810, the vessel *Harry Morris*, with David Smith as master, entered into the transport service and served in the Baltic. Michael Henley ordered Smith to report to the resident agent for transports at Yarmouth, where the ship was to enter the service as a three-month transport: 'we trust you will proceed to Yarmouth as soon as you can. You are for the Fleet in the Baltic, or elsewhere in the Baltic as may be ordered'.[52] It was accepted into the transport service on 8 October 1810.[53] The contract entered into was lengthy and detailed. The most important issue was the agreement to mutual advantage; in the words of the contract it was

> covenanted, concluded, and agreed upon this Fourth Day of September . . . the Commissioners for conducting His Majesty's Transport Service &c. for and on behalf of His Majesty, on the other Part, in the manner following; That is to say, the said Michael Henley and Son, for and on behalf of themselves, and all and every one of the owners of the said Ship

---

[48] NMM, HNL 13/20, f. 8, 4 Sept. 1810.
[49] NMM, HNL 34/30, f. 1, 3 Sept. 1799.
[50] NMM, HNL 34/30, f. 1, 25 Dec. 1800.
[51] See Admiralty to Victualling Commissioners, 2 Aug. 1759, Hattendorf *et al.*, *British Naval Documents 1204–1960*, pp. 448–51.
[52] NMM, HNL 13/20, f. 10, 5 Sept. 1810.
[53] NMM, HNL 1/20, f. 13, 8 Oct. 1810.

of Vessel, have granted, and to Hire and Freight . . . to continue in Pay for Three Months Certain . . . all such Soldiers, Horses, Women, Servants, Arms, Ammunition, Provisions Stores, or whatever else shall be ordered to be put on board her, and proceed therewith to such Port or Ports as shall be required.[54]

Specific costs were built into the contract. For example, Michael Henley purchased 150 chaldrons at the rate of 51s per chaldron, with specific allowances for miteage, lighterage and porterage, which was accepted by the Victualling Board, to be paid in ninety-day bills.[55] Once the contracts were signed, the ships entered the government service.

Once in the pay of the Transport Board, the ship was under that board's control, and could be used for a variety of purposes required by the British state. One typical contract stated that

the said Master shall and will receive and take on Board the said Ship or Vessel, from Time to Time, such a Number of Soldiers, Horses, Provisions, Powder, Provender, or any Kind or Sort of Naval Victualling Stores, Recruits, and whatever else there shall be Occasion for, for the Service of His Majesty, as he shall be directed and required, and as he can reasonably stow and carry . . . under Convoy, as the said Commissioners, or the Officer in Chief whose command he shall be under, shall order and direct, landing and delivering the same accordingly.[56]

It was essential that the ship's masters gave, received and kept Bills of Lading (specific receipts for ships) and other indents for supplies received on Board. A log-book of the wind and weather was also kept. At the end of the service, these would be delivered to the Transport Office, 'upon Oath, if required', together with all orders and instructions that he received.[57] The *Freedom* was a transport in the Baltic between April and December 1808. Its records and receipts remain, listing many receipts for supplies bought during 1808. Also kept for the ship's and owner's records were wage accounts, portage bills and receipts for dues.[58]

When under contract, and when sent to join a fleet, the transports came under the orders of the commander in chief. They could then be ordered wherever they were needed. John Stables, master of the *Ann* of Leith, reported that he left the port of Leith laden with ninety-six tons and one hundred-weight of coals for the Island of Anholt. On arriving at Gothenburg

[54] NMM, HNL 13/20, f. 8, 4 Sept. 1810.
[55] TNA, ADM 111/187, 11 June 1808.
[56] NMM, HNL 13/20, f. 8, 4 Sept. 1810.
[57] NMM, HNL 13/20, f. 8, 4 Sept. 1810.
[58] NMM, HNL 59/81, ff. 2–31, April–Dec. 1808.

he applied to the commander in chief, Sir James Saumarez, for a convoy to Anholt, when he received orders from him to stop in Hawke Roads, Gothenburg, to supply the Royal Navy ships on that station with coal. Later under the orders of Captain Reynolds of HMS *Tribune*, 'and also by verbal orders from Admiral Dixon's captain', he applied to Captain Barclay of HMS *Minotaur* for instructions, 'which he received and in conformity thereto sailed from Gottenburgh on the ninth day of January last for the port of Leith with the remainder of the coals on board'.[59] Once signed, a merchant vessel was for all intents and purposes a government vessel.

The Transport Board's relationship with contractors

For the transport service to procure shipping, they were forced to enter the open market and offer freight rates which could compete with those in the civilian carrying trade.[60] Wartime shipping profits outside government service could be considerable. In a time of unprecedented commercial prosperity, it was more advantageous for a merchant to put his ship to a trade than let it to government.[61] In practice though, the fear of capture played a part in a ship-owner's decision and could encourage him to enter into government service. Given the risk of capture, particularly prevalent in the Baltic with Danish gunboats a constant risk through the Sound, the safe, steady profits available with the Transport Board were attractive. The experience of one merchant, Michael Henley and Sons, indicates that owners were capable of making profits from their ships in most years of wartime and that their profits permitted them to enlarge their fleet.[62] This did not necessarily mean, however, that the sole incentive was financial. Added to this was the small amount of effort that went into managing a ship in the pay of the Transport Board. Ship-owners could diversify by employing some vessels in the transport service and some on commercial ventures. The chief advantage of state service was a guaranteed income in return for very little day-to-day management by the owner.[63]

Being insured for any loss was an added benefit. Ships in the transport service would sail at the risk of the government, with the Transport Board compensating the owners for any damage sustained by hostile action. Ship-

---

[59] NMM, HNL 13/17, f. 22, 14 April 1810.

[60] Syrett, *Shipping and the American War*, p. 78; Hall, *British Strategy*, p. 41.

[61] Condon, 'Administration of the Transport Service', p. 3.

[62] Ville, *English Shipowning*, pp. 29, 148–54.

[63] Simon Ville, 'The Deployment of English Merchant Shipping: Michael and Joseph Henley of Wapping, Ship Owners, 1775–1830', *Journal of Transport History* 5 (1984), 16–33, p. 22. Ville emphasises the considerable flexibility of the Henley's deployment.

owners were happy to let ships to the Victualling Board, since they could make money and at the same time protect their investment.[64] Though there was an inquiry into any given claim, with potential negligence on the part of the master investigated, compensation was regularly awarded. At the time a ship was engaged as a transport, her value was estimated jointly by the surveying officer, shipwright officer and storekeeper. It was a condition of the contract that if she was captured by the enemy during her time of service, her value would be paid by government. If a capture took place, the master would detail all the circumstances of the case. A certificate was also required from the commander of the convoy under whose protection she may have been, stating his opinion of the master's conduct. If the fault was the master's or the owner's, determined 'sea-risk', then the board could withhold compensation.[65] If upon investigation it appeared that the ship was unavoidably captured, and that no blame could be attached, a bill of sale was made out and the ship passed into the property of the crown.[66] In both June and July 1809 the treasury ledgers indicate that large payments were made on a regular basis.[67]

Although the potential profits for a merchant chartering his ship were not as great as in some of the Indies trades, nonetheless it is certain that ship-owners, not least the Henleys, made profits. The Henleys could also be paid though the Baltic winter, a time when their ships could not hope to carry trade there. The *Ann*, for example, carried coals to Anholt in 1811. The Transport Board paid Henley and Son £437 2s 10d for the freight of a cargo of coals from Leith, intended for Anholt, and a further £205 16s for demurrage after allowing ten days to unload, from 25 November 1809 to 13 January 1810 (being forty-nine days at four guineas per day as per their agreement). The coal itself cost £101 exactly, including duty, commission and stowage charges. The total owed was therefore £743 18s 10d. Further charges were added for refreight charges. The total owed to Henley was thus £728 10s. This left Henley and Son with an overall profit of £35 8s 10d.[68] It should be said that part of the freight had not been delivered, hence the relatively low profit. A more typical example is the ship *Ceres*. The following year, this vessel also transported coals to the Island of Anholt and completed the

[64] Syrett, *Shipping and Military Power*, p. 55. Morriss, *Foundations of British Maritime Ascendency*, p. 86.

[65] For the definition of 'sea risk', see the Commission of Naval Revision, Ninth Report, p. 10.

[66] A deduction was made for wear and tear, at a rate of eight shillings per ton per annum. TNA, 1/3763/515–37, 7 Feb. 1811.

[67] TNA, ADM 20/324, June and July 1809.

[68] NMM, HNL 13/17, f. 25–6, 2 April 1810.

contract fully. On 1 October 1811 they 'billed' the Victualling Board for the sum of £858 18s, for the freight of 254 chaldrons delivered to Anholt at £3 5s per chaldron, amounting to £825 10s, a further £32 for eight days demurrage at £4 per day, and £1 8s for pilotage. Henley's costs consisted of £139 12s 4d for the coal itself, and £522 9s 4d for freight costs. This left a profit of £196 16s 4d for Henley and Son over a period of three months.[69] This was a more typical level of profit. It was not excessive, especially compared to the lucrative trades being sought elsewhere, but it highlights the relatively small but reliable profits that could be made by a ship in government service.

Ship-owners lending ships to the transport service had other advantages. There were geographic constraints that could be added to a contract. Henley and Sons were keen to limit their ships and masters to northern European waters. Thus, it was written into their contracts that their vessels would operate 'in the European Seas but not to the Eastward of the Rock of Gibraltar'.[70] The war also forced a number of ships out of their regular trades and made them available for the transport service. During the years in which the Baltic was 'closed' (at least in theory) to the British, the percentage of Henley ships employed in the Baltic is very low, particularly in 1810 and 1811. Concurrently, the number of Henley ships employed in the transport service had a plateau during the years 1808 to 1811.

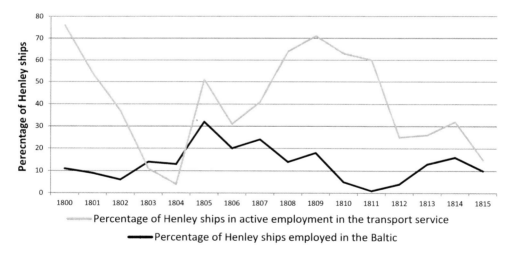

Figure 8. The deployment of Henley ships, 1800–15
Source: Ville, 'Deployment of English Merchant Shipping', p. 25.

---

[69] NMM, HNL 13/23, f. 10, 14–15, 26 July 1811, 31 July 1811, 1 Oct. 1811, 5 Nov. 1811.
[70] NMM, HNL 13/20, f. 8, 4 Sept. 1810. Although it should be added that Henley's did at one point have ships in the West Indies trade.

The Transport Board attempted to provide enough shipping for all the state's needs and achieve this at the best possible price. There were times of increasing demand, as Britain's global commitments rose throughout the war. Figure 9 shows the full tonnage employed by the Transport Board between the years 1807 and 1812. The data is collected from the Transport Board out-letters, which are irregular; unfortunately there is no data for 1811. However, the rise in transport tonnage from 1807 is clear, as is the peak in late 1808 and 1809.

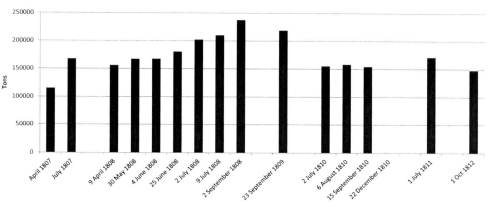

Figure 9. Tonnage in the employment of the Transport Board, 1807–12
Source: TNA, ADM 1/3754–62.

This peak was the result of expanding global commitments, including a rise in the Baltic region, creating a significant demand for transport shipping. In Figure 10, the rise in demand for shipping for the transport service in 1809 is shown by a substantial rise in the number of Henley ships in active employment in the transport service, and the small number laid up. Only by 1812, when Henley vessels were laid up for 18 per cent of the time, did the figure increase; in Ville's words, 'a reflection of the reduced demand for government transports'.[71] The relative security of a government contract (as opposed to mercantile trade) would respond to a raw financial incentive from government. When there existed a great demand for shipping, the Transport Board would raise the freight rates, hoping to encourage more shipping. Raising the financial incentive by increasing the freight rate was a tried and tested method for procuring extra tonnage. Merchants could charge increasingly higher prices as Britain became more desperate for tonnage, for example in 1809.

[71] Ville, 'Deployment of English Merchant Shipping', p. 24.

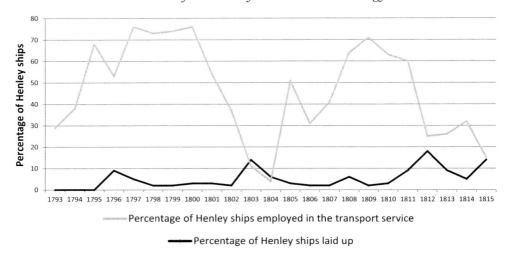

Figure 10. The deployment of Henley shipping 1793–1815
Source: Ville, 'Deployment of English Merchant Shipping', p. 25

Although ship-owners could dictate a price, there were enough ships in the British merchant fleet for there to be a proper market of shipping: the government depended upon managing this market to secure all its shipping needs. In 1807[72] and again in early 1810 the Transport Board's freight rates (the monthly rate paid per ton by the Transport Board) reached the remarkable level of 25 shillings per ton per month, owing to the demands placed on procuring tonnage to carry victuals to the Baltic fleet.[73] This rate continued throughout the rest of 1810.[74] It is clear that London merchants were doing well from the government's spiralling demands. However, paying over the odds in a time of emergency was an established procedure for raising extra tonnage. The war against revolutionary France saw major expeditions that crossed the Atlantic between 1793 and 1797, the second of which took 30,000 soldiers. The victualling needs for these expeditions were extensive: as Michael Duffy has noted, the demand 'brought the British war machinery almost to breaking point'.[75] These expeditions were seriously delayed by a lack of transports. The freight rate, previously static during the eighteenth century, was increased by two-thirds during the eight-year

---

[72] The 1807 expedition to Copenhagen took 377 transports, totalling 78,420 tons. Morriss, *Foundations of British Maritime Ascendency*, p. 342.

[73] TNA, ADM 2/158/115–16, Admiralty to Transport Board, 19 April 1810.

[74] See NMM, HNL 13/20, f. 8.

[75] Michael Duffy, *Soldiers, Sugar and Seapower: The British Expeditions to the West Indies and the War against Revolutionary France* (Oxford, 1987), p. 191.

period of the French Revolutionary War.[76] Freight rates reached a peak in 1813, when it reached 30s.[77] In April 1807, Castlereagh permitted the board to raise the rates to 20 shillings and 25 shillings per ton for vessels hired for three and six months respectively. Total hire rose from 115,157 tons in April to 167,734 tons by July.[78]

When a ship was discharged from service the owners were required to produce certificates from the necessary departments, as evidence of their having accounted for all government stores and cargoes supplied to them by the Victualling, Ordnance or Navy Boards, before the balance of freight remaining due was allowed to be paid. Only when these certificates had been handed in, considered by the sub-accountant and the general accountant, and then laid before the board for approval and allowance, was a bill made out for the balance due.[79] The Transport Board ensured this was written into every contract.[80] The Transport Board thus deferred payment, allowing it to run the transport service on credit.[81] The government always insisted on six months' payment being reserved, 'to enable Government to indemnify itself for any claims which it may have upon the owners'.[82] As the Transport Board made clear in 1811, a bill was issued for two months' hire, payable ninety days after the initial date by the treasurer of the navy. After the ship has been in service for six months, a further payment of two months' hire was made, provided a certificate under the hand of an agent for transports could be produced, stating that she was still employed, complete in men and stores and fit for the service in which she was engaged. An additional bill for two months' freight was issued at the end of ten months. Payments for two months' hire were repeated. This meant that after a transport had been in service for fourteen months, a 'reserve of six months' pay' was kept up, a deposit to cover any stores belonging to the government lost or damaged during the course of the service.[83] This ensured that the government had the means of indemnification for any time lost, whether through neglect of the master or crew, or from inability of the ship to perform the services on which she may have been employed. If a ship

---

[76] Condon, 'Administration of the Transport Service', p. 3.
[77] See TNA, ADM 108/24/53, 3 Dec. 1813.
[78] Hall, *British Strategy*, p. 42.
[79] Ibid.
[80] NMM, HNL 13/20, f. 8, 4 Sept. 1810.
[81] The Navy did a lot of its business on credit. The ability of each board to run its own system of debt-based financing was crucial to the Navy's success. See Knight and Wilcox, *Sustaining the Fleet*, pp. 40–1, 79, 145, 181–3, 196.
[82] Commission of Naval Revision, Ninth Report, p. 11.
[83] TNA, ADM 1/3763/515–37, 7 Feb. 1811.

on short-term service was delayed because of a naval order, for example from a commander in chief, the Transport Board allowed for 'Interest on Transport-Office Bills', for so long a time as the vessels continued in state service. In September 1809 the board agreed to pay the owner of the *Ann*, 'if detained more than ten days after arrival in discharging the Cargo to be paid four guineas per day demurrage'.[84] However, this could work the other way, and with much stronger penalties. Negligence on the part of masters or ship-owners meant ships could be mulcted (fined). It was agreed in the contract between the respective parties that 'upon the Loss of Time, Breach of Orders, or Neglect of Duty' by the master or owner, the commissioners of the Transport Board were permitted to mulct accordingly.[85] The *Ann* was ordered to proceed immediately, 'on the Penalty of having Four-pence per Tun a Day abated from his Freight Bill, in Case of any Neglect or Delay on his Part'.[86]

This was a serious issue. By March 1811, the *Harry Morris* reported to the notary public in Portsmouth. It had served its Baltic portion of service as contracted, with a cargo of coals bound for Anholt. It arrived at Yarmouth and received orders from the resident agent there to proceed to join the convoy for Lisbon.[87] In this latter capacity it had disappointed the board. The *Harry Morris* had missed the convoy to Lisbon and Henleys and Son was mulcted of part of its fee. Two seamen had deserted, the master had not caught the wind and the ship had missed the Lisbon convoy. The Henleys were not paid while it waited for the next convoy. Added to this, they were fined for having a vessel undermanned.[88] The Transport Board was unimpressed, writing to Michael Henley and repeating their intention to 'stop the Pay, and to charge a Mulct against the Transport Harry Morris'.[89] The Transport Board would remember this indiscretion. Three months later the *Harry Morris* once again tendered to serve for the Transport Board. On 4 June, the board wrote to Henley, refusing to accept the tender.[90] Partly this was due to the lower demand for transport tonnage. As we have

---

[84] NMM, HNL 13/17, f. 11, 9 Oct. 1809.
[85] NMM, HNL 13/20, f. 8, 4 Sept. 1810.
[86] NMM, HNL 34/30, f. 3, 5 May 1800.
[87] NMM, HNL 13/20, f. 18, 16 March 1811.
[88] NMM, HNL/13/20, f. 16.
[89] NMM, HNL 13/20, f. 19, 18 March 1811. Six months later, the Transport Board actually reduced the mulct, charging compensation only for the five days the Henley ships had cost them: 'the Board are pleased to remit, to five days, the mulct imposed upon the *Harry Morris*, Coal Transport; that being the time actually lost to Government by her not sailing under the *Hotspur's* Convoy for Lisbon'. NMM, HNL 13/20, f. 24, 5 Nov. 1811.
[90] NMM, HNL 13/20, f. 21, 4 June 1811.

seen, 1809 saw the high point of tonnage requirement but this demand had receded slightly by 1811. That said, it is interesting that it should turn down this particular Henley ship. Indeed, the Transport Board continued to hire other Henley ships: for example, the *Ceres* and the *Grape* in 1811.[91] Although the Transport Board was often needy, it refused to be browbeaten.

The Transport Board was prepared to penalise ship-owners who lent their ships. Such orders came from the very top of government. Perceval, the chancellor and later prime minister, had in 1808 highlighted, the 'very many delays, and not a few accidents . . . occasioned by the desertion, indiscipline, and want of Seamanship – both of Masters and Men in the Transports . . . I believe this is the constant complaint on every occasion when a large body of Transports is employed'.[92] The neglect of a master could absolve the board of any responsibility to buy the vessel. In early 1810, the news of the loss of the *President* victualler in the Baltic broke in London. Rear Admiral Dixon wrote to the Transport Board, complaining of the misconduct of the master of the *President* victualler, urging an investigation, 'before any Certificates be granted to enable the Owners to receive payment of the Freight'.[93] The transference of risk onto the merchant was made clear by the Commission of Naval Revision. The storekeeper signed a bill of lading, and provided blank receipts to the master of the vessel, for respective pursers to sign as provisions were handed over to Royal Navy ships. These receipts were transmitted immediately on the transport's return, accounting for the whole cargo: the ship-owner was answerable financially for any discrepancy.[94] At the same time, the Transport Board could be forgiving: it was in the board's interest, after all, not to anger potential future lenders of freight. When the *Ceres* was required to lie at the island of Anholt for the purpose of discharging its cargo for eighteen days after it arrived, as it waited for the island's boats, the Transport Board was more understanding.[95] The board did not mulct on any delays in this instance.[96]

The Transport Board's power becomes more evident if the post-hire period is considered. The crucial and most ambiguous part of the contract lay in stating the ship's duties after its term of service. For example, the *Harry Morris* was

---

[91] NMM, HNL 13/23, f. 3 25 June 1811.
[92] MA, 19/29.
[93] TNA, ADM 111/194, 12 Jan. 1810.
[94] Commission of Naval Revision, Eleventh Report, p. 74.
[95] NMM, HNL 13/23, f. 3, 25 June 1811.
[96] NMM, HNL 13/23, f. 17, 27 June 1811.

to continue in Pay for Three Months certain, and after that, for so long Time as they the said Commissioners shall require; and until they, or Agents authorised by them, shall give Notice of Discharge; such Notice of Discharge to be given at Deptford or Portsmouth, as may be most convenient for His Majesty's Service, and after the Ships arrival in one of those places.[97]

The ship was contracted to the Transport Board, but after its period in service could be continued in the transport service with or without the ship-owner's consent. This was nothing new. Syrett noted that during the War of American Independence a ship-owner could not withdraw his vessel without the consent of the board. Indeed, it undoubtedly hindered the chartering of additional vessels, since chartering a vessel with the transport service was 'tantamount to economic bondage'.[98] At the same time, there was no confiscation of shipping.[99] For this to be truly effective, the government would have needed to prevent, or at least limit, the tonnage being absorbed into 'non-essential civilian commerce', as occurred in the Second World War. This was beyond the comprehension of eighteenth-century minds.[100] That aside, the Transport Board had continued to insist on including the clause controlling the withdrawal time in contracts. The *Ann*, secured for the Transport Board in 1800, was kept on under this clause.[101] This was as close to commandeering as the eighteenth-century naval administration was prepared to go. Such was the power of mercantile interest, and indeed the threat that other merchants would be dissuaded from entering into the service in the future, that the Transport Board was reluctant to use these powers to the fullest extent.

That said, once on a station, a transport could be retained there indefinitely. In practice, there was little sense in this being done in the Baltic. Dependent on supplies *from* England, keeping transports in the Baltic made little sense. In other theatres, such as the Mediterranean, this was practised. In 1800 Admiral Lord Keith spoke of 'refraining thither, as many Transports and Victuallers as will be fit' for his purposes. Need overcame maxims of early-nineteenth-century property rights.[102] The

---

[97] NMM, HNL 13/20, f. 8, 4 Sept. 1810.

[98] Syrett, *Shipping and the American War*, pp. 102–3.

[99] As argued by Patrick K. O' Brien, 'Merchants and Bankers as Patriots and Speculators? Foreign Commerce and Monetary Policy in Wartime, 1793–1815' in John J. McCusker and Kenneth Morgan, eds., *The Early Modern Atlantic Economy* (Cambridge, 2000), pp. 250–77, at p. 274.

[100] Syrett, *Shipping and the American War*, p. 105.

[101] NMM, HNL 34/30, f. 2, 16 June 1800.

[102] NMM, KEI/L/24/207–8, Keith to Lamb, 17 April 1800.

Victualling Board condoned this practice, stating in July 1800 that vict-uallers hired for the purpose of transporting provisions to the Mediter-ranean were 'invariably taken up on monthly pay' after their terms, 'for the purpose of their being removed to such Ports, and at such times as the Commander in Chief may direct'.[103] This was not commandeering by name: however it was certainly a blurring of the line between state and private property.

The transfer of authority to the Victualling Board and Transport Board was a rationalisation of the victualling service. Each could concentrate in its areas of expertise. The supply of provisions required no little coordina-tion between the two boards; indeed, all victualling arrangements were conducted between the Victualling and Transport Boards. Only in dire circumstances would the Admiralty be forced to intervene. The Transport Board thus proved adept at managing the resources of the private sector for its own ends. Using higher freight-rates and ensuring that the ship's procurement could be extended after the length of the contract, the board took an increasingly large number of vessels into the transport service in the years 1807–12. It should be remembered that loaning a ship to the Transport Board was a more secure option than pursuing the more lucrative and more dangerous mercantile trades. To continue to procure freight, the Transport Board found it necessary to raise the freight rate to unprecedented levels for this essential service.

The procurement of transports was a crucial part of the provision-ing chain. Naval administration had two levels of concern during the Napoleonic Wars. Firstly, could they get it done, and supply what was needed? Secondly, could they provide it at the cheapest possible price? For the Victualling Board, the first was never an issue: they would spend the war attempting to achieve the best possible price for their efforts. For the Transport Board, the straightforward supply of transports could be a cause for concern. The Transport Board was anxious to avoid paying over the odds: it would be wrong to suggest economy was not an objec-tive. However, this desire could be overridden by a more basic need, the chronic want of transport tonnage. The rise in freight rates to 25 shillings demonstrated that, at times, the Transport Board did become desperate and economy was put on the back burner. As such, problems of supply could impact on the provisioning system in a way that was never an issue for the Victualling Board. It would be the failures of the Transport Board

---

[103] TNA, ADM 111/156, 11 July 1800.

that placed the greater strain on the provisioning service. During the first two years of the Baltic fleet's existence, imperfect cooperation between the two would lead to severe problems in the victualling system and intervention from above.

– 5 –

The First Year in the Baltic, 1808

IN OCTOBER 1808, towards the end of his first year in the Baltic, Vice-Admiral Sir James Saumarez visited the Swedish squadron and witnessed first-hand the devastating consequences of an ineffective victualling system. 'On board their ships', he informed the Admiralty, 'I found 1500 Sick all much affected with scurvy, accompanied with dysentery, low fever, and a few Catarrhal complaints . . . all apparently sinking under general debility and despondency; in many instances amounting to insanity, which too frequently terminated in the unhappy sufferer committing suicide'. The situation was worse on land: 'in their hospitals I found 3864 suffering under similar disease', he continued.[1] The poor health of the Swedish forces is a measure against which the efforts of the Royal Navy to supply itself through the Napoleonic Wars can be judged. Employed in the same Baltic region as the Swedish navy, how was it that the British seamen stationed there did not come to suffer from similar problems? A monthly return of sick and wounded on board the Baltic squadron at the end of 1808 found only four cases of scurvy amongst over 11,000 seamen, alongside forty-five cases of rheumatism and thirty-two cases of venereal disease.[2] While the Royal Navy fleet remained healthy, and able to pursue its objective, the Swedish fleet lay stricken in port. This contrast in the respective fortunes of the two navies was firmly rooted on the effectiveness of their logistical systems.

The victualling system in practice, 1808

In April 1808 Saumarez set sail for the Baltic, having received his orders from the Admiralty, and arrived at Gothenburg on 7 May. At its height, his command that year reached forty-four ships, of which eleven were ships of the lines, alongside two 64s, four frigates, ten sloops and five bomb vessels, specialised ships for bombarding positions on land. Two rear

---

[1] TNA, ADM 1/7/278–80, Saumarez to the Admiralty, 16 Oct. 1808.
[2] TNA, ADM 1/8/38.

Table 2. Victualling delivery, 7 June 1808

Bread	5,500 Bags [616,000 lbs]
Spirits	38,500 Gallons [385,000 lbs]
Beef	22,000 pieces of 8 lbs [176,000]
Flour	132,000 pounds
Raisins	22,000 lbs [all lbs unless stated]
Suet	11,000
Pork	44,000 pieces of 4 lbs [176,000 lbs]
Pease	2,750 bushels [154,000 lbs]
Oatmeal	2,062 bushels, 4 Gallons [115,512]
Sugar	33,000
Butter	33,000
Cheese	66,000
Vinegar	5,500 Gallons [55,000]
Tobacco	22,000 lbs
Lemon Juice	38,500 lbs
Sugar for Lemon Juice	38,500 lbs
Coals	171 Chaldrons, 4 Bushels [344,960]
Candles	1,027 dozen lbs
TOTAL	**2,430,796 lbs or 1,215 tons**

Source: TNA, ADM 111/187, 7 June 1808.

admirals commanded squadrons: one, under Sir Richard Godwin Keats, was stationed in the Sound to protect and convoy British trade; the other, under Sir Samuel Hood, patrolled the Gulf of Finland to blockade the Russian fleet at Kronstadt. Later that year, a third rear admiral, Bertie, would be appointed to command the squadron in the Belt. In 1808, the fleet numbered over 11,000 men.[3] To sustain this fleet in the Baltic, the Victualling Board arranged a series of shipments of foodstuffs to be sent to the squadron. During 1808 there were four deliveries of victuals to the Baltic fleet. The Victualling Board was always faced with a dilemma: the more deliveries it made, the fresher the food would be, reducing the risks of delays, while spreading the risk of transport loss at sea. Conversely, they were unable to send out victuallers every few weeks, as such an arrangement would be both expensive and an administrative nightmare. They settled for economies of scale. Though that term is anachronistic, the principle was well understood, with four large deliveries in 1808, representing a balance

[3] TNA, ADM 8/96.

between costliness and regularity. Each delivery provided victuals enough for two to three months. The first was ordered on 7 June 1808, the order coming from the Admiralty to 'provide with all possible expedition a proportion of Provisions of all species for two months for the squadron of His Majesty's Ships and Vessels in the Baltic reporting to their Lordships Secretary when the said Provisions are ready'. Table 2 sets out what was ordered, enough to feed 11,000 men for two months. The Victualling Board then wrote to the Transport Board for the requisite freight, calculated to amount to 1600 tons.[4] Over the following weeks, the Transport Board secured tonnage for this service, reporting to the Victualling Board as each was contracted. Thus, after the order of the 7 June, the Transport Board wrote on the 8 June, 15 June, 17 June, 21 June and 25 June 1808, reporting the state of the transports secured.[5]

On the 15 July 1808 a second shipment was requested, again for two months' provisions.[6] The Victualling Board received orders from the Admiralty to bring about a shipment of foodstuffs, calculated to provide the necessary victuals for a further two months. They then wrote immediately to the Transport Board for the necessary tonnage, requesting that the Transport Board 'will cause us to be *immediately* furnished with proper Vessels for the conveyance thereof, to the extent of 1600 tons'.[7] The Victualling Board assembled the necessary victuals at Deptford, while the Transport Board secured the necessary tonnage. On the 19 July they wrote that they had chartered the following transports: the *Adventure* (146 tons), the *Sisters* (181), the *Lively* (138), the *Margaret* (160), the *Addington* (163), the *Favourite* (125) and the *Betsey* (194), and that 'they are now at Deptford in readiness to load'.[8] Five other transports had earlier been appropriated, and the full tonnage needed had been secured. The transports procured to carry the victuals to the Baltic are listed in Table 3, giving the dates by which they were loaded with provisions. These, fully loaded, then made their way to the Baltic under convoy, arriving in late August. There was a delivery of a similar size and tonnage ordered on 6 September arriving in late October. This was another shipment of two months' provisions of similar quantities to the previous two deliveries. The only major difference was that fewer amounts of meat were sent out. This difference can be explained by the large quantity of

[4] TNA, ADM 111/187, 7 June 1808.
[5] TNA, ADM 111/187, 8 June, 15 June, 17 June, 21 June, 27 June 1808.
[6] TNA, ADM 111/188, 15 July 1808.
[7] TNA, ADM 110/58/44, Victualling Board to Transport Board, 15 July 1808.
[8] TNA, ADM 111/188, 19 July 1808.

Table 3. Transports hired between 17 and 26 July 1808

Lading	Vessel's name	Master's name
17 July 1808	*Active*	R Williams
17 July 1808	*Industry*	D Lindsay
18 July 1808	*John & Francis*	J Aaron
18 July 1808	*Harmony*	E Humphries
19 July 1808	*Diana*	J Collins
25 July 1808	*Adventure*	P Middleyand
25 July 1808	*Betsey*	R Parker
25 July 1808	*Favorite*	W Clarke
25 July 1808	*Margaret*	R Richardson
23 July 1808	*Lively*	W Batho
26 July 1808	*Addington*	N. Parnell
26 July 1808	*Echo*	J Stewart

Source: TNA, ADM 110/58/100–1, Victualling Board to Transport Board, 28 July 1808.

local procurement of fresh meat in the Baltic. Although Sweden could provide few other staples of the seamen's diet, live oxen and fresh beef were available.[9] Otherwise, these were standard deliveries. Transports were procured on 17 September, 20 September and 28 September.[10] There was an urgency to this delivery: 'it being a great importance that the Provisions directed by Minute of the 6th instant to be put on warrant for the Baltic should be shipped with every possible dispatch', to such an extent that 'the Superintendent do cause every exertion to be used to that end'. This included shipping the necessary pease without waiting for kiln drying.[11] A final delivery was ordered by the Admiralty on 23 September. On this date, the Victualling Board received orders from the Admiralty to arrange a further two months' provisions for the Baltic fleet. They then wrote immediately to the Transport Board for the necessary tonnage, estimated to come to 1500 tons.[12]

There were four main victualling deliveries, all of them transporting between 1300 and 1600 tons of victuals. Indeed it is possible to calculate the total tonnage of victuals transported to support the 11,000 men stationed in the Baltic for a year (Table 4).

[9] TNA, ADM 111/188, 15 July 1808, 6 Sept. 1808. Davey, 'Supplied by the Enemy', pp. 269–72.
[10] TNA, ADM 111/188, 17 Sept. 1808, 20 Sept. 1808, 28 Sept. 1808.
[11] TNA, ADM 111/188, 21 Sept, 1808.
[12] TNA, ADM 110/58/259/60, Victualling Board to Transport Board, 23 Sept. 1808.

Table 4. Victualling deliveries, 1808

Date delivery ordered	Total transport tonnage	Number of transports	Victuals carried
7 June	1,655	9	1,600
15 July	Not known	18	1,600
6 September	1,647	9	1,300
22 September	1,506	8	1,500
TOTAL SHIPPED		44	6,000 tons

Source: TNA, ADM 1/3755–6, TNA, ADM 110/58–9, compiled using TNA, ADM 1/3755–6 for transport detail, TNA, ADM 110/58–9 for the Victualling Board and Admiralty orders.

Each shipment carried exact amounts of provisions for the fleet for the given number of men on station. Victualling Board officials, knowing the number of men to be provided for, worked out specific amounts for a specific time. In the Victualling Board out-letters is a document from 1809, which details the precise calculations made by that board for the provisioning of the Baltic fleet, with amounts of each species calculated to last for specific periods (Table 5). It was the job of the accountant for stores to prepare an account of the quantity of provisions remaining with the respective fleets around the world, also showing the number of days this would last each squadron.[13] As such, a detailed system of receipts and note-taking was practised, with the Victualling Board keeping a strict eye on provisions. Saumarez too kept a close eye on the state of provisions, striving for accuracy wherever possible. In May 1808 he sent a memorandum observing that 'several of the weekly accounts of the squadron sent to the Commander in Chief having been very incorrect which has rendered it impossible to ascertain the quantity of each species of provisions on board'. He then directed that

> the Captains and Commanders of the squadron pay particular attention to filling up the different columns as follows. In the Column for Beef is to be expressed the no. of weeks remaining of that article, allowing it to be served agreeably to the standing orders of half flour half beef. The no. of weeks flour is to be marked in the same manner. In the column of Suet and Fruit the no. of weeks of each is to be expressed in the separate columns.[14]

[13] TNA, ADM 111/195, 1 May 1810.
[14] NMM, MKH 112, General Memorandum, 6 May 1808.

Table 5. Victualling delivery, 13 June 1809

Species	on board five victuallers which have been completed, and have sailed from Deptford	which will serve 12,000 men this number of days	to be shipped on board two victuallers to complete the above 12,000 men two months as directed by Admiralty Order of 19 May 1809	Total number of days provisioned for
Bread, cwts	3,459	32	24	56
Spirits, Gall	28,952	38	18	56
Beef, Ps 8 lbs	16,576	38	18	56
Flour, lbs	99,384	38	18	56
Raisins, lbs	16,779	38	18	56
Suet, lbs	8,280	38	18	56
Pork, Ps 4lbs	33,072	38	18	56
Pease, Bush	2,017	37	19	56
Oatmeal, Bush	1,516	37	19	56
Sugar, lbs	24,710	38	18	56
Butter, lbs	24,795	38	18	56
Cheese, lbs	49,780	38	18	56
Vinegar, Gall	4,126	38	18	56
Tobacco, lbs	16,509	38	18	56
Lemon Juice, lbs	29,008	38	18	56
Sugar for Lemon Juice, lbs	29,078	38	18	56
Candles, doz.	744	37	19	56

Source: TNA, ADM 110/60/90–1. 150–1, 'A Statement of the Provisions sent to the Baltic and of those under orders for that station'.

The masters of the respective transports kept the receipts on delivering the provisions they carried to the fleet. The master was told to collect all his papers together, including owner's accounts and receipts of the supplies delivered. The board transmitted a printed copy of the 'General Instructions' to all the pursers of ships and vessels in the Royal Navy, desiring that

> He will conform to the regulations therein required to be observed, in all cases . . . and that he will be very particular in obtaining all the requisite

Vouchers for the purchases of Provisions &c which he may at any time make as required by those instructions . . . acquaint him that he may continue to draw upon us for the proportion of three hundred men; but not to consider the same as an absolute grant, but only as a temporary allowance until the passing of his accounts in this Office, when the expenses he shall actually have sustained can be clearly ascertained. Desire therefore, that he will cause a daily account to be kept of the Expenses to which he may unavoidably be subjected in providing necessaries for the use of his Garrison.[15]

Few of these receipts remain since they were rarely kept once their use had been served. However a few have survived in the records to give us an idea of how such book-keeping was done. The *Ann*, contracted to supply coal to the Baltic fleet, kept all receipts, allowing it to record the quantity of coal delivered to the respective ships.[16] Behind each victualling delivery was an intricate layer of bureaucracy with a specific amount (measured in pounds) of food supplied to each ship, carefully receipted for, each signed by the purser of the Royal Navy vessel, and the master of the transport.[17] Exact quantities taken from transports were sometimes, though not always, recorded in the captain's log. For example, the *Centaur* recorded what it had received from the victualler *Mary* on 6 August 1808 (Table 6).

Table 6. Provisions to the *Centaur* from the *Mary*, August 1808

Flour	6,914 lbs (in 20 bags)
Rum	1,032 Gallons (in 12 puncheons)
Cheese	371 lbs
Butter	325 lbs (in 5 firkins)
Candles	66 doz.
Bread	4,368 (in 39 bags)

From the *British Volunteer* Victualler it had received further supplies (Table 7). Each shipment of provisions was checked on arrival, to see whether the amount receipted for matched that on board. Where they did not match, or where receipts or invoices were missing, the Victualling Board was quick to investigate. Smithson Waller, agent victualler in the Baltic and Gothenburg and the man responsible or auditing shipments of provisions, wrote on 20 August, observing that the invoice for the beef, pork and

---

[15] TNA, ADM 111/193, 9 Nov. 1809. TNA, ADM 111/198, 8 Jan. 1811.
[16] NMM, HNL 13/17, f. 17 14 April 1810.
[17] See 22 receipts from individual ships which had taken supplied from the *Ann* victualler, each signed by the pursers. NMM, HNL 34/30, f. 4–26, 5 May 1800.

Table 7. Provisions to the *Centaur* from the *British Volunteer*

Bread	61,040 lbs (in 545 bags)
Flour	11,806 lbs (in 34 barrells)
Raisins	2,086 lbs
Pease	249 bushels
Oatmeal	184 bushels
Beef	1,368 pieces of 8lb, 2,240 4lb pieces
Suet	960 lbs
Rum	3,416 gallons
Butter	2,948 lbs
Lime juice	47 cases
Tobacco	1,946 lbs
Coals	14 chaldrons

Source: TNA, ADM 51/1824, Log of the *Centaur*, 6 August 1808.

suet in the victualler *Favourite* was not sent, and that the *Betsey*'s bill of lading specified an incorrect amount. While the invoice specified nineteen hogsheads of sugar for lemon juice (10,640 pounds) only ten hogsheads (5,600 pounds) were on board. In the *Favourite*'s invoice 3,141 pounds of tobacco was inserted, whereas there was none in the bill of lading. The board ordered that the superintendent signify to the officers concerned 'the Board's disapprobation of their conduct in the instance alluded to', and called to the attention of those officers 'to this most unfortunate part of their duty, any future neglect of which will oblige the Board to adopt efficient measures to remedy the same'.[18] This level of involvement demonstrates the board's ruthlessness with any disparity or mistake, when a receipt for an amount of provisions, which in the grand scheme of the Victualling Board's duties was fairly small, could incur such disapprobation.

Delays in the victualling process were generally the result not of Victualling Board mistakes, but problems in securing tonnage. With regard to the delivery ordered on 6 September, the Victualling Board questioned the delay, stating that the vessels provided by the Transport Board were 'insufficient to take the whole of the said Provisions', and requested a further vessel for that service.[19] The shipment from the order on 22 September also had problems securing the necessary merchant ships. 'Not any vessels having yet been appropriated for the reception of the Provisions intended

[18] TNA, ADM 111/188, 10 Sept. 1808.
[19] TNA, ADM 110/58/263, Victualling Board to Transport Board, 26 Sept. 1808.

to be sent out for the supply of His Majesty's Ships in the Baltic, as mentioned in our letter to you of the 23rd ult.', wrote the Victualling Board with increasing frustration, 'and the orders we are under for the shipment of the said Provisions being of a very pressing nature, we have to request you will provide us with the requisite Vessels without a moments loss of time'.[20] The shipping was secured by the 14 October.[21] On reaching the Nore it made its way under convoy to the Baltic, arriving in the western region in mid-November. Below is an example of what one transport could hold. This was the *Triptolemus*, which loaded on the 1 September 1808 for the Baltic. Every quantity of provision was measured to supply forces for particular periods (Table 8).

Table 8. Supplies on board the *Triptolemus* victualler

Beef lbs	80,640	12.25 days
Pork lbs	46,064	12.25 days
Biscuits lbs	107,072	21.2 days
Spirits gallons	5123	24.25 days
Register tonnage	224	
Tonnage on board	185.75	

Source: TNA, ADM 109/106, 'Statement of Provisions shipped on board the undermentioned Victualler, showing the number of days it will supply 5,000 men at the usual rations'.

Delays could lead to much antagonism between the Victualling and Transport Boards, with the Admiralty receiving letters absolving individual departments of blame. A delay in an earlier shipment of victuals, ordered on 6 September 1808, led the Victualling Board to lay the blame solely at the door of their Transport colleagues. Although a 'personal communication' from the chairman of the Transport Board stated that a part of the tonnage would be appropriated immediately, the Victualling Board wondered whether it might be best to postpone the shipment forwarding of the supply 'as the Transport Board may not be able to furnish the remainder of the Tonnage in the due time'. They did add a more forgiving postscript, that 'the omission of the insertion in our weekly return of unexecuted orders, of their Lordships directions of the 5th inst. arose entirely from inadvertence; but in all future returns we will take care that such directions from

---

[20] TNA, ADM 110/58/277–8, Victualling Board to Transport Board, 1 Oct. 1808.
[21] TNA, ADM 110/58/328–9, Victualling Board to Transport Board, 17 Oct. 1808.

their Lordships, whilst unexecuted, shall be duly inserted therein'.[22] On 3 October these transports were ready.[23]

At no point in 1808 were entire shipments in doubt. There were four distinct 'deliveries' of supplies. Orders for the supply to the Baltic were given by the Admiralty on 7 June, 15 July, 6 September 1808 and a final shipment was ordered on 22 September, to see the ships remaining in port in the Baltic through to the melting of the ice the following spring.[24] Between shipments, a small number of victuallers remained as store ships in the Baltic. For the most part, shipments arrived quickly and without attendant difficulties. During 1808, it took an average of 51.33 days from the initial Admiralty order for the victuals to arrive with the fleet at the southern entrance to the Belt and Sound, near Hanö and Karlskrona, an impressively short time. A victualling convoy would then continue across the Baltic: it would take an average of another twenty days (71.5 days in total) to reach the eastern Baltic, to Hood's squadron, employed in blockading the Russian Baltic fleet.[25]

Speed and flexibility

At the end of 1808, both the Admiralty and Saumarez had good reason to consider the victualling operations of that year a success. The victualling system proved to be very effective, albeit with isolated problems. In August a delay in a transport shipment had worried Saumarez, demonstrating the concern all commanders had for their supplies. 'I have the honor to inform your Excellency', he wrote to a Swedish notary, 'that the contrary Winds have prevented these last five weeks the arrival of the Victuallers I expected from England with the Provisions for the Squadron under my command. It was not until four days since that they have been enabled to join Rear Admiral Sir Samuel Hood off Moen Island, and I waited here for those supplies in order to proceed off Hanö.'[26] The lack of provisions did affect operations, albeit in a limited way, notably the brief detention of the *Mars* and *Africa*, having to travel out away from their station to collect provisions. 'I send Captain Hope the account of the distribution of

---

[22] TNA, ADM 110/58/239/41, Victualling Board to Admiralty, 16 Sept. 1808.

[23] TNA, ADM 110/58/283–4, Victualling Board to Admiralty, 3 Oct. 1808.

[24] TNA, ADM 2/154/453, TNA, ADM 2/155/23.

[25] These times were calculated using Admiralty and Victualling Board orders, see TNA, ADM 111/187–8. For information regarding the arrival time of the victualling deliveries, see TNA, ADM 51/1825, ADM 52/3798. See Appendix 4.

[26] SRO, HA 93/6/1/237, Saumarez to Baron de Rajalin, 5 Aug. 1808. Hanö is on the southern tip of Sweden near Karlskrona.

provisions made, of which the *Centaur* is full', wrote Hood to Saumarez. While he noted that the *Mars* and *Africa* would return to their stations immediately, the *Brunswick* and *Edgar* would be detained even longer as they awaited supplies.[27] There was 'a material deficiency in the supply', particularly of bread. Hood's complaints stemmed from a very real and unforeseen obstacle: the delays had been exacerbated by 'Admiral Keats's detour', namely the sudden need to provide provisions for a Spanish army numbering 10,000 men. The episode demonstrates, though, the remarkable flexibility the victualling system provided.[28]

In August 1808 Saumarez was ordered to assist in the removal of a Spanish army from Denmark, and organise its transportation back to the Iberian Peninsula. Until that year, it had made up part of the French army in northern Europe. Following the French occupation of Spain, and the replacement of King Ferdinand with Napoleon's brother, Joseph, the ensuing nationalist revolt against French rule induced the Spanish commander and his men to change allegiance. Their hope of repatriation rested upon the Royal Navy.[29] The operation placed a strain on a new and untested supply system, adding 10,000 soldiers to the number to be fed, to all intents and purposes doubling the complement of mouths to feed in the Baltic. The troops were retrieved from the Danish port of Nyborg then taken to the island of Langeland, south-east of Funen, which as Keats explained, 'is a productive island and where they could support themselves till transports were ready', albeit for only a few weeks.[30] A convention was entered into between the Spanish commander, La Marques de Romana, and the governor of Langeland guaranteeing non-hostility and a sufficient supply of provisions from the island. Most important was a plentiful supply of water.[31]

The island of Langeland was not to be as productive as Keats had hoped; he was to face significant supply problems when dealing with this unforeseen operation. Indeed, the whole affair is an excellent case-study of the Royal Navy's ability to victual its men when faced with sudden demand. On 1 August Saumarez was informed that there were sufficient provisions for fifteen weeks for the number of men in the Baltic squadron,

[27] SRO, HA 93/6/1/235, Hood to Saumarez, 6 Aug. 1808.
[28] SRO, HA 93/6/1/234, Hood to Saumarez, 5 Aug. 1808.
[29] For a full account of this operation see James Davey, 'The Repatriation of Spanish Soldiers from Denmark, 1808: The British Government, Logistics and Maritime Supremacy', *The Journal of Military History* 74/4 (October 2010), 689–707.
[30] TNA, ADM 1/6/423–4, Keats to Saumarez, 5 Aug. 1808.
[31] TNA, ADM 1/6/454, Keats to Admiralty, 13 Aug. 1808. TNA, ADM 1/7/15, Keats to Saumarez, 13 Aug. 1808. TNA, ADM 80/145, Keats's Order Book, 16 Aug. 1808.

until 13 November. Both Keats and Saumarez were aware that 10,000 extra mouths to feed would reduce this dramatically, the latter noting 'the scarcity supply of Provisions for so unexpected additional force'.[32] On 8 August Keats found it necessary to introduce two-thirds rationing. The following week, as the troops remained on Langeland, despite its fertility relative to other islands, Keats was forced to reduce this to half rations for bread and spirits. There were severe concerns as to the British ability to feed their new charges. The commandant of Langeland informed the British that 'in his opinion the Island cannot afford subsistence for more than a fortnight for this Army'.[33] This was repeated by Keats, who now realised that Langeland was not the agricultural haven for which he had hoped. He informed Saumarez that 'it seems that the Island is not capable of affording Provisions for more than two or three weeks at furthest', reinforcing his decision to cut rations.[34] With some optimism, he hoped that 'every one will chearfully [*sic*] submit to this necessary reduction', having 'the strongest reason to believe it will only be requisite to continue it a *very few days*'.[35]

This was said in the knowledge that the Victualling Board had already planned to redress the shortage. On 6 August Saumarez ordered two victuallers from Gothenburg to tide Keats over and wrote to London requesting 'directions as they may deem advisable for Victualling the Spanish Troops should we be so fortunate to succeed in extricating them from their present situation'.[36] Despite the Baltic victualling system still being in its formative stages, the board demonstrated remarkable flexibility in adapting to the challenge of an extra 10,000 mouths to feed. Saumarez wrote, 'I hope the two army victuallers ordered from Gothenburg will soon arrive, they contain provisions for ten thousand men for six weeks, Bread, Spirits, Beef and Pork and I hope other articles will be sent from England with the Transports applied for the conveyance of the Spanish Troops'.[37] He need not have worried: a fleet of eighteen victuallers was already set to leave London, and they arrived a mere two weeks after rationing had been introduced.[38] Their arrival in Langeland, in Keats's words, placed 'us quite at

---

[32] TNA, ADM 1/6/382, Memorandum to Saumarez, 1 Aug. 1808, signed 'George Hope (Capt.)'; SRO SA/3/1/3/1, Saumarez to Martha Saumarez, 20 Aug. 1808.

[33] TNA, ADM 1/6/386–7, Keats to Saumarez, 4 Aug. 1808.

[34] TNA, ADM 1/7/15, Keats to Saumarez, 13 Aug. 1808.

[35] TNA, ADM 80/145, Keats's Order Book, 8 Aug. 1808. TNA, ADM 80.145, Keats's Order Book, 20 Aug. 1808.

[36] TNA, ADM 1/6/399–400, Saumarez to Admiralty, 6 Aug. 1808.

[37] SRO, HA 93/6/1/264, Saumarez to Keats, 17 Aug. 1808.

[38] The need to feed the unexpected Spanish army explains the need for four deliveries of

ease on the subject of Provisions', and enabled him to end the rationing.[39] It demonstrates how the Admiralty and its subordinate boards could respond to immediate events, and more than adequately provide for them.

There remained victualling problems, particularly at the end of the year, as the majority of the fleet began its migration back to British ports for the winter. Rear Admiral Dixon complained to Keats in December 1808 that 'the River [the Göta Älv] is Frozen and we can get no more Water'. Further to this, a supply of provisions had arrived, enabling Dixon 'to complete all the ships to 25 January, and I have gone to Two thirds allowance of Bread from this day . . . I am getting very low in Spirits and other Provisions'.[40] Keats himself reported supply issues; 'If the weather which we have had for this week past is the usual for the Season, it is time to quit the Belt . . . I am also under some embarrassment on the score of Provisions . . . tho' it is now a fortnight since I sent to Gothenburg, no Victualler or Sloop with a temporary supply has yet made its appearance'.[41]

This apparent shortage is something of a mystery and more perceived than real. Saumarez instructed Keats to remain at Marstrand during the Winter, 'for the purpose of protecting the Trade of His Majesty's subjects', and in 'constant readiness' to cooperate with their Swedish allies. He ordered all stores that could be spared from the ships returning to Britain to leave their provisions with Keats.[42] An account of the victuallers lying at Flemish Roads, near Gothenburg, on 25 October 1808 (a mere month before Keats wrote his letter), found a fleet not merely satisfactorily provisioned, but excellently provided for, with over 900,000 lbs of bread, 20,000 gallons of wine, 30,000 gallons of rum and almost 100,000 pieces of pork and beef. Table 9 shows an account of provisions with the Baltic fleet at the end of October 1808. Some of this would have been used by the returning fleet. However, there would have been vast amounts left for the small number of ships remaining in the Baltic. A basic calculation suggests that this was enough to supply 3,000 men for 151 days, until the following summer.[43]

---

victuals from Deptford in 1808, especially the two so close together, on 6 and 22 September. The former was aimed largely at replenishing the huge amounts of the previous delivery (15 July) that had been consumed by over 9,000 Spanish soldiers.

[39] TNA, ADM 1/7/56–7, Keats to Admiralty, 22 Aug. 1808.

[40] TNA, ADM 1/7/461–2, Dixon to Keats, Wingo Sound, 1 Dec. 1808.

[41] TNA, ADM 1/7/476–7, Keats to Admiralty, 12 Dec. 1808.

[42] TNA, ADM 1/7/343–4, Saumarez to Admiralty, 29 Oct. 1808.

[43] These calculations are based on one man requiring one pound of bread per day. Given that there were 10,144 men in the Baltic in November, and 6,578 in December, and assuming that they had used the supply in the victuallers for the whole of this period (itself very unlikely), that would still have left 453,026 lbs of bread for the wintering Baltic fleet,

Table 9. Provisions at Flemish Roads, Gothenburg, in October 1808

Species	Amount
Bread	961,264 lbs
Wine	20,914 gallons
Rum	36,290 gallons
Beef	33,268 pieces
Pork	59,206 pieces
Flour	177,116 lbs
Suet	16.620 lbs
Raisins	32,264 lbs
Pease	5,257 bushels
Oatmeal	3,504 bushels
Sugar	52,430 lbs
Butter	12,964 lbs
Cheese	34,302 lbs
Lemon juice	76,464 lbs
Sugar and lemon juice	58,520 lbs
Lemon juice bottles	19,110

Source: TNA, ADM 1/7/343–4, 'an account of the provisions &c on board the undermentioned Victuallers lying in Flemish Roads, Gothenburg, October 25th 1808'.

By the end of December, these provisions had been located, enough to see Keats and his small squadron that remained in the Baltic through the winter. 'As the *Superb* is nearly watered and complete in Provisions', he confirmed to the Admiralty only a week after writing his initial letter of complaint, 'I shall remain off the Wingo [the Royal Navy's station off Gothenburg] for the present, dispatch Victuallers and Duplicate Orders to recall them, and proceed perhaps in the *Superb* myself to their relief, if advisable'.[44] With the victuallers dispatched, the temporary victualling problem had been solved. Indeed, the small force that remained through the winter of 1808–9 was more than adequately provisioned. Early the following year, as the ice melted and the Baltic once again opened up to trade and the Royal Navy, Hood reported to Saumarez on the remaining

---

which numbered a mere 2,365 men. Even with the Baltic fleet using the victuallers to their maximum, the 10,144 men based in the Baltic throughout would have used 304,320 lbs, the 6,578 men based there in December would have used 203,918. Thus, from the initial 961,246 lbs, there would have been, at the very least, 453,026 remaining.

[44] TNA, ADM 1/7/520, Keats to Admiralty, 31 Dec. 1808.

provisions and stores in Gothenburg. He found 35,850 lbs of bread, 21,049 pieces of beef, 8,008 pieces of pork: a surprising amount left after a gruelling winter, confirmed in the Victualling Board minutes.[45] In April 1809, the Transport Board wrote to the Victualling Board, informing them that five victuallers had been ordered back to England, it appearing that 'their cargoes are nearly complete', and requested to be informed what orders were to be given respecting them. The Victualling Board ordered that the said victuallers proceed to Deptford and deliver their cargoes into store.[46] There had indeed been no shortage of provisions over the winter. That a fleet could have access to such a large amount of victuals, having already been at sea for six months, demonstrates the remarkable contribution an effective victualling system could make to a fleet in pursuance of its objectives, both operational and strategic.

Fears dispelled

By the end of the first year of Baltic operations, initial fears had been allayed. Problems of political hostility and geographical factors had been overcome by a supply system that left a ship in the eastern Baltic as well supplied as one in a British port. At no point had operations been drastically affected by victualling shortages. There had been temporary shortages, on occasion lasting as much as two weeks. Yet the victualling service to the Baltic fleet at this point was by no means perfect. The occasional unavailability of transports, for example, had brought delays. However, the service had reacted well to sudden demands, such as the unexpected need to feed a Spanish force.

The Royal Navy fleet stationed in the Baltic, having been on active service for six months, surrounded by hostile shores, and with a precarious supply train through the Sound and Belt, was as well supplied with provisions as if it had been in a home port. The relative ease with which the Royal Navy had set up a logistical chain contrasted greatly with the devastation brought to the Swedish fleet, as seen when Saumarez visited in late 1808. The difference between the supply of the Swedish and British fleets was so great that Rear Admiral Keats worried the British victualling prowess might demoralise the Swedes further: 'I apprehend some difficulties', he stated, 'on the part of the Swedish Government, to admit our men to

---

[45] TNA, ADM 1/8/279–80, Hood to Saumarez, 'Remains of Provisions and Victualling Stores on board the *Flora* Transport, Hawke Roads, Gothenburg' (signed Graves, agent for transports), 29 April 1809.

[46] TNA, ADM 111/191, 3 April 1809.

associate with, or live near, the Swedish Seamen, fearing jealousies and discontents might arise from the superior pay and nourishment of the English Seamen'.[47] Saumarez recommended a series of measures to help the recuperation of his Swedish allies' fleet: 'I have daily, since my arrival here devoted my best attention to promote the recovery of the numerous Swedish Sick Seamen on Board their Ships, and in their hospitals on shore', Saumarez wrote to the Admiralty:

> Scurvy is itself the most debilitating disease, the human body or mind is subject to, and vinegar when the disease is present can never cure it, and if used largely will always increase the evil, in these instances, it diseased the bowels, and scurvy is always ready to fix on any port in a state of irritation, and its aggravating influence, and great tendency to . . . prove fatal in two or three days . . . I strongly recommended a nourishing diet with a free use of vegetables and fruit and Port wine as far as the nature of their complaints would admit of.

Fortunately, the Swedish admirals and officers had taken account of his recommendations for restoring health in the fleet, and avoiding a 'future calamity'.[48]

In the second half of the eighteenth century the British naval administration made significant advances in combating the various diseases that afflicted naval seamen. The first slop-ships had been introduced in 1781, which saw new recruits washed and clothed, significantly diminishing the incidence (although not quite eradicating) typhus. Similarly, regimes of cleanliness and ventilation on board ship significantly reduced dysentery outbreaks. Maintaining a clean, ventilated ship was standard practice by the 1780s. Outbreaks of yellow fever and malaria in tropical stations were harder to eradicate, but there remained a striking contrast in hygiene and in health, as commentators noted, between British ships and French vessels captured.[49] For Britain, it was scurvy that remained the regular blight on naval service. The search for its prevention consumed the Sick and Hurt Board in the latter decades of the eighteenth century, as it continually hampered operations across the world. Ignorance of its causes meant crews away from port and fresh foodstuffs were prone to outbreaks of this disease.

By the time of the Napoleonic War, however, it was no longer the mystery to naval captains it had once been. Even before the sanctioned supply of lemon juice to ships many admirals were already converts to this method

---

[47] TNA, ADM 1/7/447–52, Keats to Admiralty, 27 Nov. 1808.

[48] TNA, ADM 1/7/278–80, Saumarez to Admiralty, 16 Oct. 1808.

[49] Rodger, *Command of the Ocean*, pp. 399, 436, 486–7. For more detail see Kevin Brown, *Poxed and Scurvied: The Story of Sickness and Health at Sea* (Barnsley, 2011).

of preventing scurvy. Admirals such as Howe, Bridport, Rainier and Keith recognised the beneficial effects of citrus juice during the 1790s.[50] This was not a complete transformation and there were still misunderstandings. The surgeon's log of the *Ajax*, 1799–1800, notes that lemon juice was ineffective in preventing scurvy.[51] Another ship's log details an attempt in 1800 to cure scurvy by burying patients up to the neck in earth.[52] Yet, for the most part, the issue of lemon juice to Royal Naval fleets had become standard practice by the late 1790s. With lemon juice issued to all fleets, scurvy became very rare. Between 1795 and 1800 scurvy accounted for only 2 per cent of British naval patients.[53] In 1801, the Admiralty ordered that lemon juice was to be furnished to every seaman in the proportion of one ounce of sugar, and one ounce of lemon juice per man per day.[54]

The appearance of scurvy therefore became an issue of supply rather than medical knowledge, its outbreak confined to occasions when the *distribution* of lemon juice failed. It was a disease that pointed to logistical deficiency. The widespread distribution of lemon juice was only achieved when supply problems were overcome.[55] Aware of the logistical challenges, the more nervous officers of Saumarez's fleet were concerned that scurvy might be an issue. Dr Jamison warned Keats that 'the fatal ravages of that formidable disease have totally unmanned the Swedish Navy, and having manifested its way at different times on board several of our ships'.[56] A close inspection of Royal Navy musters paints a different picture. At the end of 1808 there were only four cases of scurvy amongst over 11,000 seamen.[57] Given that the fleet had been at sea for eight months this was remarkably low.

The difference between the health of the British and Swedish forces was the result of medical ignorance, and also contrasting logistical expertise.[58] For the most part, the Swedish naval diet was nutritious. Lieutenant Ross

---

[50] Brian Vale, 'The Conquest of Scurvy in the Royal Navy 1793–1800: A Challenge to Current Orthodoxy', *MM* 94/2 (May 2008), p. 168.

[51] TNA, ADM 81/5.

[52] TNA, ADM 101/83/3.

[53] Rodger, *Command of the Ocean*, p. 485.

[54] TNA, ADM 111/158.

[55] Vale, 'The Conquest of Scurvy', pp. 160–75.

[56] SRO, HA 93/6/1/460, Dr Jamison to Keats, 28 Dec. 1808.

[57] TNA, ADM 1/8/38. Of the four cases, three were on board the *Prometheus*, which had spent the second half of the campaign in the eastern outskirts of the Baltic, the furthest from supply.

[58] Jamison, the physician to the fleet, was awarded the Swedish Royal Order of Wasa in the Spring of 1809, following the 'distinguished approbation' received from the Royal College of Physicians of Stockholm. MA 21/399, Jamison to Mulgrave, 29 May 1809.

wrote to Saumarez about the typical provisions supplied to Swedish seamen: 'all the Ships companies are allowed a Gall of Corn Brandy, at 7 Bread & Butter or Bread & Herrings alternately for breakfast, at noon peasesoup with Beef & Pork . . . which appears a very wholesome meal, there bread is black but good . . . they are allowed vinegar with their full meat, and as much as they can eat of everything, the water is indifferent but they have as much as they can use'. When in port, or close to land, the Swedes had access to fresh vegetables. On longer voyages, however, anti-scorbutics were conspicuous by their absence, with the result that

> 1200 sick have already been sent home in 3 ships and those still remain, 858 part of which are about to go home . . . ¾ of those are afflicted with Scurvy the progress of which seems to have been considerably checked by the effect of Lime Juice and Sugar supplied by the British Squadron. It must be difficult to say what would most effectively remedy their present distress as the officers say that the people live as they have always been accustomed to do, but I think that allowing less salt provision might have a good effect.[59]

Saumarez agreed that it was the lack of 'antiscorbutic remedies on board their fleet at sea' that explained the widespread illness.[60] Whereas the British had gained an understanding of how scurvy could be prevented, the Swedish navy had not.

This was not merely a question of diet, however. The Swedish navy did not have the infrastructure or logistical systems to support fleets at sea. As a short-distance fleet used to short missions, Sweden had little experience of long voyages and was consequently ill-prepared for the lengthy blockade of Russian ports. They had not made the same logistical improvements Britain had during the eighteenth century. The superior supply system of the British was the important difference, according to Saumarez's surgeon, Jamison: 'after a careful examination I am decidedly of opinion that Scurvy, of the most obstinate and dangerous nature threatens the safety of the whole fleet':

> In order to account for the introduction of this unfortunate complaint it will be necessary to mention that in the months of January and February last their ships were fitted out, and have since that period, continued at sea without having received any regular supplies of Fresh Provisions, and the greater part, consisting of Country farmers in general accustomed to live on vegetable diet, fully explain the origin and cause of their present state.

[59] SRO, HA 93/6/1/330, Lieutenant Ross to Saumarez, 11 Sept. 1808.
[60] TNA, ADM 1/7/278–80, Saumarez to Admiralty, 16 Oct. 1808.

In other words, it was not simply the medical issues but the logistical deficiency that had left the Swedish fleet stricken in port. As the surgeon continued,

> the rapid progress which this disease is making cannot fail to cite the greatest alarm, as already twelve hundred men have been sent to the hospital . . . all those means which our service points out – both for the cure and prevention of this formidable evil (consistent with the situation of both fleets) have been suggested and first put into practice with the utmost alacrity, by the Physician and Surgeons, many of the latter I am sorry to say are exhausted from fatigue . . . The present proportion of lime juice with which they are supplied is insufficient to affect a radical change.[61]

There would be devastating results for Swedish operational viability; as Saumarez described it, 'a melancholy proof of the inefficiency of those ships and their inability to have kept the sea'.[62]

While the Swedish fleet, sailing off its own shoreline, was devastated as a result of its inferior supply system, the Royal Navy fleet under the command of Sir James Saumarez avoided any such problems. A poor victualling system and a disabled fleet left Sweden prey to the Russian military advance. Sweden's war with Russia in 1808 revealed many weaknesses in its civil and military administration.[63] Not least was the over-centralisation of Swedish command. By contrast, the Royal Navy could provide all the necessary provisions regardless of distance, climate or military opposition. As we have seen, in October 1808, after six months at sea, the Baltic fleet could call upon 76,464 lbs of lemon juice, a further 58,520 lbs mixed with sugar, and a further 19,110 bottles of the anti-scorbutic.[64] It was supply that made the ultimate difference; the widespread distribution of lemon juice was only achieved when supply problems were overcome.[65]

Blockade and the protection of trade

An effective and successful provisioning system enabled the Baltic fleet to perform its major duties. Saumarez's first concern on arriving in the Baltic in 1808 had been to protect Sweden from a Russian invasion. The British fleet instantly gained a command of the Baltic, blockading the Russian fleet

---

[61] SRO, HA 93/6/1/333, Valentine Duke, Surgeon RN, to Saumarez, 12 Sept.
[62] Saumarez to Pole, 21 Nov. 1808, Ryan, ed., *Saumarez Papers*, p. 55.
[63] Andersson, *A History of Sweden*, p. 307.
[64] TNA, ADM 1/7/343–4, 'An account of the provisions &c on board the undermentioned Victuallers lying in Flemish Roads, Gothenburg', 25 Oct. 1808.
[65] Vale, 'The Conquest of Scurvy', pp. 160–75.

in port. Saumarez did not expect the Russian fleet to emerge. He wrote to his wife on 14 August that 'I much doubt if it will be required as from ev'ry account the Russian Squadron have no intention to leave the Port of Cronstadt'.[66] The Russian fleet did emerge on one occasion in 1808, in the words of William James 'making a very formidable appearance'. On 24 August the Russian fleet left port, only to be chased by a combined fleet that included Royal Navy vessels under Hood and a Swedish squadron. Although the two copper-bottomed British ships slowly overhauled the Russians, the Swedish fleet could not match their sailing ability, and the Russian fleet retreated into the port of Rågervik (now Paldiski, Estonia). Saumarez, arriving late after having been occupied arranging the evacuation of the Spanish soldiers on the other side of the Baltic, decided against an attack on the port.[67] The Russian fleet took the opportunity to return to Kronstadt during the winter months, and did not leave port until 1812, when it went to sea as an ally of Britain. In the intervening years, the Russian fleet remained in Kronstadt. In 1810 a merchant commented to Saumarez that 'The Russian fleet is still laid up in Cronstadt, and there are no apparent preparations for its fitting-out'.[68] The navy's brief chase had been all that was necessary to convince them of British naval superiority. During the following year, Captain Byam Martin wrote dismissively to his wife:

> As to the Russian Fleet, it is scarcely worth my while to attempt at removing they more than womanly fears – be assured they are more intent to defend themselves in Cronstadt, than of coming out to meet this fleet. All the accounts agree that they are not even half manned.[69]

Saumarez agreed: 'the apparently intended inactivity of the Russian Fleet (which it would seem is not likely to make its appearance in any Force this season) as well as the kindly disposition of the Swedes (to be encouraged by all proper means) offers results highly advantageous to HM at this conjecture'.[70]

Concerns over the viability of the Russian fleet centred upon British trading interests in the Baltic. It was decided that the most effective form of blockade was one which would limit the movements of enemy and neutral ships trading from those ports from which British ships were excluded:

[66] Saumarez to Martha Saumarez, 14 Aug. 1808, quoted in Voelcker, *Saumarez vs. Napoleon*, p. 54.

[67] See Voelcker, *Saumarez vs. Napoleon*, pp. 55–6. William James, *The Naval History of Great Britain during the Napoelonic and Revolutionary Wars*, V (London, 2002), pp. 13–17.

[68] SRO, HA 93/6/1/1407, St Aubin to Saumarez, 25 June 1810.

[69] Voelcker, *Saumarez vs. Napoleon*, p. 76.

[70] NMM, YOR/16, 9, Saumarez to Yorke, 11 Aug. 1810.

With this view it is that we have adopted a sort of qualified or half hostility with some of the powers whose territories under the control of France and who thro' that control are compelled to shut their ports against us. The Papenburghers etc. etc. are not by us permitted to trade from their own ports to the Enemy, but they may trade either from or to *our* country to any ports not blockaded, or to and from neutral ports. By means of these Flags it is that out Merchants manage to elude the operation of the French prohibitions; these flags therefore ought, I conceive, to be preserved in the same state, and possibly it will be found advisable to add to their number.[71]

The number was in fact increased to include any flag except the French.[72]

The British Orders in Council of 1806–7 imposed a blockade across northern Europe. As it stated,

all the ports and places of France and her allies, or any other country at war with His Majesty, all other ports or places in Europe, from which, although not at war with His Majesty, the British flag is excluded, and all ports or places in the colonies belonging to His Majesty's enemies, shall, from henceforth, be subject to the same restrictions in point of trade and navigation . . . as if the same were actually blockaded by His Majesty's naval forces, in the most strict and rigorous manner.

All trade deriving from such countries would be considered unlawful, and liable to capture and condemning.[73] On 9 December 1807, after Tilsit, an embargo was declared on Russian ships, which ordered general reprisals against Russian vessels.[74] The commercial effects were notable: British trade continued, but at a much lower level than before the war. A trade that in 1806 had been worth over £10 million to the British nation had been reduced to under £5 million.[75] And yet, more remarkable is that it continued at all.

Fears over Britain's trade in the region abounded as the fleet first entered the Baltic. Thornton, the British minister in Stockholm, had written to the Foreign Secretary, Canning, in June 1808, stating that he was

---

[71] British Library, Add. 49178. Spencer Perceval Papers, vol. VI (ff. 83).

[72] A. N. Ryan, 'Trade with the Enemy in the Scandinavian and Baltic Ports during the Napoleonic War: For and Against', *Transactions of the Royal Historical Society*, Fifth Series, 12 (1962), 123–40, p. 127.

[73] *Notifications, Orders and Instructions relating to Prize Subjects during the Present War*, 1810, p. 18. *London Gazette*, 1806, p. 618.

[74] Ibid., pp. 18, 75, 78.

[75] B. R. Mitchell and Phyllis Deane, *Abstract of British Historical Statistics* (Cambridge, 1962), p. 311.

Strongly inclined to believe, that the Exportation from England through this country to the Russian and other ports of the Baltic will be much less than it is hoped for in England, if I may judge from the number of licenses obtained from His Majesty in Council: and it would be very right, that the merchants of England should prepare themselves for much disappointment and much loss upon this point.

He feared for British trade in the face of Napoleon's administrative reach: 'Buonaparte is perfectly indifferent to the suffering and Privations of his Northern Allies, if he does not even take pleasure in augmenting them, and his agents pursue his system with a zeal and rigour, which I should not have expected from so corrupt and greedy of gain as all of them are whom I have seen'.[76] However, Napoleon struggled to enforce his designs at the extremities of his empire. Instead of rigorous bureaucrats, British merchants attempting to enter Baltic ports met pliable and easily corrupted officials.

The Continental System theoretically prevented the merchants of northern Europe from trading with Britain. However, the interest in continuing to trade was stronger than the political forces that worked for its prohibition. The agents and correspondents of British contractors and merchants formed organisations which defied Napoleon. Cargoes were shipped from minor ports under little scrutiny and in vessels that purported to be neutral.[77] Sir Walter Scott, a judge at the High Court of the Admiralty, said 'it is perfectly notorious that we are carrying on the whole trade of the world under simulated and disguised papers'.[78] Disguise and evasion, with trade carried largely on foreign ships with false papers meant that trade could be maintained in and out of the Baltic. A systematic smuggling operation was organised, with customs officials bribed. Officials even at the highest levels of the Napoleonic system were, as N. A. M. Rodger put it, 'eminently corruptible', and 'many honest men, not otherwise disloyal, had no patience with measures openly designed to support Napoleon's ambitions by beggaring his subjects, and particularly his non-French subjects'.[79] French customs officials were paid 500 francs a year, barely more than an unskilled worker. The chief of police in Leghorn commented on their tendency towards corrupt behaviour: 'How can you

---

[76] TNA, FO 73/48, Thornton to Canning, 11 June 1808.

[77] Richard Hill, *The Prizes of War: The Naval Prize System in the Napoleonic Wars 1793–1815* (London, 1998), pp. 10, 34–5; Albion, *Forests and Seapower*, p. 337. Alfred W. Crosby, *America, Russia, Hemp and Napoleon: American Trade with Russia and the Baltic, 1783–1812* (Columbus, OH, 1965), pp. 110, 144, 195, 230.

[78] Roland Ruppenthal, 'Denmark and the Continental System', *Journal of Modern History* 15 (March, 1943), 7–23, p. 16.

[79] Rodger, *Command of the Ocean*, p. 558.

prevent a custom officer earning 40 francs a month . . . from returning an offer of 200 or 300 francs just to pretend to be asleep for half an hour, when he is alone at his post'.[80] Despite the supposed hostility of much of the region British trade did continue in northern Germany and Russia. At Kronstadt and St Petersburg it was easy for the French ambassador to observe what was happening and to complain of infractions to the Continental System. Few British ships appeared. At Riga, on the other hand, a good deal of trade was carried on, much of it by British ships flying the flags of the United States or the Hanse towns.[81] The ports of northern Prussia, in particular Danzig, would also prove susceptible to commercial reason. The requirement to continue trading with the Baltic nations saw the foundation of a license system. To facilitate British trade, masters sailing on account of British contractors were furnished with a license, conferring immunity from the Royal Navy. Ships were then escorted across the North Sea, through the Sound, and into the Baltic. In 1808, 4,910 licenses were granted.[82] Four-fifths of licensed vessels went to the north German, Scandinavian and Russian ports.[83]

Naval convoys bringing merchants vessels into the Baltic transported vessels to a point fifty miles beyond the island of Bornholm, then released them before they came into range of Napoleon's shore batteries.[84] The Admiralty took on the organisation of these outward convoys. At a board meeting on 29 March 1808 the lords commissioners of the Admiralty requested the secretary of Lloyds put up a notice asking Baltic merchants to appoint one of their number to communicate with the Admiralty about the fixing of convoys: a gentleman named Emes was appointed to that position.[85] In the spring of each year the commander in chief, Admiralty secretaries and Emes met to discuss arrangements for the coming year.[86] As Saumarez outlined to the Admiralty at the end of 1808, 'the state of the war with respect to Russia and Prussia is maintained in a manner heretofore

---

[80] Silvia Marzagelli, 'Napoleon's Continental Blockade: An Effective Substitute to Naval Weakness?', in Bruce A. Elleman and S. C. M. Paine, eds. *Naval Blockades and Seapower: Strategies and Counter-Strategies 1805–2005* (London, 2006), pp. 25–34, at p. 29. Crowhurst, *Defence of British Trade*, p. 29.

[81] F. Crouzet, *L'économie britannique et le blocus continental 1806–1813* (Paris, 1958), I, p. 339. Anderson, 'The Continental System', pp. 71–2.

[82] 'An Account of the Number of Commercial Licenses Granted during the Last Ten Years', Parliamentary Papers, 1812, Miscellaneous.

[83] Crosby, *American Trade with Russia and the Baltic*, pp. 117–18.

[84] Ibid.

[85] TNA, ADM 3/163, 13 April 1808.

[86] Ryan, 'Defence of British Trade', p. 450.

unprecedented. An immense trade is carried on by British merchants under His Majesty's license with the different ports of those countries'.[87] An entrepôt was created at Gothenburg for 'the Admission of all British Productions, colonial or manufactured, on certain conditions, and with certain regulations, until they can be re-exported . . . in other vessels to Ports in the Possession, or under the Influence of France, from which the British Navigation and Commerce are excluded'.[88] British produce could leave on Swedish or other neutral vessels. Through such means, British trade continued to enter northern Europe.

Saumarez took particular pride in his protection of British trade; 'The very trivial loss sustained by the Merchants in the Baltic Trade, is a strong proof of the unremitted care and attention bestowed on that important subject', he commented in 1808.[89] Saumarez was constantly at pains to assure his Admiralty superiors that trade protection was his foremost concern. During the evacuation and repatriation of nearly 10,000 Spanish soldiers in August 1808, an operation of considerable importance to British war aims, he was adamant that the protection of trade was still his priority. He wrote back to London:

> I enclose herewith the Dispositions of His Majesty's Ships & Stations in the Baltic by which their Lordships will be pleased to observe I have taken the utmost use to afford protection to the Trade of His Majesty's subjects and of His ally without interfering with the measures to be pursued in rescuing the Spanish Troops from the Islands in the Belt or for weakening the Force stationed for the Defence of Sweden which has always been an object of my greatest attention.[90]

Just as British exports to the Baltic were severely impacted upon, so were imports from northern Europe. In particular, the importation of naval resources was ravaged: in 1807 Britain imported, for instance, £639,507 worth of hemp; in 1808 only £218,947 worth,[91] and imports of masts from Russia fell from 16,988 in 1807 to only 4,584 in 1808; imports of timber dropped even more sharply.[92] There was a sharp reduction in the total of Anglo-Russian trade. A British naval commander in the Baltic commented that 'it is melancholy to think of the immense trade which so lately gave consideration to these ports [i.e. the Russian Baltic ports] and

---

[87] Saumarez to Pole, 21 Nov. 1808, Ryan, ed., *Saumarez Papers*, pp. 52–3.
[88] TNA, FO 73/47, Thornton to Canning, 24 March 1808.
[89] TNA, ADM 1/7/398–405, Saumarez to Admiralty, 21 Nov. 1808.
[90] TNA, ADM 1/6/415–16, Saumarez to the Admiralty, 8 Aug. 1808.
[91] *Journals of the House of Commons* 65 (1810), 647–8, 696; 67 (1812), 766.
[92] Anderson, 'The Continental System', pp. 71–2.

now to behold the whole extent of coast from Riga downwards without even a fishing boat daring to venture out'.[93] And yet, the use of licenses, smuggling, false papers and flags meant that some Baltic mercahnts were able to continue trading with Britain. Naval stores continued to reach Britain, albeit in smaller amounts than the years before. More pertinently the presence of the British fleet in the Baltic obstructed other nations, particularly France, from trading with the Baltic at all. Normally between 3,000 and 5,000 vessels entered Russia's ports every year. In 1808, the total of all entries into all of Russia's ports was 996.[94] The logistical system supporting the fleet enabled it to cruise across the Baltic Sea between April and December without needing to return to port, or move off station. The Baltic ports were closely watched by naval vessels, particularly dozens of cruising frigates and brigs, to keep enemy privateers in ports. Convoys were gathered at Karlskrona, and later Hanö.[95] These ships too were escorted through the Baltic, navigating the Sound or Belt, and across the North Sea by British naval vessels. The great decrease in this trade, and regular delays in extracting it from the Baltic Sea, prompted severe criticism in the Admiralty. In November 1808, the secretary of the Admiralty wrote to Saumarez, 'it having been represented by the merchants that the trade was suffered to collect till the convoys became too large for protection and that this practise has prevailed throughout the season at Carlscrona and Gothenburg'. The delays though were rare, and if anything were caused by greater than expected quantities of trade entering and leaving the Baltic. As Saumarez replied, 'the cause of the convoys having sometimes collected until they became so numerous as to be almost too large for protection has arisen from the immense trade carried out by British and neutral vessels'. More serious were the losses of merchant ships to Danish privateers.[96] On one occasion alone, Saumarez was questioned by the Admiralty concerning the loss of seventeen neutral ships in a convoy under HMS *Thunderer* and *Piercer*, reflecting the pressure on government from members of Parliament representing major ports. The Admiralty wrote to Saumarez, hoping that 'the disaster which has unhappily befallen the convoy arose from unavoidable accidents, and not from any deficiency in the force allotted by you for its protection . . . use your utmost endeavors to prevent any such captures in

---

[93] Thomas Byam Martin, *Letters and Papers of Admiral of the Fleet Sir Thomas Byam Martin*, ed. Sir Richard Vesey Hamilton, II, Navy Records Society 12 (London, 1902), p. 18.

[94] Crosby, *American Trade with Russia and the Baltic*, p. 110.

[95] Ibid., pp. 117–18, 142–3.

[96] Saumarez to Pole, 21 Nov. 1808, Ryan, ed., *Saumarez Papers*, p. 53.

future'.[97] As Saumarez himself commented in 1808 with some justification, 'when it is considered that above three hundred sail of vessels have gone under convoy to the Baltic in the face of the immense flotilla which the enemy have collected in Zealand, it cannot be a matter of surprise that 16 of that number should have fallen in their hands'.[98]

Saumarez left the Baltic in 1808 content with his efforts:

> altho' it has not terminated equal to my expectations I am well convinced ev'ry thing has been done that could depend on me – and that the country will be satisfied of it, altho' I know John Bull is disappointed when success does not correspond with expectation. The Swedes who unfortunately are far more concerned, their very existence almost depending upon the reduction of the Russian Navy, are perfectly satisfied that every thing has been done that was practicable.[99]

The fleet that entered the Baltic in April 1808 faced considerable challenges that had been overcome. The victualling system worked with no little effectiveness with shipments of provisions sent to the fleet on a regular basis. Early difficulties were limited in extent and temporary; problems concerning the speed with which transports were procured were inconvenient but not devastating. Indeed the provisioning system demonstrated some flexibility in its ability to respond to unforeseen issues and obstacles. While the victualling system was not always efficient, it was effective. The challenges provided by the region – climactic, geographical and political – had been overcome. The movement of large amounts of victuals across such remarkable distances, and through such treacherous passages of water, is all the more impressive when one considers this was completed in the first year of Baltic operations. In contrast to his Swedsih allies, the British commander could look back at a year of remarkable victualling, and partial strategic success. In 1809 however, fundamental changes in government strategy and administrative overload would provide the most stringent challenges to victualling the Baltic fleet.

---

[97] Admiralty to Saumarez, 27 June 1808, Ryan, ed., *Saumarez Papers*, p. 27.
[98] SRO, HA 93/6/1/192, Saumarez to Mulgrave, 14 July 1808.
[99] Voelcker, *Saumarez vs. Napoleon*, p. 71.

6

The Escalation of Seapower, 1809

COMMAND OF THE SEA did not confer automatic dominance of the Baltic region. In early 1809, having re-entered the Baltic Sea as the ice melted, Saumarez spoke of his fears for the defence of Sweden. With a weaker army and navy than her neighbour, Sweden had 'not the means to defray the expenses of the war'. Russia invaded Sweden by land through Finland, making significant advances through the winter of 1808–9. With the Baltic Sea frozen over, the Royal Navy could do little to assist its ally. Structural inefficiencies in the Swedish administration were exacerbated by an unstable domestic political situation. Sir John Moore, during his brief expedition to the Baltic, had described the parlous state Sweden was in. While the British fleet could defend Sweden during the summer months, he did not expect Sweden to last much longer:

> The nobility are adverse to war and to all resistance, and will be glad to see the King reduced to compromise on any terms, or themselves to become subject to any other Power. The probability is that he is surrounded by persons in the interest and in correspondence with his enemies. In such a state of things we can do him no permanent good; he will not follow our counsels, and our force alone is not sufficient.[1]

Isolation, an ineffective navy and internal subversion proved a heady mixture. The Swedish military officer corps was widely discontent with Gustav IV Adolf's war policy, which they believed had brought the country to the brink of the abyss. With the Russian army threatening Stockholm, on 7 March 1809 the western army stationed in Värmland revolted against the leadership of Gustav IV Adolf, and marched towards Stockholm, prompting the king to move against the rebel army. A group of Swedish officers led by General Adlercreutz began a military coup. Desperate to avoid civil war, Gustav's palace was broken into and the king arrested.

The British Foreign Secretary, George Canning, refused to recognise the new government. Saumarez arrived in the Baltic in a difficult position. He

---

[1] J. F. Maurice, ed., *The Diary of Sir John Moore*, II (London, 1904), pp. 210–11.

complained to his wife that he had had little direction from his superiors in London: 'If not speedily attended to, my expectations of success this campaign will be annihilated and Sweden left to its fate and become a Prey to the Russian Forces from Finland'. Taking advantage of what he would later call the 'accustom'd silence' of his political superiors, he began to make his own decisions, based on his understanding of the political situation.[2] This involved pursuing a policy that catered to British interests, if not necessarily British policy. It was important that Sweden – Britain's one remaining ally in northern Europe – be maintained, and protected. Rear Admiral Nauckhoff, the commander of the Swedish blockading fleet, wrote to Saumarez outlining his fears for his country: 'We are obliged, through the remarkable revolution in Sweden, to remain strictly on the defensive with regard to our neighbours until peace is made. Russia is unwilling to make peace unless we give up Finland and declare that our ports will always be closed to England; it is necessary therefore to continue the war'.[3] The Continental System threatened to spread further.

The British response to developments in Sweden was not to escalate their maritime blockade, but to pare it back. On 16 April 1809, an Order in Council was passed which eased the restrictions imposed in 1807. France and its satellites were still under blockade, but Germany and the other Baltic states were not. Whereas before all nations party to the Continental System were 'actually blockaded in the most strict and vigorous manner', with all trade prohibited, a number of exceptions were now ordered. While the 'ports and places' of Holland, France and the northern parts of Italy would continue under this restriction, the other ports of Europe were 'released accordingly'.[4] The relaxations of 1809 in no way reduced the severity of the ban upon all direct trade between the northern nations and the ports of France and her other allies. Any ship intercepted on course for a hostile port was subject to capture.[5] However, those merchants wishing to trade with Britain had an added incentive to do so. By encouraging trade with Britain, while continuing to cut off trade with hostile nations, the British hoped to boost its own trading interests, at the same time as they undermined those of Napoleon.

The management of this trade would require a great naval presence. With doubts over Sweden's future allegiance, in 1809 Britain increased the size of the naval force in northern Europe. The decision to send naval force

---

[2] Voelcker, *Saumarez vs. Napoleon*, pp. 85–7.
[3] Nauckhoff to Saumarez, 7 June 1809, Ryan, ed., *Saumarez Papers*, pp. 77–8.
[4] *Notifications, Orders and Instructions relating to Prize Subjects during the Present War.*
[5] Ryan, 'Trade with the Enemy', p. 127.

to a region corresponded directly to the likely threat and importance the Admiralty placed on it. This meant making sacrifices elsewhere: despite the Mediterranean fleet under Collingwood having relied on a bare minimum of ships in 1808, there was a slight reduction in its size. The Channel fleet too was smaller. Northern Europe was a region in which the war could be lost. The fleet in the North Sea was also reinforced, and stationed off the Texel and Scheldt. In June 1809, a vast expedition was sent to Holland to open another front in the war against Napoleon, and to destroy the French fleet being constructed at Flushing. The British feared this might become a major shipbuilding centre for Napoleon. The Baltic fleet too would be supplemented. By July 1809, it numbered sixty-two warships, a significant increase on the previous year.[6]

As the size of the fleet was increased, so, consequently, were the demands placed on the victualling system. The great strains on the victualling system arising that arose in 1809 called into question the ability of the Royal Navy to project power in northern Europe.

A move to self-sufficiency, 1808–9

As the fleet re-entered the Baltic in April 1809, victualling officials could look back on 1808 as a relative success. During the winter months naval administrators took advantage of Saumarez's brief return to London, which provided an opportunity to correct mistakes and make improvements. The Victualling Board reported that the Admiralty were attempting to reduce the number of ships carrying provisions to the Baltic. Fewer, larger ships would be used. It was recorded in the minutes that 'it is the desire of the Lords Commissioners of the Admiralty that the said Provisions be conveyed in as few Vessels as possible; and that Vice Admiral Saumarez has *verbally expressed* a wish to the same effect to the Chairman; and request they will let us know whether it is in their power to appropriate to the said service Vessels of a greater tonnage than those they have engaged'.[7] Much victualling planning was done through unminuted conversation. Although there is no written evidence therefore, we do know that these personal conferences took place, and that improvements were made. The following winter the chairman of the Victualling Board wrote of a similar

---

[6] In October 1808, the North Sea fleet had numbered sixteen vessels. In 1809, they would transferred to the station of the Scheldt, where they were part of a force of thirty-five warships. See TNA, ADM 8/96–7. In 1808 the Baltic fleet had numbered forty-four ships at its height.

[7] TNA, ADM 111/191, 26 May 1809 (italics added).

'conference he has had with Sir James Saumarez upon the subject of the mode it may be expedient to adopt' for furnishing supplies.[8]

Over the course of 1809, more supplies would be procured locally than in the previous year. During 1808 small quantities of beef had been procured locally, organised by the agent victualler in the Baltic, Smithson Waller, and local consuls. With no cost for transport and freight, procuring supplies locally was an advantageous scheme, albeit limited in scope. The Victualling Board signed a contract with Mr Krok, a Swedish merchant, in 1808, at a price of sixpence per pound of beef, delivered at Gothenburg.[9] This works out at £7 12s per tierce (a tierce being 304 lbs). During 1808, the price of beef in Deptford was substantially higher, at £9 6s 8d per tierce.[10] Even though the price of beef dropped in 1809 to £8 2s 9d, the contract to supply in the Baltic was still significantly cheaper. The system of local procurement centred around the purchase of provisions with bills of exchange charged against the representative on that station. Bills of exchange drawn upon the Victualling Board from the Baltic increased from £19,144 in 1808 to £40,863 in 1809.[11] These were still small amounts, dealing with only one foodstuff; insufficient to deal with the greatly increased demand and strain placed upon the Baltic victualling system in 1809. The vast majority of the fleet's food would continue to come from Britain.

The first half of 1809 saw the Baltic fleet attempting to secure self-sufficiency for the most important species of all: water. The water-procurement issue had been on the commanders' minds throughout 1808. Saumarez was so concerned that he set out a 'weekly expense of water which is not to be exceeded on any account', depending on the size of a ship. A weekly return of the expense and water remaining was to be sent to him every Monday morning along with the report of sick, for the commander in chief's information.[12] It had been important to leave a portion of the fleet in the Baltic over the winter so that there would be ships on hand to protect the first merchant vessels as the ice melted the following spring. A reliable water supply had been a crucial factor in the decision of where to winter the remaining vessels of the Baltic fleet. Over-wintering was only possible because of the supplies that were organised. Keats wrote to Saumarez that

---

[8] TNA, ADM 111/194, 31 March 1810.

[9] TNA, ADM 1/6/23–4, Smithson Waller to Saumarez, 4 April 1808.

[10] House of Commons Parliamentary Papers Online, 1823 (417), 'Accounts relating to Navy and Victualling Contracts, and Pay of Shipwrights, 1790–1823', p. 12. http://parlipapers.chadwyck.co.uk/fulltext/fulltext.do?area=hcpp&id=1823-008383&pagenum=1&resultNum=6&entries=7&queryId=../session/1340976289_9998&backto=FULLREC

[11] TNA, ADM 110/61, and Davey, 'Supplied by the Enemy', p. 265.

[12] NMM, MKH 112, General Memorandum, no date but certainly May–June 1808.

I have been induced for the following reasons to order all the ships and victuallers back to Hawke Road, Gothenburg. Because, except with favorable winds it is not possible to get out of the Port, should it become necessary; Because I could not command a supply of water . . . In Hawke Roads I believe I can make sure of a supply of water . . . I should deem it under dubious circumstances preferable to be frozen up, in a situation in which I am certain of my supplies; and from which, in the case of a reverse, I should have perhaps less difficulty to extricate myself, than from Marstrand.[13]

It was already standard practice for each captain and master to list the amount of water remaining on ship. Figure 11 shows the water remaining on board HMS *Superb* between June and December 1808. The *Superb*, whose duties involved sailing the Sound and Belt protecting convoys and trade rarely let her water reserves fall below half. The swift re-watering of the ship as she entered a port is notable, as is the steady decrease as she moved away on active service.

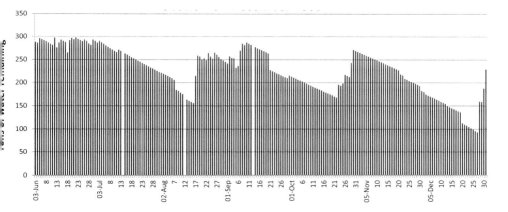

Figure 11. Water remaining on HMS *Superb*, 3 June – 31 December 1808
Source: TNA, ADM 52/3798.

Ships on more detached service were forced to cut things finer. The water supplies of the *Centaur*, stationed in the eastern Baltic, occasionally went under the 100 ton level, especially towards the end of the year. This was a natural consequence of its service: sailing for the most part far from watering ports, it did not have the same opportunities as the *Superb* to re-water regularly.[14]

---

[13] SRO, HA 93/6/1/454, Keats to Saumarez, 25 Dec. 1808.
[14] See TNA, ADM 51/1825.

Water was never far from a commander's mind. Keats suggested in February 1809 that 'sailing tanks' might be established in England, able to carry between 70 and 100 tons of water. He argued that this would be 'the means of saving a very considerable expense in the course of the summer'.[15] This proposition came to nothing, but the issue of securing a reliable water supply remained. This was brought to a head in May 1809, when eighty-three men were captured while watering on the Danish coast. Captain Honeyman of the *Ardent* recounted that

> On the morning of the 19th Instant while a party of Officers and Men were completing the wood and water of His Maj. Ship under my command, they were surprised by a considerable body of the enemy: in consequence of which, the persons named in the accompanying list were taken prisoner.[16]

It was understood that water procurement dictated the distance over which naval power could be projected: there was a clear link between operational options and supply. In early 1809, Admiral Hood looked forward to another season stationed in the far east of the Baltic, off the Gulf of Finland, blockading the Russian fleet. He warned that 'the only difficulty in the protection of the Trade being continued in the Baltic appears to be the watering of the Ships, should the ports of Sweden be shut against us which we have reason to expect must ultimately arise'.[17]

So important were reliable supplies of water to a fleet's effectiveness that in early 1809 operations were carried out to ensure continued access to drinking water. The island of Anholt at the entrance to the Baltic was captured in May 1809 and garrisoned, ensuring a constant supply of water for those in the western Baltic. In his orders for 1809, Saumarez had been told to 'investigate the lighthouse on Anholt', and examine the islands of Bornholm and Eartholm for potential occupation 'as a Commercial Depot, or Naval Station'.[18] In early 1809, Saumarez decided that the acquisition of Anholt would prove to be of 'considerable Importance in furnishing Supplies of Water to His Majesty's Fleet', while also affording a good anchorage to the merchant ships and convoys coming or going from the Baltic.[19] One of Saumarez's captains later wrote of his impressions of Anholt and its strange propensity to dispense large amounts of fresh water. 'We first went to Anholt, a small sandy island with a lighthouse', he

[15] TNA, ADM 1/8/79, Keats to Admiralty, 25 Feb. 1809.
[16] TNA, ADM 1/8/393–5, Captain Honeyman, *Ardent*, to Saumarez, 28 May 1809.
[17] TNA, ADM 1/8/282, Hood to Saumarez, 29 April 1809.
[18] SRO, HA 93/6/1/43, Admiralty Orders, 16 April 1809.
[19] TNA, ADM 1/8/360, Saumarez to Admiralty, 20 May 1809.

wrote. 'The peculiarity of this sandy island was, that fresh water was to be had at any part, even within twenty yards of the sea, we had only to sink an empty flour cask in the sand and it would instantly be filled, and with this contrivance ships would complete their water'.[20] It furnished nothing in the way of foodstuffs, grazing land or crops, however. 'In other respects', Saumarez warned, 'it can be of little use being a low sandy island with scarcely any vegetation whatever.'[21]

Nevertheless, Anholt would take on a crucial role for the British fleet in the Baltic, making up for the lack of naval bases of the size of Port Mahon or Gibraltar in the Mediterranean. Saumarez wondered about the expediency of stationing a military force on Anholt, and sent a list to the Admiralty detailing the stores on the island at the time of capture, together with a list of its inhabitants.[22] He was delighted to see the Admiralty arrange for a 150-strong party of royal marines 'with a proper Complement of officers' to be sent to the island, under the command of Captain Nicholls. The Admiralty made enquiries into the means of defence required to secure Anholt during the winter season. The Victualling Board also took on responsibility for the island's inhabitants.[23] The garrison, in addition to the inhabitants, demanded victuals for a further 500 men, dealt with by individual shipments from Deptford.[24]

In the eastern and upper Baltic a different source of water was needed. The town of Danzig was investigated, to gain intelligence on its suitability as an anchorage for merchants and whether it would supply wood and water; it was estimated that fifty barrels a day could be easily supplied.[25] The island of Gotska Sandön, near Gotland, was found to 'afford an abundant supply of water' by Captain Forest.[26] Saumarez also discovered water on Nargen Island and was delighted to discover that 'by having persevered in digging Wells in different parts', the island was 'likely to afford sufficient for all the squadron'.[27] The Baltic fleet would not have to worry about water supplies from 1809 onwards.

[20] Boteler, *Recollections*, p. 15.
[21] SRO, HA 93, Saumarez to Martha Saumarez, 19 May 1809.
[22] TNA, ADM 1/8/371–7, Saumarez to Admiralty, 23 May 1809.
[23] TNA, ADM 1/8/456, Saumarez to Admiralty, 8 June 1809; TNA, ADM 2/156/545–6, Admiralty to Victualling Board, 15 Sept. 1809.
[24] See for example the delivery of the 30 July 1810, TNA, ADM 2/158/433–4, Admiralty to Victualling Board.
[25] TNA, ADM 1/8/435–6, Captain Martin, *Implacable*, to Saumarez, 31 May 1809.
[26] TNA. ADM 1/8/499–500, Saumarez to Admiralty, 29 June 1809.
[27] TNA, ADM 1/8/548, Saumarez to Admiralty, 13 July 1809.

Victualling problems, 1809

The expanding size of Saumarez's fleet allowed him to spread vessels across the Baltic Sea. A squadron was stationed in the Sound to intimidate the Danes, now under Admiral Bertie, who had replaced Keats. Another was stationed in the eastern Baltic to guard against a Russian invasion from Finland. Saumarez was aware of the vulnerability of his opponent's supply lines, and how naval forces might be used to slow the Russian military advance. He deliberately set out to undermine the Russian enemy's logistics, 'having stationed the *Defence* and *Bellerophon* in Makiloto Bay for the purpose of interrupting the supplies of Provisions passing along the coast of Finland for the use of the Russian Troops in Aland'.[28] By 9 July Saumarez himself was anchored off Nargen Island, eight miles from Reval (Tallinn), forcing the Russian fleet to remain in Kronstadt. With this fleet neutralised, it was hoped that the presence of a British fleet would increase the chances of a compromise peace between Sweden and Russia.[29] A capture of a port was discussed, where victuallers could be protected. An unsigned memorandum on the strategic situation in the Baltic, probably written by Saumarez, recommended the capture of the Eartholm Isles on the southern tip of Sweden, to remove a nest for enemy privateers and also to provide a safe depot for store ships and victuallers, as well as a place for convoy rendezvous, in the event of Swedish ports being shut.[30] In the meantime, the Admiralty authorised a special convoy to transport victuallers to the Baltic, following a request from Saumarez.[31]

For the first few months, the fleet was well supplied and healthy. As Saumarez himself commented in June that year, 'the weather is still very cold for the season, but the men very comfortable and healthy – it is impossible for a fleet to be more healthy than that at present with me'.[32] And after a successful first year of operations, Saumarez had every reason for confidence. The Admiralty, too, believed that early fears over the ability to provision the Baltic fleet had been unfounded. In April 1809 the agent victualler in the Baltic, Smithson Waller, was removed from service. Previously the purser on the *Prince of Wales*,[33] he had been appointed by the

---

[28] TNA, ADM 1/9/7, Saumarez to Admiralty, 16 Aug. 1809.

[29] Voelcker, *Saumarez vs. Napoleon*, pp. 89–1.

[30] SRO, HA 93/6/1/1248. For the authenticity of the letter see Voelcker, *Saumarez vs. Napoleon*, pp. 86–7.

[31] SRO, HA 93/6/1/763, Admiralty to Saumarez, 19 May 1809.

[32] SRO, SA 3/1/2/1, Saumarez to Martha Saumarez, 5 June 1809.

[33] TNA, ADM 111/187, Victualling Board Minutes, 2 May 1808. Indeed, after leaving his position as agent victualler to the Baltic fleet, he returned to the *Prince of Wales*. TNA,

Admiralty in April 1808, charged with procuring and sending supplies of fresh meat and vegetables for the squadron, with a salary of £400.[34] During the previous years, small amounts of fresh meat had been procured locally, though in relatively small amounts. The burden on this task had largely fallen on British consuls.[35]

Waller had something of a reputation. James Anthony Gardner served with Waller seven years earlier on HMS *Brunswick*, and painted a lively picture of the purser. Whereas Gardner's other mess-mates are recalled respectively as 'generous', and 'worthy', Waller is described as 'a very generous fellow' who 'kept it up too much':

> Our purser was a glorious fellow for keeping it up; and taking his full share of Madeira would then turn upon rum and water, and about two or three in the morning would give his last toast, 'A bloody war and a sickly season!' and then retire in a happy state. I once told him when he had the dry belly-ache after drinking port wine, that it was likely he'd go to the palisades (the burying ground), but that I would be happy to do anything for him in England that lay in my power. He gave me a look that expressed everything but thanks.[36]

While there is no evidence that his social peculiarities bothered his commanding officers, there are hints that suggest he was not well thought of. Keats himself was unsure as to the role of Waller, often describing him as a naval storekeeper rather than an agent victualler.[37] Indeed, he had severe doubts about Waller's ability to manage even this simple task. That month he sent around a memorandum to his captains, stating that 'it is my direction, that all Demands for Provisions and Naval Stores are transmitted to me for my approval, before they are sent to the Agent Victualler, or Naval Storekeeper'.[38] Keats's distrust appears harsh: the records show Waller was reliable and precise with his accounts. On one occasion in 1808 he had been criticised by the Admiralty for taking out two clerks with him, when one clerk would have been 'fully sufficient for the purpose'.[39] This small indiscretion aside, which perhaps reveals much more about Admiralty pernicketiness than it does about the agent victualler's conduct, leaves the

---

ADM 111/194, 6 Feb. 1810.

[34] TNA, ADM 111/187, Victualling Board Minutes, 4 April 1808.

[35] Davey, 'Supplied by the Enemy', pp. 275–78.

[36] J. K. Laughton and R. V. Hamilton, eds., *Recollections of James Anthony Gardner*, Navy Records Society, vol. 31, (London, 1906), pp. 241, 248.

[37] TNA, ADM 1/7/172, Keats to Admiralty, 9 Sept. 1808.

[38] TNA, ADM 80/145, Keats, Memorandum, 4 Sept. 1808.

[39] TNA, ADM 111/188, 23 July 1808.

impression that for all his colourful behaviour, Waller was a competent official. It is possible that Keats's negative opinion was transmitted to the Admiralty through unofficial channels, perhaps during the private winter conversations. There was a precedent for removing incompetent officials: David Heatley, agent victualler in Lisbon, had been charged by the Victualling Board in 1801 with negligent behaviour, and for failing to send home his accounts. 'The want of these various accounts and vouchers for so long a period', wrote the Victualling Board to Heatley, 'at the same time that it reflects the highest discredit upon you, had involved the Department in the most serious consequences.'[40]

It seems that Waller was not discharged on grounds of incompetence, but purely because the Victualling Board found his services were redundant; he was seen as an expensive and unnecessary luxury in the Baltic. If anything, his removal was a result of the success of the victualling system in 1808. He was not replaced: 'Having taken into consideration your letter to our Secretary of yesterday's date', wrote the Admiralty, confirming his removal,

> stating that Mr Smithson Waller, whom we had directed you to appoint your Agent in procuring, and sending off supplies of cattle, fresh beef &c, for the Baltic Fleet has arrived in England, requesting to receive our directions as to your continuing Mr Waller in his present appointment: We, not deeming Mr Waller's service to be any longer necessary, do hereby require and direct you, to discontinue him, as your agent on the service aforementioned.[41]

The first year had gone well, in spite of gloomy predictions, and there was little reason to think things would be different in 1809. However, Waller's removal in early 1809 is symptomatic of the Admiralty's over-confidence.[42]

Yet 1809 witnessed a greater strain on the victualling system, one that stretched it almost to breaking point. There were fundamental changes that impacted heavily on the Baltic fleet's supply, and temporary temporary failures of the provisioning service, requiring novel measures to remedy them. In 1809, Saumarez and the Victualling Board were to face the most daunting challenge to the safe victualling of their fleet, without an agent

[40] NMM, ADM DP/31, 8 April 1801, NMM, ADM DP/21, 7 May 1800, Victualling Board to Heatley.

[41] TNA, ADM 2/156/107–8, Admiralty to Victualling Board, 25 April 1809.

[42] One potential reason is that Waller, as a reliable purser, was needed on the *Prince of Wales*, the vessel he was employed on before and after his Baltic service. Between 1809 and 1810 the *Prince of Wales* was without a captain in Chatham being repaired; perhaps an experienced purser, who knew the ship well, was required to assist in this process. See *Steel's Navy List 1809–1810*.

victualler. It is impossible to avoid the question of how much an agent victualler could have assisted the victualling effort in 1809. Certainly it did not make provisioning any easier.

In late 1808, Keats began to call for a more aggressive approach in the Baltic, and subsequently for more ships:

> As our plans of defence must be . . . proportioned to the efforts of the enemy, . . . [and] . . . on the supposition that his efforts will be doubled next year, and that that which we have employed here this year has not been adequate to the Service; besides the Ships of Line it may be found requisite to keep off Helsingborg, there should be a Division consisting of Four or five Ships from 64 (of lightest draught of water) to 32 guns, with three of four smaller vessels, stationed from Falsterbo to Landscrona, expressly for the protection of the Malmo passage . . . I have formed my estimate upon a supposition that the Enemy's force will next year be double what it has been this.[43]

In particular, and having spent much of the previous year in the Channel, he called for more warships in the Belt; 'my apprehension for the safety of the Trade arises more from the want of a sufficiency of Cruizers in the Baltic, to keep Privateers from interrupting the ships in their passage from the Russian and Prussian Ports to Carlscrona, than from any other cause'.[44] Saumarez agreed: in his first two months in the Baltic in 1809, he constantly petitioned the Admiralty for more naval forces to be sent out to the Baltic:

> I propose to proceed without Delay off Carlscrona, where I expect to fall in with the Rear Admiral [Keats], and I shall anxiously hope for the junction of such further Force from England as their Lordships may have thought proper to place under my orders, the present Force both of Line of Battle Ships and Heavy Frigates, being way inadequate to the important Services incident to this station.[45]

The following month, in a letter concerning the most recent convoy which had sailed to England, he wrote that

> the whole consisting of about one hundred and sixty sail . . . It is not without considerable anxiety that I find myself impelled to order so numerous and important a convoy to sail from the Baltic with so few ships for their Protection, but the attention required for the security of the Trade that is daily assembling off Carlscrona from the Southern Ports of the Baltic, together with the other important Services required upon

---

[43] TNA, ADM 1/7/447–52, Keats to Admiralty, 27 Nov. 1808.
[44] TNA, ADM 1/7/444–6, Keats to Admiralty, 26 Nov. 1808.
[45] TNA, ADM 1/8/416, Saumarez to Admiralty, 30 May 1809.

the station, will not admit my placing a greater Force under the orders of Sir Richard Keats.[46]

The importance of the Baltic theatre is clearly shown by the Admiralty's positive response to the calls. August and September 1809 saw more ships in the Baltic than at any other point in the Napoleonic War. This also meant that there was a significant rise in the number of men that would need feeding. Whereas the summer of 1808 saw just under 12,000 men needing to be victualled in the Baltic, during the summer of 1809 this had risen to over 16,000, and during one month to over 17,000.[47]

The increased size of the Baltic fleet came as the British Cabinet began to ratchet up the war effort under the premiership of Portland, and continuing when Spencer Perceval became prime minister in October 1809. It was in 1809 that the expedition to Walcheren set out, and the British commitment in the Peninsula increased. The former expedition would bring serious problems for the victualling system, leading to a severe shortage of transports, both in the Baltic and the Mediterranean.[48] In April 1809, the Transport Board had reported that it did not have enough transport tonnage to fulfil all of its tasks. A shipment to Rio de Janeiro could not be organised without 'interfering with other pressing services'.[49] The next station to suffer was the Mediterranean. In July that year the Transport Board struggled to find the necessary shipping for transporting provisions there, as they were 'under the necessity of appropriating to the present Expedition [Walcheren] all the Transports they can now possibly bring forward'.[50]

Walcheren placed increasing demands on the transport tonnage procurement. In November 1809, the operation was accounting for eighty-six transport ships, with a total tonnage of 23,153.[51] An Admiralty order to provide and send out 'with as little delay as possible' provisions for 25,000

---

[46] TNA, ADM 1/8/449–50, Saumarez to Admiralty, 4 June 1809, ADM 1/8/449–50.

[47] TNA, ADM 8/95–199. This level of commitment, in terms of both ships and men, continued throughout 1809–12.

[48] During the parliamentary enquiry into the failings at Walcheren, the chairman of the Transport Board, Sir Rupert George, answered questions levied against the administration for not launching the expedition earlier in the year when the weather would have been more favourable. This would have been impossible, he argued, emphasising the difficulty in procuring the huge amounts of shipping required by the expedition – requisitioning of neutral ships had even been considered; sufficient shipping could not be provided until July 1809, months later than had been expected. See Bond, *The Grand Expedition*, pp. 145–6.

[49] TNA, ADM 111/191, 24 April 1809.

[50] TNA, ADM 111/192, 11 July 1809.

[51] TNA, ADM 1/3759, 12 Nov. 1809.

men for one month of all species for the ships and vessels in the Scheldt saw transports organised within three days.[52] The needs of other stations receded. With so many transports tied up in this venture, procuring tonnage and freight for Baltic deliveries became much harder to come by. For example, a small delivery ordered on 16 August had to wait until 6 September for the sole transport needed to be procured by the Transport Board.[53] Attempts were made to cut down on transport usage. In September 1809, the Transport Board 'directed Vice Admiral Wells to provide conveyance to Anholt for the twenty five or thirty Tons of Provisions' mentioned in the board's letter to them 'on board such Ship of War as may be appropriated to take charge of the Baltic Convoys', and not on a transport.[54] Keats had urged the appointment of an agent of transports as early as February 1809. 'I have of course felt it in my duty to remedy or at least to endeavour to remedy, abuses wherever I have met them. . . and I would certainly recommend an Agent of Prisoners and of Transports being appointed'.[55] Captain Thomas Graves was belatedly appointed as an agent of transports, yet this proved too late. The summer of 1809 witnessed the first major victualling failures of the war in the Baltic.[56]

There were four deliveries of victuals to the Baltic fleet in 1809, and each would suffer from victualling difficulties. Saumarez's first request for provisions came on 10 May 1809. Using a speedy sloop, by 19 May it had reached the Admiralty, which then ordered the necessary victuals, this order arriving with the Victualling Board the following day, which then ordered the respective transport tonnage.[57] Already the effects of the Walcheren expedition were becoming apparent. It took until 10 June before transport tonnage was secured, a total of twenty-one days.[58] There was then a serious delay in loading the victualling shipments. Many of the victuallers were not loaded until 4 July.[59] For the first time in the Baltic, major victualling

---

[52] See Victualling Board minutes, TNA, ADM 111/192, 22 Aug. 1809.

[53] TNA, ADM 111/192, 6 Sept. 1809.

[54] TNA, ADM 111/192, 28 Sept. 1809.

[55] TNA, ADM 1/8/39, Keats to Admiralty, 10 Feb. 1809.

[56] How official Graves's role as agent for transports is is, however, unclear. A 'Return of Officers in His Majesty's Navy who are employed as Agents for Transports', compiled in February 1811, lists the various agents at Gibraltar, Malta, Grenada, Martinique, Halifax and the Cape of Good Hope, along with assorted home ports, but does not mention one for the Baltic. See TNA, ADM 1/3762/77–80, 4 Feb. 1811. A similar return, for October 1812, also fails to list an agent for transports in the Baltic; see TNA, ADM 1/3763/427, 1 Oct. 1812.

[57] TNA, ADM 2/156/185, see Saumarez to Admiralty, 10 May 1809, Admiralty Order, and TNA, ADM 110/60/1, Victualling Board to Transport Board, 20 May 1809.

[58] TNA, ADM 111/191.

[59] TNA, ADM 111/192.

problems were the result of faults in the victualling service. The Transport Board's difficulties in securing tonnage and fundamental problems in the Victualling Board system for remote supply combined to bring severe problems to the Baltic fleet. Saumarez was deeply concerned, and was certainly greatly inconvenienced. 'Not having received any accounts of any Victuallers being on their way from England for the Squadron, make me most particularly anxious for their arrival', he wrote to the Admiralty in June.[60] A major victualling shortfall, as he well knew, could have devastating effects on operational viability.

The first transports to be loaded were sent with an early convoy. These victuallers had sailed from the Nore on 13 June 1809, arrived in the Belt on 1 July and reached Saumarez in the eastern Baltic (Nargen Island) on 21 July.[61] Convoys of victualling deliveries continued to make impressive time from Deptford to the western Baltic. The time taken from the Nore to the western Baltic was a mere eighteen days, and only thirty-nine days to reach Nargen Island further east. The arrival of a convoy of victuallers brought enough food to last 'till the latter end of September'.[62] The remaining victuallers, however, would not arrive in the eastern Baltic until the 26 August.[63] In June the cumulative effect of additional seamen upon an insufficiently flexible victualling system contrived to bring about massive delays in distributing provision.

As the victualling system began to break down, the subordinate boards began to report to the Admiralty, distancing themselves from blame. The Victualling Board wrote to the Admiralty:

> Having been pleased by their Order of the 19th inst. to direct us to send out, with as little delay as possible a supply of Potatoes and Onions, for the use of His Majesty's ships under the command of Rear Admiral Dixon in the Great Belt, and finding it impracticable at this time to procure Freight, on any terms for the conveyance of the said Vegetables, we have to request you will move their Lordships to signify to us whether there is a probability of our being enabled to forward about eighteen or twenty Tons of the aforementioned articles by any of His Majesty's Ships.[64]

The problems securing tonnage are all the more remarkable when one considers that this was for only a small amount of foodstuffs that needed transporting. In 1809 the strain on the victualling system began to worry

---

[60] TNA, ADM 1/8/499–500, Saumarez to Admiralty, 29 June 1809.
[61] See convoy of *Curlew*, TNA, ADM 7/791/118.
[62] TNA, Saumarez to Admiralty, 21 July 1809.
[63] TNA, ADM 51/2345, ADM 51/1979.
[64] TNA, ADM 110/60/285–6, Victualling Board to Admiralty, 22 Aug. 1809.

the commanders in the Baltic. In July the captain of the *Ruby* moved his squadron off station in search of a victualling convoy:

> Being given to understand that the Victuallers for the Fleet were in the Convoy, I lost no time in joining it, and having this morning ordered the Victuallers each alongside their respective Ships, have completed the *Ruby*, *Majestic*, *Vanguard* and *Ardent*, to Six Months Provisions, except Butter and Cheese, Flour and Suet, of the former, to two months, the latter to Four, and have to inform you that I shall return immediately with the *Ruby* and *Vanguard* to Sproe, leaving the *Majestic* to accompany the convoy on, the moment the wind will permit.[65]

That he was willing to go out of his way in search of victuallers demonstrates the worries commanders had over provisioning.

A second smaller shipment of provisions was ordered on 16 August 1809. Again, it took a long time to find the necessary transport tonnage.[66] The secretary of the Admiralty, John Barrow, passed on the Admiralty's anxieties on 11 September, inquiring as to 'when the Provisions will be ready which were ordered for the Baltic Fleet by their Lordships Order of the 16th ult.' The Victualling Board was quick to blame the Transport Board, making it clear they had applied to the Transport Board weeks before, and only recently been furnished with them. The transports were being loaded as they wrote.[67] In 1809 the average time taken for an order to arrive in the eastern Baltic was eighty days, significantly slower than the year before.[68]

A third delivery ordered on 6 September followed a request from Saumarez calling for further supplies of provisions, sent on 25 August. Again the Transport Board began to procure tonnage, appropriating larger transports and therefore allowing fewer to be hired. The transports procured were all at least 300-ton ships, as opposed to the previous year, when transports to the Baltic were rarely more than 200 tons. Out of necessity rather than by choice, economies of scale had been brought in. This greatly increased the speed with which tonnage could be procured. This delivery of provisions arrived in the western Baltic on 18 October.[69] Thus, the time difference between Saumarez ordering supplies and those supplies arriving, was less than two months. The speed with which naval administrators could receive

---

[65] TNA, ADM 1/8/506–7, captain of the *Ruby* to Saumarez, 1 July 1809.

[66] Twenty-two days. See ADM 111/192.

[67] TNA, ADM 111/192, 12 Sept. 1809.

[68] For the Admiralty and Victualling Board orders, see TNA, ADM 111/191–3. For information regarding the arrival time of the victualling deliveries, see TNA, ADM 51/1958, ADM 51/2345, ADM 51/1979, ADM 52/2976, ADM 51/1996. See Appendix 4.

[69] See TNA, ADM 1/9/76, 192.

and deal with a victualling order from a commander was in this case less than a month.

The long-term issues securing tonnage had not been solved through this measure. Again towards the end of the year, delays would cause severe concerns for the Baltic fleet. Saumarez was deeply worried about his supply line, and the consequent effect:

> As the Ships to be left upon this station for the Protection of the Trade to the 1st December are very short of Provisions', he wrote in November, 'I request their Lordships will be pleased to give Directions that a supply of the articles mentioned in the enclosed may be sent as speedy as possible to Hawke Roads, no Victuallers having arrived since the supply sent out in the vessels named in the margin [*Blessing, Hawke, Henry*] which had been very inadequate to the Demand of the Squadron.[70]

Problems procuring transport tonnage continued to plague the victualling system. The final victualling delivery of 1809 was ordered on 20 November. At the end of the year, the Victualling Board again wrote to the Transport Board pleading for tonnage to be secured quickly:

> There being an urgent and pressing need for a quantity of Provisions being forwarded with the utmost expedition to Hawke Road Gothenburg for the use of His Majesty's Ships under the command of Vice Admiral Sir James Saumarez; we have to request you will provide us with a suitable Vessel to convoy the same without a moments delay, observing that the Tonnage of the Provisions is about three hundred and fifty tons.[71]

Three days later, the two transports *President* and *Flora* had been provided for service by the Transport Board.[72]

The harsh realities of navigating to the Baltic had a direct repercussion on the victualling system. Rear Admiral Dixon, remaining on the station through the winter, wrote to Saumarez, reporting the unfortunate fate of the transports. 'I am seriously concerned to acquaint you that the *President* Vict. one of two under the escort of the *Osprey* & considerably the largest was wrecked on the night of the 11th during a very heavy Gale of wind, on the Tisleraes . . . she sailed upon the Rocks & in a very short time was dashed to pieces'. The *Theo* victualler arrived with the *Osprey* and entered port also in great peril.[73] By December, there were severe victualling shortages. Table 10 gives an account of the victuals available in the Baltic

---

[70] TNA, ADM 1/9/215, Saumarez to Admiralty, 7 Nov. 1809.
[71] TNA, ADM 110/61/57–8, Victualling Board to Transport Board, 20 Nov. 1809.
[72] TNA, ADM 110/61/67–8, Victualling Board to Transport Board, 23 Nov. 1809.
[73] SRO, HA 93/6/1/1227, Dixon to Saumarez, 14 Dec. 1809.

in December 1809. These amounts would clearly not be enough to last through the winter. The 36,736 lbs of bread would last the remaining 2,800 men planned to be in the Baltic for only thirteen days.

Table 10. Provisions remaining on Baltic victuallers, December 1809

	1st *Flora* victualler	2nd *Flora* victualler
Bread lbs	9,296	27,440
Rum gallons	1,415	4,621
Beef lbs	1,826	1,848
Flour lbs	33,057	11,088
Raisin lbs	3,927	
Suet lbs	3,354	1,800
Pork 4k pieces	3,144	3,692
Pease bags	113	230
Oatmeal	548	172.4
Vinegar gallons	2,236	
Tobacco lbs	8,129	
Lemon juice	12,667	
Butter, cheese lbs	32 days	5,566

Source: TNA, ADM 1/9/306–7. 'An account of Provisions remaining on board the 1st and 2nd *Floras*', the two remaining victuallers in the Baltic in December 1809', 14 December 1809.

The naval administrators moved quickly to limit the damage. The Transport Board immediately found new transports to replace the quantities lost on board the *President*. 'In consequence of the loss of the *President*, 278 tons, Hawke Road, Navy Victualler', wrote the Transport Board to the Admiralty, 'we have been under the necessity of appropriating, in her room, the *William*, 349 tons, Mediterranean Navy Victualler, and *Mary*, 122 tons, which are laden and ordered to the Nore; and we request you to move their Lordships to appoint such convoy for their protection to Hawke Road as they may think proper.'[74] This was completed a mere eleven days after the actual incident. Taking into account the time delay for the news to travel to London, this was remarkably fast. Once again the victualling system had proved adept at reacting quickly to potentially disastrous circumstances.

[74] TNA, ADM 1/3759, Transport Board to Admiralty, 25 Dec. 1809.

The naval administration had once again shown itself to be able to react swiftly to unforeseen mishaps; conversely, it had proved unable to organise and manage a system that could deal adequately with the challenges of scale and distance, unable to organise reliable supplies of transport freight. This was not merely a transport problem, however: the delays had spread across the victualling system. The problems of 1809 were not limited solely to transport shortage. A retrospective letter written in 1811 from the Victualling Board is worth quoting in full:

> We have to acquaint you that as the arrangement formed for sending out supplies to the Baltic Fleet at periods fixed upon by the Commander in Chief, has been grounded upon an order from the Right Honourable the Lords Commissioners of the Admiralty we cannot presume to deviate from it, nor is it for us to question its propriety; the more especially when we consider the great inconvenience to which the Baltic Fleet was subjected in the year 1809 from the want of the arrival of supplies in due time, occasioned not only by delays which probably were unavoidable, but also by many of the King's Ships having sailed very short of the quantities of Provisions they were expected to take out, a circumstance against the recurrence of which it is not in our power to provide.[75]

The Victualling Board, for all its attempts to place the blame at the door of the Transport Board, was also at fault. In leaving for the Baltic under-supplied, many of the Victualling Board's subsequent calculations were thrown out.

It was traditional for ships assigned to Channel service to be victualled for four months, East Indies eight, whilst ships heading to medium-distance stations, such as off Africa, West Indies and North America, were provisioned for six.[76] The Baltic was perhaps in a curious position; certainly it was for victualling planners. Saumarez was used to six months' provisions. In April 1808 he wrote to his wife that 'I am well equipped for a six months cruise'.[77] On the other hand, the Victualling Board was less clear on the standard amount of victuals a Baltic fleet should possess on leaving port. On one occasion in August 1808 the commissioners wrote to the Admiralty that four months' provisions were all that were necessary for the Baltic fleet.[78] Other ships leaving to join the Baltic fleet in May 1808 were ordered to be supplied only 'to as full a proportion of all species

[75] TNA, ADM 110/64/11–12, Victualling Board to Transport Board, 13 June 1811.
[76] Baugh, *British Naval Administration in the Age of Walpole*, p. 431.
[77] SRO, HA 93, Saumarez to Martha Saumarez, 18 April 1808.
[78] TNA, ADM 1/7, Victualling Board to Admiralty, 22 Aug. 1808.

as they can stow'.[79] A Victualling Board minute recorded an order that other ships on their way to the Baltic should be 'completed at Yarmouth to five months of all species including Wine and Spirits'.[80] In August 1808, the Victualling Board made a calculation for 11,000 men 'presuming that the ships when they left this country, had on board a proportion equal to four months consumption'.[81] Clearly, commander and administrator had differing ideas about what constituted the correct victualling reserves.

These problems were not isolated incidents. Both the sloops *Diligence* and *Alonzo* had severe problems assembling provisions at Chatham in early 1809. The captain of the *Diligence* wrote apologetically to Saumarez:

> In answer to your order of the 12th inst: I have to acquaint you that it is uncertain when the Sloop under my command will be ready to Drop down the river, in consequence of the uncertainty of our being supplied with water and Provisions, I sent a demand to the Victualling Office for Casks and Water, to stow our ground tier on the 3 April and it is not complete yet; I have had a demand in that Office for six months Provisions, several days, and it is quite uncertain when we shall be supplied with them, although I have attended every day in order to hasten them.[82]

The captain of the *Alonzo* too complained about poor provisioning: 'his Majesty's ships has been detained in consequence of a want of Stores and Provisions at the Victualling Office, and them having received orders to supply those Line of Battle Ships fitting here first; I have received the greater part of my sea provisions and tomorrow I expect the remainder'.[83] Indeed, into the winter of 1809–10, problems at the Victualling Board continued, as ships in the Baltic waited impatiently for their supplies. Three vessels were forced to wait owing to delays in loading stores.[84]

Delays loading vessels naturally impacted on the quality of the provisions. On two occasions, Mr Holt, the accountant for stores at Deptford, had reason to complain about provisions shipped on board victuallers to the Baltic. On 15 June he reported a claim made on passing the account of Thomas Nicholls, the master of the transport *Ceres*. Between 14 July 1808 and 28 April 1809, 626 lbs of bread were condemned in a survey of 17 February 1809. It was ordered that the claim be placed to the credit of

[79] TNA, ADM 111/187, 13 May 1808.
[80] TNA, ADM 111/187, 23 May 1808.
[81] TNA, ADM 111/188, Victualling Board to Saumarez, 22 Aug. 1808.
[82] TNA, ADM 1/8/227, Captain Smith, *Diligence*, 13 April 1809.
[83] TNA, ADM 1/8/223, Captain Barker, *Alonzo*, 13 April 1809.
[84] TNA, ADM 110/61/291–3, Victualling Board to Admiralty, 30 Jan. 1810.

the master's account.[85] That same day, Holt also reported a similar claim by the masters of the *Boreas* transport, between 2 July 1808 and 26 April 1809, 'for Bread 152 pounds, Oatmeal 40 gallons, Pot Barley 80 pounds, returned into store at Portsmouth and there condemned 19 April'. Again it was ordered that the master's account be credited.[86] Errors at the store office were not limited to quality concerns. Later in 1809, the purser of the *Vanguard* in the Baltic reported short measures of certain species sent out.[87] These were small quantities: 626 pounds of bread lost among deliveries of hundreds of thousands of pounds of bread were not enough to impact seriously upon a fleet's operational viability. Yet it is notable that errors came in 1809, without doubt a low point for the Victualling Board.

Victualling and operations

The victualling system was struggling to function as well as it had done the year before. It should be emphasised that 1809 was not a story of continuous provisioning disasters. Shipments did get through to Saumarez, if occasionally the margin was cut fine. In neither June nor December, when victualling deliveries were seriously delayed, was Saumarez forced to abandon any of his key objectives; the navy continued to blockade the Russian fleet, protect British trade and assist the Swedish navy against the Russian forces. The provisioning system reacted quickly to victualling shortfalls: Royal Navy fleets were never forced to return to port, or worse, to return to Britain. The incredibly low rates of scurvy seen the year before were replicated throughout 1809. On the 27 December 1809, Jamison wrote to the Admiralty, listing the numbers sick on the hospital ship *Gorgon* between 5 and 27 December 1809. Of the twenty men listed, none had scurvy. Fever and debility were present, as was rheumatism, but not scurvy.[88] Jamison was a very competent physician to the fleet, sending back monthly returns listing the respective numbers of sick. During the entire year, in a fleet averaging over 16,000 men, there was only one recorded case of scurvy.[89]

Despite widespread concerns over the provisioning system, it allowed the naval fleet to pursue its objectives. The relaxation of the Orders in Council in early 1809 opened up northern Europe for trade. The Continental System

---

85 TNA, ADM 111/191, 15 June 1809.
86 TNA, ADM 111/191, 15 June 1809.
87 TNA, ADM 111/192, 17 Oct. 1809.
88 TNA, ADM 97/88, Jamison to Transport Board, 27 Dec. 1809.
89 TNA, ADM 102/241.

could do little to shape the allegiances of Baltic merchants who relied on Britain for their livelihoods. The license trade blossomed in 1809: having given 4,910 in 1808, merchants were presented with 15,226 in 1809, the majority of which (four-fifths) went to Baltic merchants.[90] In 1809, 1,685 ships were convoyed to the Baltic. These went to destinations across the Baltic Sea: to Memel, Liebnau, Karlskrona, Gothenburg. Many had Germanic names, hinting at their likely ownership.[91] Russia confiscated the cargoes of forty-nine vessels that arrived in 1809.[92] These was a small proportion of an otherwise free-flowing trade. The year 1809 saw British trade flowing once more at its peace-time volume. A Russian imperial *ukaz* of May 1809 ordered that the genuinely neutral character of all ships arriving in Russian ports under neutral flags should be carefully certified and that their papers should be sent to St Petersburg to be scrutinised there. This had little effect and the Russian authorities frequently accepted as genuine ships' papers and captains' declarations as to ports of origin and destinations which were false.[93] A combination of licenses and naval protection saw British trade entering and leaving the Baltic in vast quantities. Nothing demonstrates this more clearly than Admiral Dickson's accounts between 25 June and 9 November 1809, which point to fifteen separate convoys passing through the Belt, numbering 2,210 ships in total, without any losses.[94]

The need to secure naval stores from the Baltic was ever present. In 1809 Russia attempted to cut off all commerce between herself and England. On 7 May the tsar ordered sweeping sequestrations, 'whereby British property to a large amount and stores for the use of His Majesty's Navy and paid for by the said British merchants are now under arrest and at the discretion and disposal of the Russian government'.[95] There was, however, difficulty in executing it properly when neutrals and the populations of St Petersburg, Kronstadt, Riga, Reval, Archangel etc. were intent on subverting it.[96] The relaxation of Britain's Order in Council only encouraged merchants in the

---

[90] 'An Account of the Number of Commercial Licenses Granted during the Last Ten Years', Parliamentary Papers, 1812, Miscellaneous; Crosby, *American Trade with Russia and the Baltic*.

[91] TNA, ADM 7/791–2. The first convoy was on 9 March 1809, the last on the 3 December 1809.

[92] Crosby, *American Trade with Russia and the Baltic*, p. 144.

[93] Anderson, 'The Continental System', p. 72.

[94] TNA, ADM 1/9/249, 'A List of Convoys that have passed within the Limits of Rear Admiral Dickson between the 25th Day of June and the 9th November, off Sproe', 9 Nov. 1809.

[95] Albion, *Forests and Seapower*, p. 341.

[96] Crouzet, *L'économie britannique et le blocus continental*, II, p. 889; Crosby, *American Trade with Russia and the Baltic*, p. 144.

Baltic ports to consider risking Napoleon's wrath and trade with Britain. For all that Riga and St Petersburg were supposedly sealed off, shipments continued to come thence, though they were subject to long delays as the papers were considered.[97] Isaac Solly, the main supplier of hemp from the Baltic to the Royal Navy operating out of Danzig, worked with more pliable officials, but even he moved his operations of supplying the navy with shipbuilding resources elsewhere. Drusina, the British secret service agent who operated under the name of Hahn, reported in May 1809 that 'Notwithstanding the many impediments laid in the way of Trade, several ships have cleared out from these ports [Königsberg and Memel] actually bound for Great Britain with cargoes of hemp, flax, linseed, bristles, timber, staves etc. – The French Consul takes a fee of 1 per cent for himself and a douceur to his secretary for his certificate d'origine.'[98]

In April 1809, Saumarez had written to the Admiralty promising to 'pay every attention' to 'affording protection to the Ships employed by him in obtaining Hemp for His Majesty's Service in this passage up and down the Baltic'.[99] Isaac Solly was able to ask the comptroller of the navy for individual convoys for his ships, or at least that they should not be kept waiting for the accumulation of a large fleet.[100] Solly's similar (and repeated) requests of 22 August, 31 August, 8 September 1809 and 4 July 1810 suggest that his requests for special convoys were repeatedly accepted.[101] Solly employed ships flying the flags of the United States, Russia, Prussia, Denmark and Danzig. The strictures of the Continental System could also be avoided by using entrepôts, not least neutral Gothenburg. Cargoes were sent from Memel and Pillau to Gothenburg under neutral colours, from which they could be sent to Britain.[102] Saumarez too could take advantage of opportunities as they arose. On one occasion in 1809, he skipped over the usual procedure for supplying trading licenses, such was the need for these essential commodities for the Royal Navy. With boats laden with hemp and flax awaiting licenses, he anticipated the government's orders, awarding licenses to those vessels laden with naval stores and bound to a port in Great Britain.[103] Indeed, one can see Saumarez's delight when reporting Captain Martin's success

---

[97]   Albion, *Forests and Seapower*, p. 342.
[98]   TNA, FO 80, Drusina to Foreign Office, 19 May 1809. Quoted in Albion, *Forests and Seapower*, pp. 341–2.
[99]   TNA, ADM 1/8/219, Saumarez to Admiralty, 14 April 1809.
[100]   SRO, HA 93/6/1/586/4, Isaac Solly to the comptroller of the navy, 8 April 1809.
[101]   SRO, HA 93/6/1/1070/1–2, 1091, 1113, 1427, Isaac Solly to the comptroller of the navy, 22 Aug. 1809, 31 Aug. 1809, 4 July 1810.
[102]   Albion, *Forests and Seapower*, p. 343.
[103]   TNA, ADM 1/8/487, Saumarez to Admiralty, 20 June 1809.

in requisitioning from the enemy large quantities of naval stores in 1809, and on discovering fir trees on Nargen Island ideal for spars.[104] In August, Saumarez found himself organising the removal of pine sticks for spars, 5,188 of them in total, from the eastern Baltic back to Britain, at a time when 'a supply of so useful an article could be so readily obtained for the service of His Majesty's dockyards'.[105] The importation of naval stores remained a matter of opportunism and naval vigilance taking advantage of corrupt officials and the commercial instincts of the Baltic mercantile population. In 1809, 2,697 ships were convoyed back from the Baltic. These included large shipments, sometimes numbering over two hundred vessels, from St Petersburg and Riga, the two major sources of hemp.[106] Britain imported twice as many naval stores from the Baltic as it did in 1808.[107]

In one crucial respect, however, the Baltic fleet could do little to stop the Russian advance across Finland. Swedish military defeat would lead to peace negotiations, signed at the Treaty of Fredrikshamn on 17 September 1809, which presented the whole of Finland to Russia. The naval fortress of Sveaborg, which had been taken in the spring of 1808, was handed to Russia, a strategic advantage that Russia would benefit from for the rest of the nineteenth century. Sweden was forced to join the Continental System. For Britain, this was devastating news. The British were reliant on Swedish goodwill, to allow all British ships – naval and merchant – to leave port, even allowing shelter in the case of bad weather. Platen, a Swedish councillor of state, declared to Saumarez:

> As the conclusion of the peace, hard as it is, we cannot yet deny that in an high degree we are indebted to you for our existing as a state . . . our ports are open to so brave an ally, to so successful a protector, for so many sails as your brave excellency judges fit to send into them for the remaining of the harvest.[108]

For all this, the loss of Sweden meant that Britain was now completely isolated in northern Europe.

---

[104] TNA, ADM 1/8/525–6, Saumarez to Admiralty, 9 July 1809, TNA, ADM 1/8/582–3, Saumarez to Admiralty, 21 July 1809.

[105] TNA, ADM 1/9/33, Saumarez to Admiralty, 16 Aug. 1809. See also TNA, ADM 1/12/209, Saumarez to the Admiralty, arranging for Victuallers use to transport Timber back to England, 2 Aug. 1811.

[106] TNA, ADM 7/791–2. One convoy amounted to 255 ships, another 274, all predominantly from St Petersburg and Riga. There were additional convoys in the hundreds. From other ports across the Baltic, much smaller convoys were organised. The average convoy size this year from the Baltic was sixty-five vessels.

[107] Crosby, *American Trade with Russia and the Baltic*, p. 144.

[108] Voelcker, *Saumarez vs. Napoleon*, pp. 91–2.

The victualling system in 1809 found itself under great strain, yet it was a strain they were able to withstand. Unclear organisation in the Victualling Board, communication problems emanating from the supply of such a remote fleet, the loss of a transport, the sudden increase in the size of the Baltic fleet and the difficulty in procuring tonnage worried commanders and concerned the Admiralty. The victualling system had proved adept at reacting quickly to avoid disastrous food shortages in the Baltic fleet. It had proved less able to organise regular, timely shipments in advance. Following a damaging year in which the victualling of the Baltic fleet had been called into question, changes needed to be made.

7

The Navy, Reform and the British State

T HE FRENCH REVOLUTIONARY AND NAPOLEONIC WARS saw long years
of bitter contest between the two major powers of Europe, Britain
and France. Both were forced to throw off ingrained traditions in a quest
for greater military effectiveness and governmental efficiency. The British
state was reshaped by the needs of war. The collection of customs and excise
duties and taxes grew in scale and efficiency, while the first income tax
was introduced. Government sought to gain an effective control over its
workings and outputs, in the process undermining traditional hierarchical
arrangements.[1] There was an enormous expansion of taxes, public debt
and central-government agencies. This was characteristic of the whole
of the Napoleonic War, though it was under the government of Spencer
Perceval, 1809–12, that the country's capacity to raise and spend revenue
grew extensively. As revenue rose, the state's central offices grew in size.
Whereas at the beginning of the eighteenth century these stood at 12,000
employees, by 1797 this had risen to 16,267. By the end of the Napoleonic
War in 1815 the figure was 24,598.[2] The growth of the central infrastructure
was particularly evident in the naval offices. In 1793, the Treasury, Home
Office and Foreign Office contained seventeen, nineteen and nineteen
personnel respectively. By comparison, the year before, the Navy Office
had 98 permanent staff and 10 extra clerks, which by 1813 had grown to 151
with 80 extra clerks, a total of 231. The Admiralty Office's 45 employees in
1797 grew to 65 in 1815, while the Victualling Office too had grown from
65 to 105 employees between the beginning of the Great Wars and the
Battle of Trafalgar (1805).[3]

The growth in the size of the state encouraged serious attacks on its
ostensible extravagance and the greed of its ministers: its efficiency was

---

[1] John Brewer, *The Sinews of Power*. John Gascoigne, *Science in the Service of Empire:
Joseph Banks, the British State and the Uses of Science in the Age of Revolution* (Cambridge,
1998), pp. 1–2.

[2] Harling and Mandler, 'From Fiscal-Military State to Laissez-Faire State'.

[3] Morriss, *Foundations of British Maritime Ascendency*, pp. 8–9. Roger Knight, 'Politics
and Trust in Victualling the Navy, 1793–1815', *MM* 94/2 (May 2008), 133–49.

called into question by the opposition in Parliament and the radical press, in particular over how it allocated resources.[4] From the 1780s there were persistent if irregular calls for 'economic reform'. Criticism was directed against the management of public finance, with repeated parliamentary committees of accounts to examine expenditure and methods of accounting.[5] Even after Britain's greatest victories at sea the civil administration of the navy suffered from almost continuous criticism because of its alleged corruption and inefficiency.[6] Herein lies a paradox: how could a state where patronage, favouritism, privilege were rife order itself to fight and win a global war in which unprecedented revenues were collected and government expenditure exceeded all previous records? A more complicated picture emerges. The raising and managing of exceptional amounts of revenue required an overhaul of the British state's administrative machinery. Perceval refused to give in to those arguing for economic reform. 'We cannot without absolute reduction of army, or navy, make any such saving as would justify this expression', he said, stating that absolute reductions were impossible under the circumstances.[7] Nonetheless, a degree of reform was necessary, not merely to appease critics of government spending, but also to improve Britain's war-fighting machine. Given a choice between defeat and reform, British governments unsurprisingly chose the latter: war was a lever for organisational change.[8]

The eighteenth-century state has always been seen as contrasting greatly with the mid-Victorian 'laissez-faire' polity. The purchase of offices, lifetime tenure, the concept of offices as personal property, the existence of fees and perquisites rather than fixed salaries, and political influence over appointments, all characterised the eighteenth-century political world. A 'rational' civil service, with strict salaries, formal superannuation agreements and the political office as a position of public trust came only in the mid-nineteenth century, a far cry from the 'extraordinary patch-work of administrative efficiency and waste, of probity and abuse' that characterised the eighteenth century.[9] Furthermore, while the mid-Victorian state was

---

[4] Harling, *Old Corruption*, pp. 2, 75. Christie, *Wars and Revolutions*, pp. 290, 296.

[5] M. J. Daunton, *Progress and Poverty: An Economic and Social History of Britain 1700–1850* (Oxford, 1995), p. 516.

[6] Bernard Pool, 'Navy Contracts in the Last Years of the Navy Board, 1780–1832', *MM* 50/3 (1964) 161–76, p. 161.

[7] Perceval to Wellesley, Jan. 1810, British Library, Add. 37295, quoted in Harling, *Old Corruption*, p. 133.

[8] B. D. Porter, *War and the Rise of the State: The Military Foundations of Modern Politics* (New York, 1974), pp. 36–9, 58–9, 72–121.

[9] Harling, *Old Corruption*, p. 24. Gerald Aylmer, 'From Office-Holding to Civil

characterised by 'cheap government' and low expenditure compared to other European states, the eighteenth century 'fiscal military' state witnessed very high levels of public expenditure. Spending was £4.9 per capita in 1801 and £4.5 per capita in 1811, compared to £2 per capita in 1851.[10] While there can be no arguing with the fact that the eighteenth century state was one of high public expenditure, the issue of governance is more debateable. Size did not necessarily equate to inefficiency. The inefficiencies and corruption have certainly been overstated. Patronage was a crucial component of appointments, but it is easy to exaggerate the extent of government patronage. There was a growing tendency to appoint men on the grounds of ability, merit and experience, in other words a professionalisation of the naval departments. In some naval departments it was difficult to avoid political influence. The Admiralty ensured that its make-up changed with every change in government, although the secretaries tended to survive the change.[11] The rest of naval administration did not see dismissals on political grounds, at least not after 1714. Hence, the commissioners of the Navy, Victualling, Transport and Sick and Hurt Boards were much more akin to modern civil servants than those of the Admiralty. The navy was less burdened, in Baugh's words, by 'the useless younger sons of great families' than other governmental departments. The chief reason for this was that so many naval jobs required very particular skills and experience.

What is unusual about naval patronage was that so much of it was internal to the naval establishment. The comptroller of the Navy Board was always a Royal Navy captain on half-pay, who acted as the chairman and leader of the board. The surveyor was always a former dockyard master shipwright: he was the navy's principal warship designer. Powerful influences on naval appointments still came from outside the naval establishment. For all that, however well qualified for promotion a man might be by capacity or seniority, it was expected that he should be recommended by someone of rank and status.[12] The years of the French Revolutionary and Napoleonic War would provide further strains on the machinery of the eighteenth-century state. Britain, involved in war for national survival unprecedented in scope, made continual reforms to its

Service: The Genesis of Modern Bureaucracy', *Transactions of the Royal Historical Society*, 5th series, part 30 (1980), 91–108. Harling, *Old Corruption*, p. 10.

[10] Harling, *Old Corruption*, pp. 9–12, 14.

[11] From 1807 it was formalised that the first secretary of the Admiralty would be a political appointment, chosen by the prime minister, while the second secretary was a permanent official known also as the 'Secretary'. Rodger, *Command of the Ocean*, p. 484.

[12] Baugh, *Naval Administration 1715–1750*, pp. 1–5. Rodger, *Command of the Ocean*, pp. 291–311.

administrative bodies. Nowhere was this seen more clearly seen than in the naval departments.

The outbreak of war in 1793 found naval administrators defending themselves from accusations of corruption and waste. The Victualling Board had long been criticised for corruption: in 1782, there had been a lengthy scandal involving the chief clerk to the secretary of the Victualling Board, a man named Wilkins, who had divulged confidential information to a naval agent. Lacking support from the Admiralty, George Philip Towry, at this time secretary to the board, was forced to reinstate him. An outraged Burgoyne resigned from the board and wrote to Towry, 'My good friend, I fear you are likely to have a troublesome life of it, & will I fear soon experience how impossible it is to stem the tide of *jobbs* & *dishonesty*'. Towry, tasked with restoring the good name of the board, saw it as 'absolutely necessary to restore the Victualling Office to the good opinion of the Public', and was under no illusions as to 'how low it had fallen'.[13] The pressure of war would force continued inquiries into the state of the navy and its administration. Calls for reform of the Victualling Board in 1788 following the Commission on Fees were not heeded. Successive governments refused to publish the reports, and the commission's reports remained hidden until 1806, when Pitt's death allowed their release. There were a number of commissions into specific parts of the naval infrastructure, for instance the Commission on Naval Timber of 1792, and select committee investigations into the financing of the naval departments in 1797 and 1798.[14]

Dissatisfaction with the course of the French Revolutionary War would prompt further change. St Vincent's tenure as First Lord in the years 1801–4 brought passionate, if wayward, attempts to reform the civil administration of the navy. St Vincent hoped the Commission of Naval Enquiry in 1803 would cut public expenditure and eradicate corruption in the Navy Board and dockyards, promising to 'enquire and examine into any Irregularities, Frauds and Abuses, which are of have been practised by Persons employed in the several naval departments'. This did more harm than good, with St Vincent's high-handed measures (including cancelling timber contracts) devastating timber, hemp and planking stocks, and

---

[13] Knight, 'Politics and Trust', p. 134.
[14] Their full titles were 'The Commission on Naval Timber Reports of the Commissioners appointed to enquire into the State and Condition of the Woods, forests and Land Revenues of the Crown', and the 'Reports from the Select Committee on Finance 1797–1798', Commons Reports, XII, 36 reports. There were concurrent investigations of the military branches of government, not least the 'Commission of Military Enquiry, reporting from 1806 to 1812'.

temporarilly discredited the case for reform. It did little to assuage popular (or indeed governmental) discontent. The naval departments struggled to cope with the expansion of the war after the Peace of Amiens. Charles Middleton wrote on becoming First Lord in 1805, 'our naval Boards are in such a weak state, that they cannot be relied upon for either advice or execution, but I trust they may be amended. There is no lack of willingness, but we are all worn out, and more active officers must be found as opportunity offers to succeed them.' Thomas Grenville, First Lord in 1806, agreed: 'the civil departments are as it appears to me in the most wretched state: the Victualling Board cannot go on as it is, & the difficulty is to find the right frame to put in & proper persons to conduct it'.[15] The Commission of Naval Revision was created to investigate the 'civil affairs of the navy' in their entirety. Set up in 1804, the Ministry of Talents refused to publish the reports, and the Tenth, Eleventh and Twelfth Reports were not released until April 1809. Although its commissioners were aware of the commission's public role, it was a genuine attempt to reconfigure and improve the naval administration.[16]

The character and competence of the individual office holder was a central part of these investigations. A motion was proposed by Admiral Sir Charles Pole, chairman of the earlier Commission of Naval Enquiry, on the necessity to appoint 'professional' and 'indefatigable' commissioners.[17] Patronage remained an important lever on appointments. The letters of Lord Mulgrave, First Lord of the Admiralty between 1807 and 1810, are dominated by concerns about patronage, both of naval and political appointments.[18] A typical letter, from Captain Courtney Boyle, reminded Mulgrave of 'the interest which my friends have made with your Lordship to obtain me a civil situation in England, and the kind manner in which you have received their applications in my favour'. He stated 'how grateful I should ever feel, to your Lordship, should you think proper to appoint me to one of the additional Commissioners, proposed for the Victualling Board'.[19] Yet the same time as Boyle's application was accepted men of talent were increasingly being brought in. Nicholas Brown, appointed in 1808, had been Nelson's secretary in the Mediterranean for eight years, and later Lord Keith's, where he had organised the supplies for 15,000 seamen on a daily basis. Here was a man who knew his business.

[15] Knight, 'Politics and Trust', p. 139.
[16] Ibid., p. 141.
[17] Macdonald, *Management Competence and Incompetence*, p. 113.
[18] MA 19–20.
[19] MA 20/151, Captain Courtney Boyle to Lord Mulgrave, 12 Oct. 1808.

In 1809 the discovery of misdeeds by the victualling office led to the replacement of three commissioners, creating embarrassment in Parliament. The Victualling Board 'purged' itself, as elderly, ineffectual commissioners were removed in favour of younger, more dynamic – and most importantly competent – officials who were appointed on merit. Commissioners Marsh, Budge and Moody were all removed from service on the board, and replaced with younger more able employees. Accordingly, the naval departments were bodies which over time gained a monopoly on expertise within their fields. Each possessed knowledge, publically acknowledged and achieved by experience, not readily available to everyone, and therefore distinguishable from common practitioners.[20] The Victualling and Transport Boards possessed unrivalled knowledge of the food and shipping markets. They knew how to manage contractors, and oversee contracts.[21]

These changes went hand in hand with the gradual reform of sinecures, reversions and pensions between 1805 and 1815 that marked an important step in the slow transformation of the legal character of office from private property to public trust.[22] Staff remuneration changed from a system based on gratuities and perquisites to one of established salaries with regular long-service increases. The 1780 Commissioners for Examining the Public Accounts laid down the principle that public revenue and private income should be completely separated, although it was not until 1800 that their salary recommendations for the Victualling Board and its staff were put into effect.[23] Soon after its establishment in 1794 the Transport Board made efforts to eliminate abuses that still existed. One of the first resolutions passed by the Transport Board stated that no person belonging to or under the direction of the board should have any property vested in transports, or share or shares of any ships or vessels employed as a transport, directly or indirectly, under pain of dismissal from office.[24] The Commission of Naval Revision ensured that any form of corrupt behaviour was rooted out. It stated that 'No Commissioner, Officer, Clerk, or other person belonging to the Victualling Department shall receive for his own advantage any fee, gratuity, perquisite, or emolument whatever, from any person having, or

---

[20] For this definition of 'expertise' see Eric H. Ash, 'Expertise and the Early Modern State', *OSIRIS* 25/1 (2010), 4–8.

[21] See Knight and Wilcox, *Sustaining the Fleet*, and Chapter 4.

[22] Harling, *Old Corruption*, p. 123.

[23] Roger Morriss, *Naval Power and British Culture, 1760–1850* (London, 2004), p. 31. Commission on Fees, Eighth Report, pp. 695–706, quoted in Macdonald, *Management Competence and Incompetence*, p. 127.

[24] TNA, ADM 108/31, 26 Aug. 1794, quoted in Condon, 'The Establishment of the Transport Board', p. 82.

had, any transactions with the Victualling Department', and ordered that all victualling office employees take an oath, supported by a bond worth three times their respective salaries.[25] Every person entrusted with making purchases, 'or other expenditure of public money abroad' was to 'attest on oath . . . that he neither has received, nor expects to receive, directly or indirectly, any benefit whatever from such expenses', again under penalty.[26] In April 1808 for example, ten Victualling Board employees, including the accountant for cash, were sacked for the simple crime of receiving presents from contractors.[27] This was an unusual event: the Commission of Naval Revision had testified that the 'highly commendable disinterestedness in the Commissioners still continues'.[28]

The Commission of Naval Revision

In April 1809 the Ninth, Tenth, Eleventh and Twelfth Reports of the Commission for Revising and Digesting the Civil Affairs of His Majesty's Navy or more simply the 'Commission of Naval Revision' were published, though its contents had been understood in governmental circles for the two preceding years. The reports would have a great influence on the reforms being introduced to improve the victualling system during the winter of 1809-10. Instead of focusing on personnel the Commission of Naval Revision brought about fundamental systematic change. The impulse for reform came from a variety of sources. While it was partly a response to the scrutiny of public criticism, it performed specific and important roles for the government. Administrative efficiency, or at least a reputation for it, was needed to maintain the credit-worthiness of the fiscal-military state.[29] It was the immediate pressure of war, and the prospect of defeat, that worried those in government. The main concern of the tenth report of the Commission of Naval Revision was 'the pressure of current business': the Napoleonic War.[30] Britain was committed to war until France was defeated. Accordingly, the conflict required unprecedented means to win. As the threat to the country evolved, so did the measures to deal with it: the state was looking for efficiency and stepped in where it did not exist. While the commission was charged with investigating the whole of naval administration, it spent much of its time recommending changes to

[25] Commission of Naval Revision, Tenth Report, p. 21.
[26] Ibid., p. 22.
[27] TNA, ADM 111/187, 23 April 1808.
[28] Commission of Naval Revision, Tenth Report, p. 16.
[29] Daunton, *Progress and Poverty*, p. 517.
[30] Commission of Naval Revision, Tenth Report, pp. 1–3.

the Victualling Board. Throughout 1809 the results of these reports had been implemented; in early 1810 they would begin to take shape. New procedures and systems were brought in after the Commission of Naval Revision had made its recommendations. The report brought in wholesale changes to the way in which victualling services were conducted. Efficient control of ships from shore required accurate reports and timely returns of information to the Admiralty and Victualling Board: this entire process was completely overhauled. The report, advocating as it did a more accountable and streamlined civil service, began to reform the entire culture of naval administration.

The main focus of the Tenth Report was 'the numerous instances of mismanagement', and the huge backlog of accounts. The Commission estimated that there was a total of £10,985,100 worth of cash accounts yet to be paid off and remaining 'unliquidated'. 'We cannot avoid remarking, that when it becomes notorious that the Accounts delivered into any Office generally lay there for a considerable time, and sometimes years before they are finally settled', they wrote. This was put down to 'a lack of sufficient space to employ more clerks' and 'the pressure of the current business', by which they meant the pressure of war. The report stated that 'nothing short of an entire new system [is] likely to be effectual'. The members of the board were divided into committees of correspondence, accounts and stores.[31] Operational issues also caused contemporary concern. 1808 to 1809 was a particularly sensitive time for the Victualling Board. The failure of the Walcheren expedition, deriving from logistical issues, furthered the reformer's remit. The problems the Baltic fleet had faced only added to the sense that the victualling system needed to improve its operational performance.

The Eleventh Report considered the victualling system abroad, at British out-ports and for foreign fleets. As it observed, the business of victualling 'is conducted in a loose and confused manner without system, clearness, regularity or method'. The accounts for stores, which were involved in loading supplies for foreign fleets, were 'unnecessarily intricate and voluminous, without providing any sufficient check'. The Baltic fleet that had been over-supplied in 1808, and would suffer in 1809 from the opposite problem, bore witness to this. With so many of the board's staff involved in rendering accounts, there was some doubt 'who is to be considered really responsible for the Stores'. Books, accounts and returns were 'unnecessarily multiplied', full of defective information, often 'formed from probable calculation, but

---

[31] Ibid., pp. 3–5, 8, 13–14, 36.

not from fact'. There were others that were entirely fictitious. Vouchers and returns of information were therefore often useless. They 'omitted to describe the numerous useless Forms and Accounts kept relating to the supply of provisions to Your Majesty's ships in ordinary – a branch of duty which we found in much unnecessary perplexity'. It is not hard to see why the Victualling Board had occasionally miscalculated when sending supplies to the Baltic fleet in 1808 and 1809. These criticisms aside, the commission's report was not one of blame: instead it targeted 'the consequences of defects, which have gradually and imperceptibly arisen in the course of the last century'. They took advantage of the opportunity to bring in an entirely new system, replacing the piecemeal reforms of the eighteenth century.[32]

The recommendations of the commission were lengthy and wide-ranging. The main objective was a significant improvement in the board's distribution of provisions. All forms of wastage were discouraged. A clerk from the victualling office was to attend the issue of provisions to ensure supplies were correct, while each clerk was to be given a daily issue book in which all issues would be written, including the species and the quantity. Precise amounts of foodstuffs were to be sent to fulfil the needs of exact numbers of men. They were also to ensure all casks were sent off perfectly full. These daily issue books were to be regularly compared to pursers' receipts by the resident agent. The system whereby receipts, vouchers and bills of lading were regulated was improved, with one 'clerk of the check' placed in charge: 'In shipping Provisions and Stores for [foreign] Service, the two clerks shall attend and take an exact Account of the quantity of each species of Stores laden in any Transport, in their respective Daily Issue Books'. These would be forwarded to the clerk of the check, and then the agent, who would compare them quarterly. Great care was taken to document and take account of stores lost by leakage and waste: again it would be recorded in various accounts and ledgers, to be double-checked at regular intervals by the storekeeper. Most importantly complete accounts were to be kept of all stores received, issued and expended. By doing so (and checking that what was coming in was similar to what was going out) they aimed to place the entire victualling establishment on a much more efficient footing, and to target wastage. There would be a quarterly examination of these accounts. Weekly accounts 'of the progress made in shipping off provisions' were ordered, so ensuring that they 'at all times know the progress made in shipping Provisions and Victualling Stores . . . on distant service'.[33]

---

[32] Commission of Naval Revision, Eleventh Report, pp. 4, 6–7, 24.
[33] Ibid., pp. 74–6, 81, 82, 86, 90.

The delivery of foodstuffs to fleets stationed abroad was now regulated, precise and accountable. As the Victualling Board explained, 'it being essentially requisite in the shipment of Provisions from this Department at Deptford to the Foreign Stations that the Commander in Chief, Agent Victuallers and other persons, to whom the said Provisions &c may be consigned, should be made acquainted, as early as possible, with the respective quantities laden on board each vessels'. At the other end of the system, under the new regulations issued to the 'Agents for the Victualling Establishments at the Home Stations', as soon as the masters of the vessels had signed the receipts for the quantities of provisions and victualling stores shipped on board them, the receipts and invoices were to be forwarded immediately to the accountant for stores, 'to the end that an abstract of the articles shipped may be forthwith laid before the Board by him'. The board wanted to oversee all levels of the victualling system. It gave warning of the penalties 'in the event of its at any time occurring that the Masters of the Vessels omit to timely sign the receipt, which the Agent at Deptford is by every means in his power to prevent'.[34] Quantities shipped and delivered were noted, so as to inform future decisions. Great care was taken to ensure the most efficient service. As the commission wrote, 'the Storekeeper is to issue first the provisions that are the oldest, or in the worst condition for keeping, and to this end he is to regulate the conveyance of them to the respective ships, that the Provisions which it may be proper to expend first may be the last received into the Ships, and thereby stowed uppermost, and most readily got at for being first expended'. Those dealing with public money were to be carefully regulated. The chief clerk of the Imprest Office would examine rates of exchange on which bills of exchange were drawn.[35]

The commission found little wrong with the Transport Board. On the contrary, the Ninth Report of 1809, which focused on the workings of the Transport Board, complimented them on the success of the board since its inception in 1794. The Ninth Report stated that 'much Money and Time have also been saved by transferring Ships from one Service to another, according to the demands of each, instead of suffering them to remain unemployed, as was before the practise'.[36] The transport tonnage crisis that had impacted on the Baltic fleet in 1809 did not enter this investigation.

Nevertheless, the commission would leave an important legacy that would impact on the Transport Board. The environment of reform brought

---

[34] TNA, ADM 111/193, 27 Oct. 1809 .
[35] Commission of Naval Revision, Eleventh Report, p. 74.
[36] Commission of Naval Revision, Ninth Report, p. 14.

by the Commision of Naval Revision brought widespread systematic changes were brought to the victualling system during the winter of 1809–10. Performance measurement was at the heart of the administrative changes. Admirals' and captains' correspondence informed those in London. Inter-departmental letters were passed between naval boards, highlighting inef-ficiencies and inaccuracies. Large amounts of information were collected, for instance the 'state and condition' of fleets, and were returned from foreign stations. Occasionally this was recorded in the Victualling Board minutes, but often it was not. Every winter, with Saumarez back in London, changes to systems and procedures could be recommended and executed. On 12 April 1810, for instance, he wrote to the Victualling Board proposing changes to the supply system, advocating fewer, larger shipments planned precisely months in advance.[37] Ships would no longer leave ports under-supplied. The Admiralty made it clear that in the Baltic, fleets were to be provisioned initially with six months' provisions.[38] Notice was given to the officers and agents at Deptford, Chatham, Portsmouth, Plymouth and Dover, and on board the depot ships *Lancaster* and *Harmony* at Sheerness and the Downs'.[39] Never again would ships leave port lacking provisions.

The wide-ranging overhaul of the victualling system was also prompted by the problems of 1809. In April 1810, as the Baltic fleet left for its third year on station, the Admiralty allowed the Transport Board to raise its tonnage rates for the hire of freight:

> Whereas you have transmitted to us in your letter to our secretary of the 12th Inst. the copy of a letter you had received from the Victualling Board upon the subject of the Tonnage that will be required for conveying Provi-sions to the fleet in the Baltic, under the orders of Vice Admiral Sir James Saumarez . . . it will be necessary to increase the rate of hire, to twenty five shillings per Ton, per month, for three months certain, which is the rate of hire you have given for some time past, in cases of emergency; we have taken the same into consideration, & do hereby require and direct you, to procure the Tonnage which may be required for the service in question, on the most reasonable terms in your power, in sufficient time to load the vessels of the period specified in your letter for the Transport of Provisions for the Baltic Fleet accordingly.[40]

The rate of hire was increased: the Transport Board had paid for more transports to solve the problem. Difficulties securing tonnage in the future

---

[37] TNA, ADM 2/158/115–16.
[38] TNA, ADM 2/157/464–5, Admiralty to Transport Board, 30 Jan. 1810.
[39] TNA, ADM 111/194, 31 Jan. 1810.
[40] TNA, ADM 2/158/115–16, Admiralty to Transport Board, 19 April 1810.

had been comprehensively reduced. Additionally, the Board was helped by a narrowing of the nation's strategic involvements. With the operations to Corunna and Walcheren now at an end demand for transports decreased. This, in line with the raising of the freight rate, meant that by 1810, any crisis that might have existed concerning the procurement of transport tonnage was over. The Transport Board issued increasingly detailed demands by select shipping. Whereas in 1809 they were hiring almost desperately, by 1810 they could be choosier. In 1810, three tenders by Henley and Son were offered: the vessels *Mary*, *Freedom* and *Norfolk* were each rejected, the secretary to the board writing to Henley that 'I am directed by the Board to acquaint you that she is not wanted'.[41] By September 1810 the board had more than enough shipping for its need. On the same date, two other Henley ships, the *Zephyr* of 372 tons and the *Trusty* of 487 tons, tendered for 'six months Coppered Transports', were also rejected by the Transport Office.[42]

Crucially, and a sign of the Victualling Board's increasing competence and expertise, decision-making was centred at the board's central office. This enabled it to take a longer-term view of what was needed. Knowing the numbers of men in the Baltic and the daily ration, whilst also being aware of the transport tonnage situation, they were better placed to make the decisions of when and how much to send. In what was essentially a centralisation of the victualling process, Saumarez still played a role, but a more subsidiary one. By 1810, the Victualling Board was in complete control of all remote supply to the Baltic, deciding when shipments were sent as well as the quantities of foodstuffs to be sent.[43] Deliveries became known as 'moieties', with two main shipments of victuals planned for each year. The term moiety had previously been used to describe payments of species to the Swedish government, as part of their subsidy.[44]

Saumarez was of course still in correspondence with the Victualling Board, and was of great assistance in advising or correcting its knowledge of the number of seamen in the Baltic. The Victualling Board wrote to the Transport Board that same month, acknowledging his advice that his fleet had grown in size, requiring an extra 900 tons of provisions to be forwarded.[45] Moreover, this demonstrates the remarkable flexibility available to the Baltic victualling system in 1810. The supply was increased

[41] NMM, HNL 13/22, f. 2, 14 Sept. 1810.
[42] NMM, HNL 14/5, f. 1, 5–6, 14 Sept. 1810.
[43] SRO, HA 93/6/1/1362, Victualling Board to Saumarez, 5 June 1810.
[44] See TNA, FO 73/49, Thornton to Canning, 9 Aug. 1808.
[45] TNA, ADM 110/62/131, Victualling Board to Transport Board, 5 June 1810.

from 2,000 to 2,900 tons in a matter of weeks without any complications or delays. Such an arrangement could avoid the issue of procuring transports, which was the delaying factor of the previous year. 'In order to afford the Transport Board timely notice of the Tonnage required for this service', wrote the Victualling Board, they would be informed in advance, 'stating that the Tonnage necessary for the first moiety, consisting of 2000 Tons, will require to be at Deptford, in perfect readiness to load by the first week in May next; and that the second Moiety consisting of the like number of Tons, will be required to be in readiness, at the same place, by the first week in July'.[46] The board also decided that the 'respective Cargoes of the different Ships should be comprised of equal proportions of each particular Species of Provisions'. Up until then victuallers had not carried equal proportions of all species.[47] It is highly likely that the loss of the *President* had caused serious deficiencies of particular foodstuffs, which were then greatly missed. The agent at Deptford was directed to take special care that such regular assortment of the different species be 'duly apportioned and punctually attended to'.[48]

The commanders in the Baltic could still have an impact on decision-making about victualling. For instance, the Victualling Board responded quickly to a hastening latter from the George Hope, first captain to the Baltic Fleet (in modern parlance the chief of staff, and the man responsible for such planning), who urged that the second moiety of the provisions be urgently forwarded. They asked the Transport Board when the necessary tonnage might be ready.[49] The planning remained the Victualling Board's responsibility. The Victualling Board was outlining specific times for victualling delivery, up to six months in advance, corresponding with the Transport Board to ensure food and transport were coordinated.[50] In the first months of 1810, the Victualling Board could state to the Transport Board that the forthcoming supplies for the Baltic fleet

> will amount in the whole to about Four Thousand Tons, the first variety of which it is essentially requisite should be so timely shipped as to be forwarded from Deptford by the 1st day of June next, and the other variety by the first day of August following, we have to request that you will cause us to be furnished, by the 1st day of May next, with suitable Vessels

[46] TNA, ADM 111/194, 31 March 1810.
[47] Note for example the *Flora* victuallers, see p. 141. In neither of those ships for example was there wine, spirits, sugar or butter.
[48] TNA, ADM 1/9/306–7, TNA, ADM 111/194, 31 March 1810.
[49] TNA, ADM 110/62/199–200, Victualling Board to Transport Board, 14 July 1810.
[50] TNA, ADM 110/64/90–1, Victualling Board to Transport Board, 20 July 1811.

for the conveyance of the first variety to the extent of 2000 Tons, and that you will take such previous measures for providing tonnage for the remaining variety or 2000 Tons as you may judge expedient, observing that it is indispensably necessary that the vessels to be appropriated should be at Deptford in perfect readiness to load by the 1st day of July next.[51]

By planning so far ahead, and with knowledge of the changing availability of transports at their fingertips, the Victualling Board solved the problems that could arise from temporary shortages of both tonnage and specific victuals.

The contrast with three years earlier was marked. In 1808, there had been four small shipments of victuals, sent at Saumarez's bidding, often amounting to little more than short-term solutions to the problem of provisioning. Dependent on communication from Saumarez, these deliveries could be hamstrung by the need to prepare at short notice; in times of transport shortage this posed problems. Following the changes made in the winter of 1809–10, this would no longer be the case. But by centralising the victualling system, the naval administration had ensured that huge shipments of victuals could be prepared in advance. With time, and extra money for securing freight, delays in shipments would be a thing of the past. Two large shipments were organised by the Victualling Board; they could be brought forward, if, for example, the numbers of seamen in the Baltic changed. And so it was done; this became the regular system for victualling service. In March 1810, it was agreed to send four months' provisions for 15,000 men, the first moiety to leave during the first week of June, the second to be ready to be shipped by the first week in August that year.[52] For this first moiety, the Transport Board was securing tonnage far in advance, as early as 28 April and 1 May 1810.[53] Ships would be sent when loaded: hence the first two victuallers, ready on 11 May, joined the first convoy. The next ships fully loaded were ready on 21 May, the last on 2 June.[54] The majority had already been loaded before 1 June, the time limit set for the transports given in the letter of 31 March 1810.

Small misjudgements could be rectified. Captain Garret, the agent for transports at Deptford, complained that the vessels furnished by the Transport Board for the conveyance of provisions for the use of the Baltic fleet had been 'found incapable of taking the whole proportion required to be sent out by about 700 Bags', and 'it being absolutely necessary that

---

[51] TNA, ADM 110/61/460–1, Victualling Board to Transport Board, 31 March 1810.
[52] See TNA, ADM 111/194, 31 March 1810.
[53] TNA, ADM 111/195, 28 April 1810, 1 May 1810. Also the 3 and 4 May.
[54] TNA, ADM 111/195, 11 May 1810, 21 May 1810, 2 June 1810.

the said Bread should be forwarded, and that a proportion of other species should be shipped therewith on order to Ballast the Vessels that may be appropriated to convey the same'. Within two days the Transport Board had obliged, securing the *Elizabeth* transport of 162 tons for the service, thereby completing the full amount of the first moiety.[55] The second moiety was arranged similarly, though this time supplies for 17,000 men were sent, in line with the increase in size of the Baltic fleet. The full complement of transports was ready by 7 August 1810, only a few days later than planned.[56]

Further changes were made. Permanent victuallers were sent to aid fleets heading to the Baltic, again at the bidding of the Admiralty rather than the commander in chief, carrying fresh water.[57] Another victualler was sent there to furnish other provisions.[58] Increased use was made of other British out-ports, in particular Yarmouth. In 1808 and 1809 supplies had come only from Deptford, despite Yarmouth's proximity to the Baltic, in sailing time as well as distance. Both the 1801 and 1807 expeditions to the Baltic had sailed from Yarmouth, though it had not previously been used by Saumarez's fleet. In 1810 it began to be used to supply certain victuals to the fleet. This was initially suggested by Admiral Dixon in 1809, and passed on by the Victualling Board to the Admiralty. He asked that supplies of live oxen and vegetables might occasionally sent from Yarmouth for the fleet. The Victualling Board was initially sceptical. There were no instances of live cattle being sent to Yarmouth, and there were concerns that 'it would be very difficult if not impracticable, to preserve vegetables on such a Voyage'. Nor was the Admiralty were keen on the idea.[59] However, the following year, Yarmouth began to be used to cater for the increasing victualling needs of the Baltic fleet.[60] Fairly large amounts were sent, 'as opportunities occur in his Majesty's Ships'. The majority of the supplies came to Yarmouth from Deptford itself with victuals redirected from the capital. In a further example of the Victualling Board expanding its supply base, it also took on responsibility for the island of Anholt's provisioning on a permanent basis. An ongoing arrangement was agreed to supply the troops at the island.[61] With the Victualling Board controlling the

---

[55] TNA, ADM 111/195, 24 May 1810, 26 May 1810.

[56] It is not clear from the archives, but as occurred with the first shipment, it is highly likely that the first transports to be loaded would have left much earlier than 7 August. ADM 111/196, 7 Aug. 1810.

[57] TNA, ADM 2/160/259–60, Admiralty to Victualling Board, 5 April 1811.

[58] TNA, ADM 2/160/466, Admiralty to Victualling Board, 28 June 1811.

[59] TNA, ADM 110/60/281, Victualling Board to Admiralty, 18 Aug. 1809

[60] TNA, ADM 2/159/58–9, Admiralty to Victualling Board, 30 Aug. 1810.

[61] TNA, ADM 110/62/137–9, Victualling Board to Admiralty, 8 June 1810.

distribution of victuals to the Baltic fleet, Saumarez could concentrate on his operational objectives rather than spending time on managing the provisions for his fleet.

The victualling system improved

Contemporary opinions about the performance of the victualling service were rooted in the immediate concerns of administrators and commanders. The first concern was effectiveness. This was not a word familiar in the early nineteenth century, though its meaning would have been: ensuring a system that worked and achieved the intended objectives. Commanders' comments on supply consisted almost solely of complaints: only at crisis points did victualling as a subject explicitly enter the correspondence between commanders and administrators. In 1809, it was evident to all that the provisioning system was not working, and the travails of that year were referred to in later years as examples to avoid. For the Victualling and Transport Boards, effectiveness meant ensuring that supplies arrived on time, in the right amounts, at the designated locations. In 1808 and 1809, despite delays and encumbrances, the victualling system was effective in getting the basic task done: keeping men at sea fed adequately. Instead, it was the quest for efficiency, a more nuanced concept, that was at the heart of critical pamphleteering and rigorous government commissions. The government, and indeed the public, strove for more. With effectiveness achieved, 'efficiency' became the target of administrators. Applied to the provisioning system this meant ensuring delays were minimal, and that wastage was rooted out. Efficiency is a much more measurable concept, quantitatively determined by the ratio of output to input, or rather, the quality of service attained for the money spent. Judging efficiency is therefore a means of testing the improvement of the victualling service in terms of speed and wastage.

The Commission of Naval Revision brought fundamental systematic changes to the vicualling system. The reforms carried out during the winter of 1809–10 reconfigured the way the Baltic fleet was supplied, improving the speed and efficiency of the logistical effort. Firstly, it was vital to ensure that provisions arrived in the Baltic quickly. An appropriate designation is 'timeliness': provisions needed to arrive quickly but not before they were needed. Because administrators were dealing with perishable supplies, foodstuffs arriving too early would be rotten by the time they were needed. The effective management of provisions required cooperation and co-ordination across more than one government body. The speed with which provisions were distributed can be separated into several categories: the time taken, on receiving orders from the Admiralty, for the necessary tonnage to be ordered from the Transport Board and for the necessary victuals to be ordered from the victualling stores; the speed in which tonnage is secured; and the period taken to load provisions and arrange a convoy. It is also possible to judge victualling efficiency: to what degree were shortages and wastage an issue?

Admiralty to Victualling Board orders

On receiving orders from the Admiralty, or a request from a fleet commander, the Victualling Board would order the necessary tonnage and provisions there and then, always within twenty-four hours. Syrett commented that in the 1780s, 'for the Admiralty to transmit an order within 24 hours of receipt was rather exceptional', with delays of three to four days commonplace.[62] This was certainly not true by the 1800s. In 1805, Charles Middleton had planned a detailed distribution of duties among the commissioners of the Admiralty to promote 'economy of time' and the 'punctual discharge of duty', ever the objective of that distinguished administrator.[63] By the end of the Napoleonic Wars and certainly by 1808, the processing of letters was speedy and efficient. William Marsden, second secretary at the Admiralty, observed that 'no public letter was ever omitted (unless under very peculiar circumstances) to be read at the Board, minuted, answered and despatched, if practicable, on the day of its receipt'.[64]

Time taken to secure tonnage

Between 1808 and 1812 the average time between the Victualling Board requesting transport tonnage for the Baltic fleet and that tonnage being delivered was 9.11 days. This in itself is impressive. The speed of transport procurement becomes more illuminating if we look at the average times taken for tonnage to be supplied each year between 1808 and 1812, as shown in Figure 12. The average increase in time in 1809, the year of transport shortage, can be seen. What is more noticeable from this graph is the decrease in the average time it took for tonnage to be secured after 1809. By 1812 the time had been almost halved. Following the problems of

[62] Syrett, *Shipping and the American War*, p. 7.
[63] *Barham Papers*, III, pp. 76–8.
[64] William Marsden, *A Brief Memoir of the Life and Writings of the Late William Marsden, Written by Himself* (London, 1838), p. 97. Quoted in Morriss, *Naval Power and British Culture*, p. 19.

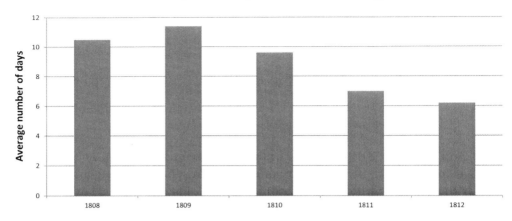

Figure 12. Average time taken to procure tonnage, 1808–12
Source: TNA, ADM 111/187–8, TNA, ADM 111/191–3, TNA, ADM 111/195–6, TNA, ADM 111/199–200, TNA, ADM 111/203–5, TNA, ADM 110/58/328–9. See Appendix 1. It is calculated by measuring the time delay between the order being given for tonnage by the Victualling Board and the last transport being procured.

1809, the Admiralty wrote to the Transport Board, recognising from the previous years' difficulties the crucial importance of securing the necessary tonnage. The Admiralty gave the Transport Board a blank cheque to raise the freight rate to 25 shillings, making ship-owners more willing to come forward and let their vessels.

Transports were secured within a week of orders being given. The speed with which transport tonnage could be procured throughout 1808–12 becomes even more marked if the Victualling and Transport Boards' performance is considered not over a short period, but throughout the French Revolutionary and Napoleonic Wars. By 1810, transport-procurement speed had increased dramatically, especially compared with corresponding times before the Peace of Amiens. The average time taken to procure transport tonnage to support Lord Keith's Mediterranean fleet between 1800 and 1802 was 29 days. The contrast with the figure for the period 1808–12 – a mere 9.11 days – was marked.[65] Although the earlier period presents data from a different fleet in a different theatre, in each case the duties of the Transport Board were the same: to hire transports as quickly as possible. The contrast between the board's effectiveness in 1800–2 and their performance by 1810 is self-evident. This was a vast improvement and demonstrates further the

[65] TNA, ADM 111/154–5, ADM 111/158–61, ADM 111/163, ADM 111/187–8, ADM 111/191–3, ADM 111/195–6, ADM 111/199–200, ADM 111/203–5, ADM 110/58/328–9. See Appendix 1 and 2.

smoother, speedier and more efficient naval administration following the report of the Commission of Naval Revision.

Time taken to load victualling shipments

Once tonnage was secured there was then the time taken to load victuallers and to arrange and join a convoy. This was a cumbersome and often laborious task. In 1808 Perceval wrote that 'everybody knows how much time is consumed getting Transports out of the River [Thames] to the Ports of Departure and how many expeditions have been delayed for weeks and sometimes months from that cause alone'.[66] This may have been related to complaints in January 1808 that the Portsmouth victualling office had taken far too long to revictual some transports.[67] Table 11 shows the average yearly time taken for this step in the process with the Baltic fleet.

Table 11. Time taken to load and arrange a convoy, 1808–11

Year	Time taken to load and arrange convoy
1808	7.25 days
1809	12.2 days
1810	13.3 days

The average time increased between 1808 and 1810, though Appendix 3 demonstrates that this process often took as little as four or five days: in 1809 and 1810 a couple of exceptional delays account for the longer period. Naval administraors were not helped by the fact that arranging a convoy depended on merchants' acquiescence and the availability of escorts. Baltic convoys were arranged between the Admiralty and interested merchants. By 1812, victualling deliveries were planned to take advantage of convoys. As the Victualling Board noted, convoys would leave 'every 14 Days from 9th July to the 15th October, in order that the Victuallers belonging to this Department may be prepared to take advantage of the several convoys, and to avoid the delay and expense occasioned by the necessity of affording protection to single ships which might have sailed with the general convoys'.[68]

---

[66] MA, 19/29.
[67] Hall, *British Strategy*, p. 40.
[68] TNA, ADM 111/204/295–7, 14 July 1812.

Wastage

It was the Victualling Board's duty to plan each individual fleet's requirements. Informed by the Admiralty of a fleet's size, the Victualling Board would also have access to the 'Admiralty Ship Lists', recorded monthly, giving the complement of men for each ship and fleet. As such they knew the number of men on each station and the daily ration required by each individual. From this they would calculate the amount of each provision that was needed each day by the fleet, and could then distribute provisions designed to last for a set period of time. Much rested upon these calculations. Sending too little would lead to shortages. To send too much would be a waste of resources. The estimates were generally very accurate, with specific quantities sent out to supply exact forces. For example, in September 1801 the Victualling Board sent out 80,000 four-pound pieces of pork with one shipment to the Mediterranean, 'being a proportion for twenty thousand men for two months'.[69] This amounted to 320,000 individual rations. This amount of pork, divided by the 20,000 seamen, meant the shipment contained 16 rations per man serving in the Mediterranean. And, since each man was given two rations of pork per week, this allowed enough pork for eight weeks, almost exactly the two months planned for by the Victualling Board. Far from being a leaden institution responding to demand at short notice, the Victualling Board practised a highly sophisticated level of planning and organisation.

Judging efficiency is a matter of judging wastage against shortage. Knowing the number of men stationed in each theatre, the board could calculate the number of rations needed over a year. The Victualling Board minutes show the number of rations sent out. If significantly higher amounts of rations were sent out than were needed, then we can talk of wastage. If there was significantly less being sent out, then there was clearly a shortage. The Baltic theatre particularly lends itself to this mode of analysis in view of its annual status. Since the majority of the fleet would return at the end of each year, annual needs can be book-ended and isolated individually. Bread was the staple of a seaman's diet. A fleet of 11,000 men required 11,000 lbs of bread per day. The provisions brought on board the fleet on leaving Deptford would maintain them for six months. In 1808 Saumarez left for the Baltic, in his words 'well equipped for a six months cruise'.[70] To keep the fleet maintained for the rest of the year required 1,777,825 lbs of bisket bread to be transported out to the Baltic. The total amount of

[69] TNA, ADM 111/160, 16 Sept. 1801.
[70] SRO, HA 93, Saumarez to Martha Saumarez, 18 April 1808.

bread sent out was 2,500,400 lbs. Supplies were also sent out to supply 10,000 Spanish troops temporarily supplied by the British fleet in the Baltic. Figure 13 shows the amount of bread required and the amount of bread delivered throughout the 1808–12 period.

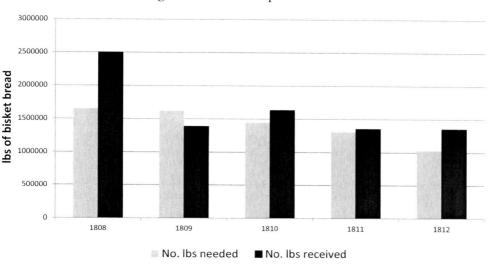

Figure 13. Efficiency of victualling deliveries, 1808–12: bread
Source: TNA, ADM 111/187–8, ADM 111/191–3, ADM 111/195–6, ADM 111/199–200, ADM 111/203–5, ADM 110/58/328–9. See Appendix 5.

In 1808 significantly more bread was sent than was needed. The large amount sent, particularly early in 1808, might have been intended not just for the Baltic fleet but also to feed Sir John Moore's military expedition sent to the Baltic in May for joint operations with Sweden. This force was withdrawn in the summer because of a dispute between Moore and the Swedish king, and was moved to support the Spanish revolt against France in the Peninsula. This left an excess of foodstuffs in the Baltic, explaining the over-supply. Despite the departure of Moore's army, further supplies continued to be sent in September. With fears for the Baltic fleet's provisioning efforts, and unsure of Britain's ability to victual them, this over-supply was a cautious move in case of large losses while going through the Great Belt. The following year, the Victualling Board made the opposite mistake. 1809 was the only year that too little was sent. Instead of sending too much, they barely sent enough: shortage instead of waste. This is a good example of inefficiency leading to ineffectiveness. The deficit can partly be explained by the surplus left over from the year before: it is no coincidence, however, that it was in 1809 that the most pronounced victualling complaints were made by Saumarez.[71]

The victualling practice reforms in the winter of 1809–10 also marked a more efficient organisation of resources. In 1810 and 1811, the difference between the provisions needed and provisions sent was far closer. In these two years increasingly accurate calculations were made by the Victualling Board between the needs of the fleet and provisions shipped.

Table 12. Bread needed and delivered to the Baltic fleet, 1808–12

Year	lbs of bread needed	lbs of bread delivered	% difference
1808	1,777,825	2,500,400	28.90
1809	1,619,199	1,388,240	−14.26
1810	1,445,610	1,631,056	11.37
1811	1,307,382	1,355,200	3.53
1812	1,027,644	1,355,200	24.17

Source: TNA, ADM 111/187–8, ADM 111/191–3, ADM 111/195–6, ADM 111/199–200, ADM 111/203–5, ADM 110/58/328–9. Appendix 5.

Table 12 refers only to bisket bread but these sorts of accurate provisioning estimates were made for all species of foodstuffs. Only beef, which on most stations could be procured locally, was exempt from these calculations. Even here reductions in beef transported to the Baltic or Mediterranean were made only when secure local supplies had been organised. Figure 14 shows the amount of spirits needed and sent between 1808 and 1812. The graph shows a similar pattern to bisket bread, although more pronounced in the first two years. In 1808 there was a vast over-supply, to an even greater extent than with bread. Spirits having greater longevity than bisket-bread meant much more would keep until the following year. It is possible the following year's shortage was planned to be covered by the previous year's over-supply. However, we know that in 1809 there were shortages of spirits, as Saumarez complained of that specific deficit and was forced to purchase spirits locally.[72] Between 1810 and 1812, the quantity of spirits required and the amount transported became increasingly congruous. In 1810 and 1811 the Victualling Board's calculations were almost exactly right, with only 19.32 per cent and 6.61 per cent extra being sent. This slight wastage on the part of the board was understandable. Given that transports could be lost,

[71] This was exacerbated by ships leaving for the Baltic with less than the original six months' rations. See pp. 142–3.
[72] TNA, ADM 111/193, 29 Nov. 1809.

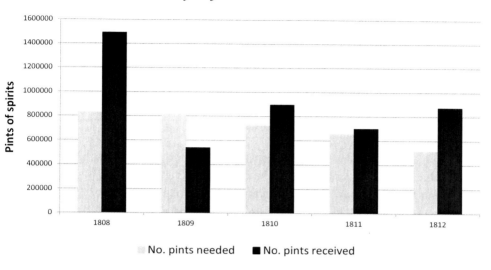

Figure 14. Efficiency of victualling deliveries, 1808–12: spirits
Source: TNA, ADM 111/187–8, ADM 111/191–3, ADM 111/195–6, ADM 111/199–200, ADM 111/203–5, ADM 110/58/328–9. See Appendix 6.

Table 13. Spirits needed and delivered to the Baltic fleet, 1808–12

Year	Amount needed	Amount sent	% difference
1810	722,805 lbs	895,992 lbs	19.32
1811	653,691 lbs	699,992 lbs	6.61
1812	513,822 lbs	873,396 lbs	41.16

Source: TNA, ADM 111/187–8, ADM 111/191–3, ADM 111/195–6, ADM 111/199–200, ADM 111/203–5, ADM 110/58/328–9. Appendix 6.

and that provisions could go off, it was logical that the naval administration would allow a degree of error with their calculations. The figure for 1812 is less precise, although there are good reasons for this. The 'amount sent' column is slightly skewed since Britain in 1812 was supplying the Swedish forces with victuals, now that they were once again allied with Britain. Secondly Russia ceased to be a Baltic antagonist in 1812: Royal Navy ships were ordered away from the Baltic to other theatres throughout the year, reducing the amount needed, particularly at the end of the year.

A key tenet of the British state was its ability to reform itself, under pressure of fighting a war unprecedented in scale. With appointments made on grounds of merit, and traditional eighteenth-century throw-backs of gratuities and perquisites removed, the British state was showing itself to be a more flexible institution than has previously been supposed. Fundamentally, the state proved adept at enacting systematic change. The Commission of Naval Revision prompted an overhaul of the victualling system with immediate effect, and a legacy of reforming agency. From 1809 transports were procured more quickly than ever before and exact quantities of provisions were distributed. The delays of 1809 would not be repeated again. The key logisticical improvement during the Napoleonic War was the gradual – yet crucial – improvement in speed with which deliveries of foodstuffs were ordered, arranged and loaded. Delays might not have always been the fault of naval administration: this did not stop it improving its performance. The timely arrival of provisions would have telling consequences for British seapower.

8

Logistics and Seapower, 1810–1812

T HE REFORMS during the winter of 1809–10 made crucial and lasting improvements to the victualling service. The planning of victualling shipments was now centralised at the Victualling Board, in the hands of those with expert knowledge and experience of arranging supplies. Planning ahead, unheard of in 1808–9, meant tonnage could be secured in advance, with increased amounts of money available for transport hire. The Victualling Board was organising the distribution of resources before commanders requested them; efficiency became the overriding objective of the board. If 1809 had been a year in which shortage had become a significant issue, from 1810 wastage was the concern. Far from being short of supplies, the Baltic fleet was over-supplied throughout 1810–12. The Victualling Board in 1810, having made a detailed account of the quantities already sent, and those about to be sent, suspended the shipment of 400 tons of food, so as to avoid 'considerable expense and loss to the public in the event of the same not being required for the supply of the beforementioned squadron'.[1] Again, the contrast with the previous year was marked. Whereas in 1809 the Victualling Board had been desperate to requisition any tonnage available, and struggled to send ships out fully supplied, in 1810 they were asking permission to suspend shipments. In reply it was ordered that 'the whole of the Provisions remaining due upon warrant for the supply of the Squadron in the Baltic be countermanded'.[2]

By 1811, the Admiralty had all but ceased writing to the Victualling Board.[3] The lack of any correspondence at all concerning provisioning

---

[1] TNA, ADM 110/62/275–6, Victualling Board to Admiralty, 9 Aug. 1810.

[2] TNA, ADM 111/196, 11 Aug. 1810.

[3] A careful study of the Admiralty out-letters finds two examples of Admiralty–Victualling Board correspondence. One informed the board they were sending two transports to act as permanent victuallers in the Baltic, the other concerned a shipment of provisions ordered to Wingo Sound for the benefit of Saumarez's fleet. Saumarez wrote to the Victualling Board to urge that a supply be hastened; the board wrote back that this was already taken care of. TNA, ADM 2/160 and ADM 1/161, TNA, ADM 110/64/425–6, Victualling Board to Admiralty, 2 Dec. 1811.

is a telling demonstration of the thorough improvement the provision-ing system had undergone by 1811. There was no longer any need for the Admiralty to intervene. On only one isolated occasion during these years did administrators raise concerns over a victualling delivery. In the summer of 1811, the Victualling Board wrote concerning the procurement of shipping. The board complained to the Admiralty, and wrote to the Transport Board, referring them to their previous letters to remind them of the application made earlier, strongly impressing on them 'the neces-sity of suitable vessels being immediately furnished for the service'.[4] They were less than impressed with the Transport Board, also complaining of 500 tons of shipping still required for the fleet in the Mediterranean.[5] Echoes of the issues in 1809 returned to the Victualling Board in 1811, with worries once again that inadequacies in the Transport Board would bring about delays. The Transport Board was more competent than their administrative peers in Somerset House had expected. On 12 June they replied, stating that 'as two ships making together 461 Tons have already sailed, and one of 392 Tons is now ready to load in aid of the Baltic Service, they trust that no inconvenience will arise from the time which has been necessarily required for providing for it, especially as the Baltic Fleet has so recently sailed from this country; but that there will be no delay on the part of their Department in completing such Service'.[6] It was a problem of communication rather than organisation.

Like the previous year, 1811 revealed a victualling system coping well with demand. For the second shipment of 1811, the Transport Board had procured shipping before the foodstuffs had even been ordered. The same day the Victualling Board ordered the second moiety to be put on warrant they received a letter from the Transport Board stating that the transport *Urania* of 206 tons was already appropriated to load cargo for the Baltic 'in aid of the 1,392 Tons of Navy Provisions for which conveyance was required to the Baltic'.[7] Their calculations as to what was needed were proved to be correct. As they wrote, 'the Provisions on board His Majesty's Ships in the Baltic, together with what are on board Victuallers there, and on the way thither, being, as the Committee conceive, sufficient to serve to the end of December next'. As such, they ordered that 'no further supplies are to be forwarded to His Majesty's Ships and Vessels in the Baltic', and requested the accountant for stores 'for his causing the Provisions remaining due on

[4] TNA, ADM 111/199, 12 June 1811.
[5] TNA, ADM 111/199, 3 June 1811.
[6] TNA, ADM 111/199, 12 June 1811.
[7] TNA, ADM 111/200, 27 July 1811.

warrant from Deptford for the Baltic to be countermanded'.[8] In 1811, Dr Jamison, the physician to the Baltic fleet, wrote to the Transport Board, complaining that the fleet had perhaps too much lemon juice.

> To be persevered in during long voyages, it often forms the remote cause of other diseases, such as water in the chest, general Dropsy, Dysentery, or Debility of the digestive organ . . . a large use of Lemon Juice will debilitate the most healthy and when persevered into perhaps a necessary extent to cure frequent returns of Scorbutic action, and the want of necessary nourishing Diet encourages its debilitating powers, Hence the diseases of debility which I have mentioned frequently follow its lavish use in the previous reduced constitutions from vicissitude of Climate described in the notation.[9]

That the physician to the Baltic fleet was able to use a word like 'lavish' to describe the supply of lemon juice to the fleet says much about how the system had been improved.

In 1812, the supply of the Baltic continued as it had done in 1810 and 1811, that is to say, without drama or controversy. Transport tonnage was procured on schedule, victualling convoys left on time.[10] Convoys were fixed to the Baltic 'every 14 Days from 9th July to the 15th October, in order that the Victuallers belonging to this Department may be prepared to take advantage of the several convoys, and to avoid the delay and expense occasioned by the necessity of affording protection to single ships which might have sailed with the general convoys'.[11] If there were shortages of manpower loading, the Victualling Board provided extra manpower: 'it being of the utmost importance that the Victuallers loading for the Baltic should be all completed by the end of the next week' they wrote, 'write to the Agent at Deptford and direct him to cause every exertion to be used for that purpose, and if it shall be deemed necessary, to employ a part of the men during Extra hours upon the said service.'[12] The Victualling Board, with decision-making centralised in its offices, and confident in its abilities to adapt to changing circumstances, was managing a flexible system, fit for purpose. Of course, no system was perfect. Eighteenth-century communication times, the regularity of adverse weather and currents and the unpredictability of winds meant that even the best-laid plans could come awry. James Yeo,

[8] TNA, ADM 111/200, 18 Sept. 1810, 20 Sept. 1810.
[9] TNA, ADM 1/3761, Dr Jamison to the Transport Board, 4 Nov. 1810.
[10] TNA, ADM 111/203.
[11] TNA, ADM 111/204/295–7, 14 July 1812.
[12] TNA, ADM 111/204, 1 Aug. 1812.

the agent victualler at Minorca during the 1800s, had highlighted the difficulty in planning complex operations amidst challenging conditions: as he pointed out, 'in great and multiplied concerns it's possible for an oversight to happen'.[13] Victualling operations required careful planning, deliberate calculations and inter-board organisation. They also needed flexibility to deal with unforeseen events.

On only one occasion was a ship forced off station due to victualling concerns. In 1811, HMS *Plantagenet* was stationed off Rostock escorting merchant vessels on their way to and from the Baltic. Its captain, Eyles, wrote on 28 July speaking of 'the expense of Provisions as stated in the weekly account, having now not more than fifty nine days Bread & Spirits at two thirds allowance'. He added that the 'victualling also of the *Woodlark* and *Fly*', two ships also in his squadron 'will reduce me more'. He stated that he could 'not rely upon any supply from the Transports gone up, for what are the Contents of two amongst so many'.[14] The lack of supplies meant he was forced off his station. As Dixon explained to Saumarez, 'In consequence of the very reduced state of the Water and Provisions of that ship. I have directed Captain Williams of the *Dictator* to succeed Captain Eyles on that station, and intend taking the *Plantagenet* to Anholt to compleat her water and afterwards send her to Wingo Sound for her Provisions'.[15] The two other ships previously mentioned, although smaller, would remain on station: Eyles mentioned that 'the *Woodlark* & *Fly* [would remain] to Cruize here until my return which movement I trust you will approve'.[16] This was an isolated occasion and one whose operational effects were negligible. The ship's station off Rostock was relatively close to British victualling bases: both Hanö and Anholt were 120 miles away. Ships from stations away from Hanö, Gothenburg, Karlskrona and Anholt in the eastern and lower Baltic (for example off Rostock) were most at risk from running out of victuals. However, as Eyles commented, transports would still reach them. Although the *Plantagenet* left its station, the *Woodlark* and *Fly* remained, and the *Dictator* would soon join them: operational effectiveness was not compromised. It is telling that fifty-nine days' worth of victuals provoked such concern: the bar of provisioning standards had been set very high. That this constituted the only major occasion when operations were influenced by victualling speaks volumes about the overall effectiveness of Baltic provisioning in these years.

[13] NMM, KEI/L/2/212, Yeo to Keith, 29 May 1800.
[14] SRO, HA 93/6/1/1810/2, Captain Eyles to Dixon, 28 July 1811.
[15] SRO, HA 93/6/1/1810, Dixon to Saumarez, 4 Aug. 1811.
[16] SRO, HA 93/6/1/1810/1, Captain Eyles to Dixon, 25 July 1811.

This incident aside, the story of victualling from 1810 to 1812 was one of unremitting success. Shipments from Britain arrived quickly and on time, and there were no shortages. Scurvy would barely appear for the rest of the fleet's time in the Baltic. The following year, the incidence of scurvy was limited to two individual ships: the *Hannibal* (two cases) and the *Calypso* (four cases).[17] The sloop *Osprey* was involved in convoying merchant ships across the Baltic. The journal of Mr Gamble, the surgeon on board, survives for the period 30 September 1810 to 1 October 1811. Throughout this period and despite many entries describing the various ailments of seamen on board, there was not one reported case of scurvy on board. His abstract for the period reveals that there were twenty-three cases of flux, four wounds and accidents, three of rheumatism, seven of venereal disease. Of a total fifty cases, not one was linked to scurvy.[18] The management of shore leave, rather than supply, became the great determinant of a seaman's health.

The contrast with three years earlier was evident to everyone. By 1811, the problems of 1809 were a thing of the past, an unpleasant but distant memory. The mistakes of 1809 would not be made again. By 1811, both the Victualling Board and Saumarez testified to the quality of the provisioning system, enabling the commander in chief to concentrate on his operational and strategic objectives. In a 'Report of the State and Condition of His Majesty's Ships named in the margin [the *Hannibal, Ardent, Vanguard, Orion, Mars, Dreadnought*]', Saumarez commented in 1811 that he had 'great pleasure in stating the Crews are in general very healthy to which the occasional supplies of Fresh Provisions have greatly contributed'.[19] Contemporaries were agreed that the supply system was now flourishing.

The system devised for the provisioning of a fleet of over 16,000 men, surrounded by hostile states, with a vulnerable supply line, was a remarkable achievement of administration and logistical ingenuity, and a testament to the flexibility of the naval bureaucracy, and the reforming instincts of the British state at war. The Baltic Sea had been opened up to the full potency of British naval power. Operations that were beyond contemplation a generation before were being executed deliberately and successfully. The improvements in the victualling system brought a strategic flexibility no other nation could match; no other nation in the world would have been able to supply a fleet in such dangerous waters, for so long, and with such

---

[17] TNA, ADM 97/88, 'State and Condition of the Baltic fleet, May-August 1811'.

[18] TNA, ADM 101/111/4, 'Medical and Surgical Journal of His Majesty's Ship *Osprey* between 30 September 1810 and 1 October 1811'.

[19] TNA, ADM 1/12/139, Saumarez to Admiralty, 7 July 1811.

success. Herein lay the contribution of the victualling service to Britain's victory in the Napoleonic Wars. The success of the victualling system guaranteed operational effectiveness. Supply, after all, was the means to a strategic end.

Seapower and supply: the consequences of a superior provisioning system

The Royal Navy fleet in the Baltic pursued crucial objectives, made possible only by the supply system that sustained them once there. The Baltic fleet's primary duty was defensive: ensuring the vast export trade to northern Europe continued. On this the British economy, and the fiscal state, rested. Equally important was the importation of shipbuilding resources from the Baltic region. It also had a more offensive function: undermining Napoleon's Continental System.

The protection of British trade

The Royal Navy's immediate responsibility was the protection of British and neutral trade in that region. Having escorted vessels through the Sound or Belt, it was charged with seeing these ships safely across the Baltic Sea, protecting against French and Danish privateers. This was a careful balancing act as British merchants did not wish the ships laden with their property to appear off the Baltic ports in convoy with the Royal Navy, as this would have defeated the precautions taken to disguise the origin of the cargoes.[20]

The situation was made more complicated by the ambiguity of Sweden's position. When Saumarez arrived at Gothenburg in May 1810, understanding the country to have submitted to the Continental System, he found 'everything much in the same state as when I left it last year – the Swedes as disposed to be friendly to us as ever, but apprehensive that we will not let them preserve their neutrality much longer'. Saumarez was 'concerned to find that these Northern States are more than ever attached to the French Alliance and I can see no prospect of detaching them from it'. And yet, Sweden remained to all intents and purposes neutral. Fotö, a small island north of Vingö, became a significant smuggling centre, containing shops, warehouses and markets all staffed by Britons and protected by Saumarez's fleet. From there English and colonial goods were shipped out in vast quantities to the ports of northern Germany and Swedish Pomerania, while 'the local commissioners turned a blind eye'.[21]

---

[20] TNA, ADM 1/6/ 28 July 1808. Ryan, 'Defence of British Trade', pp. 449–50.
[21] Voelcker, *Saumarez vs. Napoleon*, p. 108.

This advantageous relationship would survive changes in monarch. In the summer of 1810, the death of Crown Prince Karl August of Augustenborg threw Sweden into turmoil. Karl August had been elected crown prince of Sweden after the deposition of Gustav IV Adolph, his death raising questions as to his succession. By late August it was becoming clear that Napoleon's choice, his former marshall Bernadotte, would shortly be crowned. Sweden, already a member of the Continental System, seemed to be sliding further into the Napoleonic camp. On the contrary, Bernadotte played a more nuanced game. He promised 'very strict instructions relative to English commerce', but in reality, aware that the Swedish economy rested on trade with Britain, he hid commercial dealings with Britain. In November 1810 diplomatic and military pressure from Napoleon forced Sweden to declare war on Britain. Yet Bernadotte did not let this obstruct economic interests. Count von Rosen was instructed by the Swedish government to 'give his strongest assurances . . . that it was by no means the intention of the Swedish government to follow up its declaration by any act of hostility'. Any of the declarations measures were 'perfectly contrary to the Swedish government, and particularly those of the Crown Prince'. Throughout 1811 cordial relations between Saumarez and Swedish government officials ensured their respective national interests were achieved. While Sweden was forced to make temporary displays of allegiance to Napoleon, these were token efforts: the war between Britain and Sweden would remain a 'phoney' one. Between 1810 and 1812, a settlement was built on the island of Hanö off Karlshamn, unknown to the French, complete with water supplies and a slaughterhouse, solely for the use of the Royal Navy. It became the rendezvous point for convoys returning from the Baltic, and also allowed small amounts of beef to be supplied to the British fleet.[22]

Elsewhere the situation was more clear-cut. In early 1810, the king of Denmark withdrew all restrictions on the operations of Danish privateers and authorised them to capture the vessels of any nation sailing under British convoy, stating that all such vessels were to be considered lawful prizes without further proof of their being enemy property.[23] During 1810, Danish privateers did record successes against British merchant ships. In July the Danes captured forty-seven sail off the Skaw.[24] In 1810 British shipping losses reached their peak, with 619 vessels lost. More important

---

[22] For a full account of the respective diplomatic positioning, see Voelcker, *Saumarez vs. Napoleon*, pp. 109–13, 121–3, 141–54, 159–63. For an analysis of the local supply arrangements see Davey, 'Supplied by the Enemy', pp. 279–82.

[23] Voelcker, *Saumarez vs. Napoleon*, p. 108.

[24] Rodger, *Command of the Ocean*, p. 558.

were the effects of these losses on insurance rates. Baltic rates that in 1806 had been between 3 and 5 per cent, rose as high as 20 per cent by 1808. At their highest, in 1811, they reached 22 per cent.[25] The Admiralty forwarded complaints to Saumarez from the insurers Lloyds who were deeply concerned at these losses: 'The Chairman of a committee appointed by the underwriters of Lloyds to enquire into the losses . . . that have lately taken place in the Baltic, having respected that you may be permitted to give them such Information on the subject as you are in possession of'.[26] Shipping losses of this magnitude went straight to the heart of the mutually reliant relationship between the government and the City. The Danish threat provoked a greater naval presence in the Sound and Belt; the squadron under Dixon was reinforced. By 1811 the Danish privateer threat had been neutralised. As Fenwick commented, 'the vigilance of your cruisers and the formidable convoy's sent thro' the Belt have completely disheartened the Danish privateers who making few or no prizes now will be all ruined'.[27] As a result, Fenwick commented that the Danish government was 'also thereby deprived of the large revenue which it last year obtained from the amount of goods condemned'.[28] The Royal Navy's dominance of the Baltic Sea was beginning to effect a political outcome on land.

The conduct of convoys was remarkably successful. The entrepôt at Gothenburg and then Hanö, the widespread use of neutral fleets and licenses and neutral flags, combined with the liberal attitudes of continental custom officials meant that by 1809 and in 1810 British trade was once again flowing at something close to its peacetime volume. 1810 was the peak year of the English license trade. In total, 18,536 licenses were given to merchants compared to 15,226 the year before, and 4,910 in 1808, the majority of whom were trading in the Baltic.[29] Additionally, in 1810 there was a vast increase in the number of ships convoyed by the Royal Navy into the Baltic. Whereas in 1809 1,685 ships were convoyed in, in 1810 3,001 merchant vessels were escorted into the Baltic. Convoys as a result were far larger: the average size rose from thirty-three to sixty-six vessels.[30] The increase in the volume of trade required a greater naval protection, which

---

[25] Ryan, 'Defence of British Trade', p. 461.

[26] SRO, HA 93/6/1/1654, Admiralty to Saumarez, 10 Dec. 1810.

[27] SRO, HA 93/6/1/1787, Fenwick to Saumarez, July 1811.

[28] SRO, HA 93/6/1/1787, Fenwick to Saumarez, July 1811.

[29] 'An Account of the Number of Commercial Licenses Granted during the Last Ten Years', Parliamentary Papers, 1812, Miscellaneous.

[30] TNA, ADM 7/793. The first convoy sailed on the 3 April 1810, the last leaving on 22 November 1810.

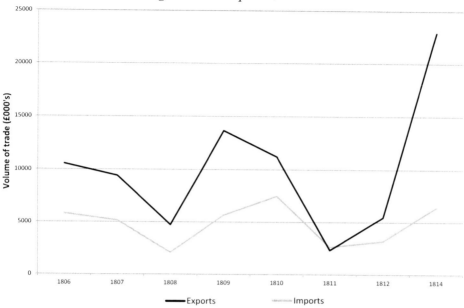

Figure 15. British volume of trade with northern Europe, 1806–14
Source: Mitchell and Deane, *Abstract of British Historical Statistics*, p. 311.
There is no data for 1813, which explains the rather sharp rises in 1814.

in itself was reliant on a victualling system that could sustain fleets across the Baltic the year round. These were operations beyond the remit of the navy even ten years before. The results were startling: British exports to northern Europe in 1810 amounted to £13,857,946, again a greater volume than the peacetime year of 1806.[31] Here was the navy directly combating the Continental System.

Napoleon was not unaware of the difficulty in applying his economic policies in northern Europe. In response to its lax enforcement, towards the end of 1810 Napoleon heightened the continental blockade. Frustrated with his allies, he insisted that 'no colonial goods must arrive in ports controlled by me, even with certificates of origin, which are valueless'. Convinced that British merchants were desperate for peace, he re-iterated that only by attacking the British economy could it be defeated: 'I have no other means of waging war on England', he wrote. On 19 October 1810 he issued a decree from Amsterdam that reinforced the Berlin decree of 1806, prohibiting all goods from English manufacturer, and ordering that any found should be confiscated and burnt. He included goods that existed 'in actual entrepôt,

---

[31] *Journal of the House of Commons* 67, p. 766, quoted in Crosby, *American Trade with Russia and the Baltic*, p. 230.

or in the magazines of our customs'. He subsequently wrote to Alexander I and warned him: 'Six hundred English ships wandering round the Baltic have been kept out by Mecklenberg and Prussia, and are heading from your lands. If you admit them, the war continues; if you receive them and confiscate their cargoes . . . the blow that this will strike England will be fearful.'[32] His position was strengthened by France's annexation of many of the little states whose flags were utilised by smugglers for cover severely limited the English merchants in their choice of disguises.[33]

In the last months of 1811, greater quantities of English property were confiscated than ever before. Napoleon had set his customs agents and those of his obedient allies to making great bonfires of all the British goods they seized.[34] In Baltic ports some 240 ships with British cargoes were seized and their contents condemned.[35] These confiscations account for the small decrease in the volume of British exports to northern Europe in 1810 from the year before. However, these enormous confiscations of shipping on the continent would have great impact, causing profound disillusionment with the license trade in the mercantile community. In 1811, many merchants withdrew from the trade.[36] Only 1,927 ships entered the Baltic, compared to 3,001 the previous year. The Admiralty continued to organise convoys, but noticed a diminution in the number of ships wishing to enter the Baltic. These were much smaller convoys, on average thirty-six vessels.[37] One concerned pamphleteer wrote that year that 'in the ports of the Baltic, our losses by confiscation have been ruinous beyond all precedent, and the real extent of their injurious effects on our maritime interest remains yet unascertained'.[38]

It was in 1811, the worst year of the war for Britain economically, that Napoleon came closest to severely harming British exports in the Baltic. The economist J. Oddy wrote in 1811 that 'the late stoppages to that exportation [to the Baltic] has occasioned . . . increasing Commercial embarrassment in the Commercial World, whilst the Merchants warehouses & Stores are full: but which they cannot sell at even depreciated value, from the want

---

[32] Voelcker, *Saumarez vs. Napoleon*, p. 119.

[33] Crosby, *American Trade with Russia and the Baltic*, p. 197.

[34] Ibid., pp. 195–6.

[35] Christie, *Wars and Revolutions*, p. 314.

[36] Crosby, *American Trade with Russia and the Baltic*, p. 196.

[37] TNA, ADM 7/795. The first convoy left on 16 April, the last on 30 November.

[38] *An Inquiry into the State of Our Commercial Relations with the Northern Powers, with Reference to Our Trade with them under the Regulation of Licenses, the Advantage which the Enemy Derives from it, and its Effects on the Revenue, the Course of the Foreign Exchanges, the Price of Bullion, and the General Prosperity of the British Empire* (London, 1811), p. 4.

of Exportation'.[39] The Continental System began to threaten Britain. British exports to northern Europe fell to only a quarter of the level of 1806, to £3,483,091 in total.[40] Even the Swedes were forced to demonstrate their allegiance to the Continental System, confiscating the cargoes of eighty-two vessels in an incident that became known as the 'Carlshamn Cargoes', valued at £923,375.[41] The trade that the British state relied on the most was being undermined. That British exports continued to northern Europe at all was due to the work of the naval fleet in the Baltic. For all that exports to northern Europe fell in 1811, each British cargo contributed to the weakening of the Continental System.

The procurement of naval stores

The war in northern Europe had severe implications for the procurement of the most valuable of commodities: naval stores. Prices began to rocket, on account of rising freight rates. Hemp that in 1807 cost £66 per ton had risen to £118 by the end of 1808.[42] Memel fir costing £7 in the autumn of 1806 had risen to £16 by 1809. Danzig plank that had cost £12 in 1806 cost £24 in 1809, and could barely be obtained. The freight rates of hemp rose from a peacetime rate of £2 per ton to £30 in 1809.[43] The price rises are a useful indicator of the declining ability to procure shipbuilding resources from the Baltic region. From the summer of 1810, the obstacles in the way of this trade steadily increased, remaining very formidable until 1812. This was exacerbated by Napoleon's heightening of the Continental System in 1810. That year, 137 British ships loaded on account of British merchants were seized in Russian ports, and the greater part of their cargoes confiscated and sold. In 1811 the Continental System was at the highest pitch of its effectiveness.[44]

The year 1810 saw a great deal of naval stores importation. 2,695 vessels were convoyed from the Baltic, bringing home crucial shipbuilding resources. This was almost exactly the same number as the previous year.

[39] TNA, FO 22/63/7–11, J. Oddy, extract from Oddy's *Treatise on European Commerce*, 11 March 1811.

[40] *Journal of the House of Commons* 67), p. 766, quoted in Crosby, *American Trade with Russia and the Baltic*, p. 230.

[41] For a more detailed account see Voelcker, *Saumarez vs. Napoleon*, pp. 128–40.

[42] Anderson, 'The Continental System and Russo-British Relations during the Napoleonic Wars', p. 71.

[43] Hall, *British Strategy*, p. 89.

[44] Anderson, 'The Continental System and Russo-British Relations during the Napoleonic Wars', p. 73.

Napoleon's increased vigilance meant that there were fewer convoys, but those that did sail were larger. There were thirty-four convoys (as opposed to forty-one the previous year) and the average convoy size was seventy-nine vessels. Like the year before there was a contrast between small collections of merchant ships from across the Baltic and vast shipments from the ports of Riga and St Petersburg , the latter numbering in the many hundreds.[45] Large convoys continued to leave the Baltic. One captain remembered, 'at one time, with over 400 vessels, under charge of the *Hero*, ourselves, two frigates and a bomb, we never saw the head of the convoy from the time of leaving Wingoe Sound'.[46] This was the reality of British maritime and commercial power, a point not lost on foreign observers. Sir John Ross described one such witness to British maritime strength:

> On arriving in the Belt, with a convoy of no less than a thousand sail homeward bound, it was intimated that the French Prince of Ponte Corvo, the newly elected successor to the throne, was at Nyburg, and permission to cross the Belt was demanded and obtained from the Admiral for his yacht to pass unmolested, which he did on the 14 October at the time this immense fleet was at anchor of Sproe. A scene so novel to a French General, and so interesting to his Royal Highness under the present circumstances, could not but make a deep impression, while it conveyed some idea of the wealth and power of the British nation.[47]

The French general in question, Bernadotte, was shortly after named King Karl XIV Johan of Sweden. Having seen such a spectacle, he needed little convincing that Swedish national interests chimed more with Britain than France.[48]

Sweden's disregard for the Continental System, the pecuniary interest of Baltic merchants and the accommodating character of officials across northern Europe meant naval stores continued to be imported from the Baltic. Increasingly they were collected at Danzig and smaller ports in northern Germany rather than Russia. In 1810 Britain imported £725,295 of hemp, more in value than in any year since 1807.[49] Naval stores continued to arrive in British dockyards. In 1810, imports of timber rose dramati-

[45] TNA, ADM 7/793. The largest convoys that year consisted of 198, 210 and 173 ships. One shipment appears in the records that consisted of 468 vessels.

[46] Boteler, *Recollections*, p. 10.

[47] John Ross, *Memoirs and Correspondence of Admiral Lord de Saumarez, From Original Papers on Possession of the Family* (London, 1838), pp. 214–15.

[48] Voelcker, *Saumarez vs. Napoleon*, pp. 117, 145, 157–60.

[49] Crosby, *American Trade with Russia and the Baltic*, p. 195. Mitchell and Deane present slightly different figures of £752,000: Mitchell and Deane, *Abstract of British Historical Statistics*, pp. 289–90.

cally from £500,000 to £800,000.[50] A report to Yorke of 1810 showed that stocks of hemp in store for the navy were 20,249 tons against an annual consumption of 12,000 tons.[51] In 1811, the need for naval stores grew as exports from the Baltic were dramatically cut. Whereas the previous year 2,695 ships had been brought out of the Baltic, in 1811 only 1,406 were extracted. Only twenty convoys were organised from the Baltic, though these were often very large, one numbering 212 ships. The average convoy size was seventy ships.[52] The Royal Navy was forced to use alternative means to secure supplies. There had been long-standing ideas of raiding Baltic ports for supplies. While in the Baltic Captain Watkins of HMS *Majestic* volunteered for a service, 'which I think can be performed, and desirable on account of the great scarcity of Riga Spars in our Dock Yards. My plan is to attempt carrying away . . . some vessels as well as a quantity that may be now at Memel (with I conceive very little risk) should your Lordship approve I will enter farther into my plan of proceeding.'[53]

Over the following years, the naval commanders in the Baltic would spend considerable time locating and transporting shipbuilding resources back to Britain. Saumarez continued to search for naval stores. As he wrote in 1811, 'I enclose . . . intelligence which I have received of a considerable quantity of oak timber laying in the Island of Oesel in the Gulf of Finland intended for the use of the arsenal at Cronstadt. Should their Lordships think it an object of sufficient importance to use Endeavors to have it conveyed to England, I request the Commissioners of His Majesty's Navy may be directed to send Transports furnished with proper Materials for removing Timber.' The Admiralty replied positively, asking Saumarez to make use of such victuallers and store ships for this purpose as he had available.[54] Through such actions, the Royal Navy in the Baltic ensured that quantities of naval stores were arriving in British dockyards. There is no doubt, however, that the ratcheting up of the Continental System threatened serious consequences for British trade to and from the Baltic. At the same time the Continental System, and indeed the British blockade, was having reciprocal effects across the nations of northern Europe.

---

[50] Peter Padfield, *Maritime Power and the Struggle for Freedom: Naval Campaigns that Shaped the Modern World, 1788–1851* (London, 2003), p. 286.

[51] NMM, YOR/17.

[52] TNA, ADM 7/795.

[53] MA 21/846, Captain Frederick Watkins, HMS *Majestic*, to Lord Mulgrave, 5 March 1809.

[54] TNA, ADM 1/12/110, Saumarez to Admiralty, 20 May 1811.

The attack on the Russian economy

British policy in the Baltic revolved around competing economic and political interests. It was vital that British goods continued to enter the Baltic, and equally important that imports of naval stores endured. For all that, there was an awareness that the economies of northern Europe also depended on their exportation of raw materials. Britain received 91 per cent of Russian's flax, 61 per cent of its hemp, 76 per cent of its tallow and 75 per cent of its iron.[55] Naval power in the Baltic ensured that Russia's maritime trade could be cut off. Before the war, 35 per cent of the imports and 63 per cent of the exports of St Petersburg were handled by British merchant houses.[56] In a game of brinksmanship, it was not clear who would blink first. The British naval presence ruled out any form of export to any European nation. All ships without a British license – ships with a British destination – were liable to capture and confiscation. Exports to France were thus eradicated. There were instances of license abuse, when ships with British licenses failed to arrive in Britain once leaving the Baltic. In 1810, thirty-seven vessels from Archangel went to Amsterdam.[57] For the most part though, vessels leaving the Baltic were convoyed by naval vessels through the Sound or Belt and then across, giving little scope for abuse. Baltic merchants were thus caught in the middle of two economic blockades – that of Napoleon and that of Britain. It was these merchants that suffered the most.

The British Orders in Council that declared a state of blockade across the Baltic Sea in 1806–7 had economic objectives. It was decided that the most effective form of blockade was one which would limit the movements of enemy and neutral ships, and would at the same time allow them to trade under the protection and control of the navy between Britain and those ports from which British ships were excluded. The relaxations of 1809 in no way reduced the severity of the ban upon all direct trade between the northern nations and the ports of France and her other allies. Any ship intercepted on course for a hostile port remained subject to capture.[58] Any cargoes thought likely to benefit an enemy were, subject to law, confiscated. Britain's Orders in Council, and their command of the Baltic Sea, forced neutrals to trade with Britain, or not trade at all. The ability to undermine the Russian economy was a vital weapon in Britain's offensive strategy.

[55] J. Oddy, extract from Oddy's *Treatise on European Commerce*, FO 22/63/7–11, 11 March 1811.
[56] Oddy, *European Commerce*, p. 132.
[57] *An Inquiry into the State of Our Commercial Relations with the Northern Powers*, p. 30.
[58] Ryan, 'Trade with the Enemy', p. 127.

There were good grounds for perceiving such economic consequences. The Russian aristocracy was seriously affected by the loss of income from their trade in timber, hemp and other products that they had supplied to the British navy for many years. During the second half of the eighteenth century Britain became Russia's most lucrative trading partner.[59] British contractors also had given long-term credits to both merchants and gentry in Russia which made them largely dependent on trading with Britain. William Coxe noted the precariousness of Russia's situation. The entire revenue of the Russian state was 6,144,986 roubles. Of this, customs represented 760,000 roubles, stamp duties and other taxes 500,000 roubles, and the poll tax 1,362,935 roubles. These revenues were seriously affected by the British navy in the Baltic, which ensured there were no outlets for Russian exports.[60] The full value of Russia's exports constituted a quarter of her annual revenue.[61] This amount had been almost entirely eradicated by the British blockade, a critical mass that threatened financial devastation. Savoy, the French minister in St Petersburg, had reported it most unlikely that France could take England's place for imports to Russia, and 'what is more, I fear that if measures are taken against England, the Emperor Alexander will have to take severe measures to silence the dissaffected'.[62]

Throughout the eighteenth century, logistical improvements had furthered the possibilities of blockade. During England's war with France between 1744 and 1748, the navy had twelve ships off Ushant with which 'to annoy the enemy's ships and commerce'. Maritime blockade was pursued effectively during the War of American Independence and was the cornerstone of Britain's naval strategy in the war against revolutionary and Napoleonic France.[63] It had the greatest potential in northern Europe, where the nations of Denmark and Russia were particularly susceptible to blockade. Sir Stephen Shairp, British consul general in St Petersburg, had predicted in 1807 that the removal of trade with Britain would force Russia out of the Continental System.[64] It followed that the relaxation

---

[59] Kaplan, *Russian Overseas Commerce*, p. 51.

[60] William Coxe, *Travels into Poland, Russia, Sweden, and Denmark, Interspersed with Historical Relations and Political Inquiries* (Dublin, 1794), particularly book VI, p. 470. The farming of 'spiritous liquors' made up 1.8m roubles.

[61] Anderson, 'The Continental System and Russo-British Relations during the Napoleonic Wars', p. 77.

[62] Alexander C. Niven, *Napoleon and Alexander I: A Study in Franco-Russian Relations, 1807–1812* (Lanham, ML, 1979), pp. 59–61.

[63] Brian Arthur, *How Britain Won the War of 1812: The Royal Navy's Blockades of the United States, 1812–1815* (Woodbridge, 2011), pp. 11–17.

[64] TNA, FO 65/71, Sharp to Canning, 9 Sept. 1807, 18 Sept. 1807.

of the Order in Council of 1809 brought some criticism from those in the Baltic who could see the effect it would have. Louis Drusina, the former British consul in Memel, who continued to act in the capacity of a secret agent, wrote in July of 1809, that 'It was ever my decided opinion that the Russian ports should have been strictly blockaded last year. The dissatisfaction in the country was very great upon the prospect of not having any trade; and, if they had not been allowed any, I am convinced the government must have changed their system, and then there would have been a free trade this year.' Later that month, Saumarez wrote in a similar vein to his wife that 'it is more to be regretted than ever that we have not long before this declared the ports of Russia in a state of Blockade as it must have changed the Politics of that Country. My opinion has been confirmed by that of Persons whose interest militates against the measure but are obliged to avow it. Our minsters will see their Error when it's too late.'[65] A full blockade precluded any acquisition of stores from the Baltic, and any chance of exporting goods into northern Europe. It remained a last resort and a latent threat.

In late 1810, Saumarez argued for greater economic sanctions to be forced on Russia. In a letter to the First Lord of the Admiralty he wondered whether 'it were possible for us to go on without any trade to the Baltic, I am convinced it would soon reduce Russia to the necessity of making peace'.[66] The British merchant John Mordaunt Johnston wrote to Saumarez a few weeks later: it is likely that Saumarez and Johnson had discussed the matter privately:

> For, either we are independent of the trade with the northern nations, or its is indispensably necessary to us; if the former be the case we ought to act a part worthy if a nation like ours, and if the latter, we can command commerce, and render it ultimately secure and profitable, by withholding it altogether for a time; that this system would produce the desired effect is evident to all those who give themselves the trouble to examine the state of the finances of different governments in the north of Europe.[67]

The intensification of economic warfare in 1811 saw these ideas realised. The escalation of the Continental System saw a great decline in mercantile activity; at the same time, British command of the Baltic Sea reduced

[65] Drusina (Hahn) to Saumarex, 11 July 1809; Saumarez to Martha Saumarez, Voelcker, *Saumarez vs. Napoleon*, p. 89.

[66] SRO, HA 93/6/1/1625, Saumarez to Yorke, 5 Nov. 1810.

[67] SRO, HA 93/6/1/1641, Johnson to Saumarez, 27 Nov. 1810. See Voelcker, *Saumarez vs. Napoleon*, p. 125, for the likelihood of conversations between the two informing their respective opinions.

French imports from Russia still further.[68] In 1811, Napoleon recognised the futility of trying to secure timber direct from the Baltic. Napoleon created 'Hanseatic licenses', which permitted the export of grain to England and allowed the export of timber and naval stores to France in the same ships. In reality, it was optimistic to expect that Britain would allow any materials to leave her ports for France.[69] He launched a longer-term project, to create a canal from the Baltic to the Seine. As he stated, 'of all connections from the Baltic to the Rhine, the best, shortest, and most economical is the sea. But the sea being closed by superior forces, there comes the idea and the necessity of an interior connection.' This was a five-year plan, never realised. For the moment, Napoleon relied on covertly removing naval stores through Kiel, though these were subject to a perilous journey, and insufficient for his designs.[70]

In Britain there were calls for a knock-out blow. One pamphlet urged Britain to 'regulate our commercial relations by the maxims of a more vigorous and decisive line of policy. As the prohibitory system, which is now so rigidly enforced on the continent, precludes us from the benefits of an export trade to it, it is indispensably requisite, that we should endeavour to counteract this evil, by opposing to it similar measures.'[71] A document in the Foreign Office files describes the decision that could be taken: a full blockade of the Baltic 'would have harassed the Russian government, and compelled her to choose out of two disastrous alternatives, either to risk a revolution in maintaining the continental system, or precipitate rupture with France in receding from it, at a time too, when the consequence of such a rupture must have been fatal. Looking forward as we then did, and as we have now every reason to do, to a more favourable occasion for such an exertion of her power, there remains little question as to the most preferable of these two expedients.'[72] One powerful interest discouraging such a measure were the ship-owners who depended upon the trade, and who constituted a powerful political group.[73]

By 1811 the British government was now willing to forgo their need for naval stores, and to restrict trade with Russia and the other Baltic

---

[68] A. Chabert, *Essai sur les mouvements des revenues et de l'activité économique en France de 1798 à 1820*, 2 vols. (Paris, 1945–9), II, 321, cited in Davis and Engerman, *Naval Blockades*, p. 46.

[69] Albion, *Forests and Seapower*, p. 344.

[70] Voelcker, *Saumarez vs. Napoleon*, p. 156.

[71] *An Inquiry into the State of Our Commercial Relations with the Northern Powers*, p. 107.

[72] FO 22/63/22–7, anonymous letter, tagged 'Preliminary Considerations', summer 1811 (no date).

[73] Ryan, 'Trade with the Enemy', pp. 131–2.

countries, and thus bring home to them the degree to which they depended economically on their ability to export to Britain. In July it decided that British merchants applying for a license to import Baltic commodities must undertake to export a cargo of British goods to that area as a condition of receiving one. Only 550 licenses for trade with the Baltic were issued in 1811 as against 1,689 in the previous year.[74] This was not a declared blockade in the official sense, but it was a strengthening of the economic pressure being placed on Russia. Russia, and indeed the whole of northern Europe, was coming to see that they were facing an economic crisis. The traditional export trade of raw materials to Britain had been undermined by Napoleon's strictures.[75] For the mercantile classes, it was a severe blow to see timber, grain, flax and hemp from their fields rotting in ports.[76] Small amounts continued thanks to the navy's efforts, but this was a significant decrease on the years of peace. Crucially, exports of these same goods to France, Holland and Spain had been cut off by the Royal Navy efforts in the Baltic Sea.

The Russian tsar, Alexander I, well understood the economic burden forced upon his country. Since 1810 he had been reconsidering his alliance with France, as the Russian economy went into severe decline. Between 1806 and 1812 exports dropped approximately two-fifths, the result of the eradication of Russia's maritime trade. Customs revenue had fallen from 9 million roubles in 1805 to 3 million in 1809.[77] The paper rouble (virtually the only currency in the Russian empire's heartlands) crashed in value. In June 1804 the paper rouble had been worth more than three-quarters its silver equivalent, but by June 1811 it was valued at less than one quarter. There was a general collapse in business confidence sparked by economic and political uncertainties. It had severe implications for the Russian state. By 1809 state income was less than half of expenditure. That year the government's tax income was 73 per cent of what it had been five years before. The cost of sustaining the Russian army rocketed. To continue the French alliance was to undermine the financial and economic basis of Russia's European position.[78] The tsar faced economic ruin across his kingdom that threatened to undermine both his fiscal situation and his throne. Opposition to his rule became ever more open. 'It was', wrote the

---

[74] Crouzet, *L'économie britannique et le blocus continental*, II, p. 656. Anderson, 'The Continental System and Russo-British Relations during the Napoleonic Wars', pp. 73, 76–7.

[75] Charles Esdaile, *Napoleon's Wars: An International History* (London, 2007), pp. 423–4.

[76] Albion, *Forests and Seapower*, p. 344; J. H. Rose, 'Napoleon and English Commerce', *English Historical Review* 8/32 (October 1893), p. 724.

[77] Esdaile, *Napoleon's Wars*, p. 434.

[78] Dominic Lieven, *Russia against Napoleon: The Battle for Europe, 1807–1814* (London, 2009), pp. 63–5, 73, 78–9, 100.

Lithuanian Countess Tisenhau, 'impossible for Alexander to close his eyes any longer to the sad condition to which the absolute cessation of commerce had reduced the empire.'[79]

As a final insult trade with France had become embarrassingly unequal: by 1811 the ratio of Russian exports to imports was 1:170.[80] Popular anger resulted in French goods being burnt in Russia. Alexander began to retreat from the Continental System. In December 1810, Russia increased the tax on goods coming by land (predominantly French), but reduced them on those coming from sea (mostly British and colonial goods, albeit under American, Prussian and other neutral flags). Neither of these nations was mentioned directly, but it was clear that British colonial goods were allowed to enter, while effectively French manufactured goods into Russia were prohibited. Russia had demonstrated it was no longer willing to submit to the economic restrictions Napoleon had tried to impose on it.[81]

Such pro-British policies dented Russian relations with Napoleon, already angered by the secretive British trading in the Baltic. Napoleon began to consider a Russian invasion. The Russian ambassador, Caulaincourt, reported in June 1811 that:

> His Majesty received me coldly, and at once began heatedly to enumerate his . . . grievances against the Tsar Alexander . . . He spoke of the ukase prohibiting foreign imports, and of the admission of neutral . . . ships into Russian ports, which, he said, was an infringements of the Continental System. He went on to say that the Tsar was treacherous, that he was arming to make war on France.

Napoleon promised that 'one good battle' would 'knock the bottom out of Alexander's fine resolutions'. Napoleon, determined to force Russia to accede once more to the Continental System, and confident of victory over the Russians, saw no reason to back down from confrontation.[82] The Russian economic policy of reducing land imports and encouraging overseas trade was crude but effective in raising the value of the rouble: it rose 30 to 40 per cent in value in the financial marts of London, Hamburg, Paris and Amsterdam.[83] But the hardening of British economic policy in 1811 added extra pressure on Alexander and his state coffers, devoid of export and revenue. Late in 1811, Alexander opened up his ports to Britain.

---

[79] Esdaile, *Napoleon's Wars*, pp. 434–5.
[80] Ibid.
[81] M. S. Anderson, 'The Continental System and Russo-British Relations during the Napoleonic Wars', p. 71; Esdaile, *Napoleon's Wars*, p. 435.
[82] Esdaile, *Napoleon's Wars*, pp. 435–6, 444–5.
[83] Crosby, *American Trade with Russia and the Baltic*, pp. 212–13.

Napoleon's reaction to this was characteristically violent, and directly related to the tsar's economic decisions. In June 1812 he declared war on Russia and the Grande Armée began its march on Moscow. With Sweden leaving the Continental System in 1812, the Baltic was once more open to the full extent of British trade. British exports doubled from the previous year. In addition, naval resources became freely available. In May 1812, Byam Martin looked forward to reconciliation with Russia, which would give 'naval stores at half the present cost . . . to say nothing of the good timber we should get, in any quantity, instead of the rotten stuff from America'.[84] With Russia soon an ally of Britain, all of her resources were made available. In 1812, the Admiralty advised the Navy Board to take advantage of the state of relations with Russia immediately and 'to procure the greatest possible supply of Riga spars and other naval stores'. Within six months the dockyards stores were well filled.[85] In 1812, fewer convoys were needed; only sixteen were organised and only five in the Baltic.[86] Not only was the Baltic trade reopened, but the Continental System had been undermined, and Russia had been extracted from her French alliance.

In the final instance logistics are a means to a strategic end and in this the supply to the Baltic fleet provided a platform on which Britain could execute operations that changed the course of the Napoleonic War. The operational viability of the Baltic fleet relied upon an effective supply system. Without regular and timely supplies the British fleet could not have remained at sea for up to ten months at a time without returning to a victualling base in the Baltic, let alone one in Britain. As a consequence, the Baltic fleet was able to fulfil its strategic obligations. The Russian fleet was blockaded in port: one incident in 1808 notwithstanding, it was to remain there for the entire war. Added to this, the British fleet managed and protected the vast trade into northern Europe, blowing a hole in the Continental System. In addition, the rigorous policy of attacking trade not bound for Britain heaped additional pressure onto a Russian economy already creaking under Napoleon's strictures. Frustrated at Russian fickleness and unwillingness to submit itself to economic ruin, in 1812 Napoleon invaded Russia. It would prove to be his undoing.

---

[84] Byam Martin, *Letters*, II, p. 176.
[85] TNA, ADM 3/259, 3 Aug. 1812. TNA, ADM 106/2095, ADM to Navy Board, 20 Jan. 1813. Albion, *Forests and Seapower*, p. 344.
[86] TNA, ADM 7/795.

Conclusion

The Napoleonic War became a conflict between rival economies. Napoleon's assault on British mercantile trade, the life-blood of its financial system, threatened the relationship between the state and the City that underlay British naval and political might. In response, the last ten years of this war saw a global projection of naval power. Fleets were sent to North America, the Caribbean, the East Indies, the Cape of Good Hope and the Brazils to protect British trade routes. The principal naval effort though remained in European waters. No sooner had Bonaparte started an economic conflict than it was escalated by the British, announcing their own blockade on the Napoleonic empire. This contest would not be decided by a naval battle, but by a broader conception of seapower. Fleets in the Mediterranean, the Channel, the North Sea and the Baltic Sea were charged not only with trade protection, but also attacking and undermining Napoleon's Continental System. This effort required a constant and rigorous application of naval force around the European coastline. Fleets were required to remain on station the year round, marshalling trade, escorting ships and attacking enemy shipping. This rested on a victualling system that could support naval forces long enough to maintain British strategic objectives.

The provisioning service was but one part of the British war machine: however, it was a crucial one. If the Victualling Board or Transport Board failed, the Royal Navy could not hope to execute its strategic and operational designs. The Victualling Board was rarely short of provisions in Deptford: the huge London food market meant the main challenge did not concern the acquisition of foodstuffs, but how much they would pay for them. Keeping fleets supplied depended on how well these foodstuffs could be distributed. Throughout the eighteenth century there had been an evolution within the British victualling service. The series of wars against the French, beginning with the War of Austrian Succession and ending with the Napoleonic Wars, witnessed a cumulative development of a system able to supply fleets away from British out-ports. This was by no means continuous progression: on the contrary, on multiple occasions, the naval administration struggled to marshal resources effectively, resulting in serious operational issues. As late as 1807, Richard Strachan was forced from his station off Rochefort due to delay in a delivery of victuals. The procurement of tonnage, management of resources and exact provision calculations were for long periods beyond the means of bureaucrats. There was, however, a clear correlation between an improving victualling service and widening operational capabilities. In the same way that Napoleon's decision to live off the land revolutionised land warfare, the Royal Navy's ability to provision fleets across the globe, using remote transports to continually revictual fleets, gave it a strategic flexibility none could match.[1] A ship sitting in the eastern Baltic would be as well provisioned as one lying off Deptford; therein lay the new-found strategic flexibility.

The naval administration that managed the provisioning of the Royal Navy was not perfect. In 1809, the Baltic fleet's provisioning system came under direct scrutiny, as shipments were delayed and both the Victualling and Transport Boards struggled to adapt to the escalation of the war. It is easy to be critical of the administrators.[2] Yet, these were individuals organising a war, unprecedented in scope, in which national survival was at stake. Backlogs of accounts paled in comparison to ensuring fleets were adequately supplied. What is remarkable is the degree of flexibility inherent in the victualling system, and the giant strides taken to ensure problems were fixed and not faced again. Systematic reform of the victualling system during the winter of 1809–10, centred around the Commission of Naval Revision, saw procedures centralised and streamlined. The British state had proved adept at instituting reforms that greatly improved the nation's ability to wage war.

From 1810 the timely arrival of victuals, carefully calculated to fit precise numbers of seamen, became commonplace. The reforms of the years 1809–10

---

[1] Napoleon's decision to live off the land, though never wholly relied on, enabled his corps to be dispersed over much wider areas, converging when necessary at the 'decisive point'. As Howard argues, the French armies 'had to a large extent to live off the country . . . Napoleon expected his troops to fend for themselves, which indeed they did, though they did make the French cause very unpopular in the process'. This policy worked less well as Napoleon penetrated the less fertile areas of Europe into Poland and Spain. See Michael Howard, *War in European History* (Oxford, 1976), pp. 84–5. Napoleon did not entirely 'live of the land', and frequently, such as in 1800, 1807, and again in 1812, laid down great magazines for the supply of the army. Yet Napoleonic strategy was based on rapid movement forcing the enemy into decisive battle. Large wagon trains, even if they had existed, struggled to keep pace. At Austerlitz in 1805, the French army carried a mere eight days worth of rations with it, spread over a wide frontage, able to subsist of the country. See Gunther Erich Rothenburg, *The Art of Warfare in the Age of Napoleon* (Bloomington, IN, 1981), pp. 129–30. See also Martin van Creveld, *Supplying War: Logistics from Wallenstein to Patton* (Cambridge, 1977), pp. 40–61, and John Morgan, 'War Feeding War? The Impact of Logistics on the Napoleonic Occupation of Catalonia', in the *Journal of Military History* 73 (January 2009), 83–116.

[2] Macdonald *Management Competence and Incompetence*, pp. 215–20, 224.

came at the end of decades of systematic change to the victualling system, showing regular, if fitful, reform of administrative practices. The period 1808 to 1812 saw the final phase in this development. In these years, a Baltic fleet, facing unknown waters and a vulnerable supply lines, could be sustained the year round. Early in the century procuring transport tonnage for a victualling convoy took months to arrange. By 1810, transport tonnage could be procured in a week. Operations conducted during the Napoleonic War could not have been carried out even twenty years earlier. The evolution of the victualling service instituted something of a strategic watershed. To describe it as a strategic 'revolution' is too strong: the ability to sustain fleets regardless of location was the culmination of decades of development in the victualling service. In this, long-term logistical development allowed a transformation of naval strategy.

The British victualling service provided a significant advantage over other European navies. The solidity and strength of each navy's infrastructure and its flexibility in response to unprecedented stresses was the difference between naval successes and failures.[3] It was in this that the Royal Navy was to have a critical advantage. Comparing naval administrations of different countries along national lines is not an easy task.[4] There is little literature on French naval administration so making a judgement is difficult; accordingly, it is difficult to measure the comparative performance of French naval administration, particularly the victualling service. French failure in the war at sea can in no way be explained by lack of interest from the governments or lack of material resources. Policy-makers were strong supporters of the navy, as the French shipbuilding efforts after Trafalgar testify. Instead, 'it was the organisational side of the navy which failed and this in turn must be explained as a result of naval policy which failed to explore the French potential as a sea power to its full extent'.[5] A comparison between Britain and Sweden though is instructive. While the Swedish fleet, sailing just outside its own ports, was devastated because of its inferior supply system, the Royal Navy fleet under the command of Sir James Saumarez was never faced with such problems.

Paul Kennedy argued that the most significant military and naval changes during the eighteenth century were 'probably in organisation', owing to the enhanced activity of the state. However, he states that seldom did this lead to national advantages, explaining that such administrative efforts were

[3] Rodger, *Command of the Ocean*, p. 379.
[4] Baugh, 'Naval Power', p. 236.
[5] Glete, *Navies and Nations*, vol. II, p. 388.

easily copied.[6] Administrative developments could be replicated, but this was a process that took years, if not decades, to realise. Throughout the wars against Napoleon, Britain possessed a telling advantage in its ability to supply its fleet, with far-reaching consequences. The victualling service allowed Britain to fight on the defensive: protecting against invasion, advancing its maritime economy and furthering its imperial interests at the expense of France. British and neutral trade was protected and enemy fleets blockaded. It also enabled offensive functions, attacking the Napoleonic empire and its economic foundations. The victualling system enabled fleets to patrol European waters, hundreds of miles from the nearest out-port. This was not merely occurring in northern Europe: in Holland, Portugal, North America and through the Mediterranean, the Royal Navy continued to protect and advance British trading interests.. However, it was in northern Europe that seapower could have a decisive impact on the course of the Napoleonic War. As naval power secured a grip on the waters around the continent, naval ships continued to secure British commercial interests while at the same time forcing Russia to leave the Continental System. Here was the ultimate justification for Britain's northern European strategy.

---

[6] Kennedy, *The Rise and Fall of the Great Powers*, p. 75.

APPENDIX I. TIME TAKEN TO SECURE

TRANSPORT TONNAGE TO THE BALTIC, 1808–12

VB order	Tonnage ready*	Time taken (days)	TNA reference
1808			
7 June	17 June	10	ADM III/187
15 July	19 July	4	ADM III/188
5 September	20 September	14	ADM III/188
22 September	7 October	14	ADM III/58/328–9
		10.5	
1809			
20 May	25 May	5	ADM III/191
20 May	10 June†	21	ADM III/191
16 August	7 September	22	ADM III/192
6 September	12 September	6	ADM III/192
20 November	23 November	3	ADM III/193
		11.4	
1810			
31 March	1 May	5	ADM III/195
31 March	4 May‡	4	ADM III/195
5 June	25 July	20	ADM III/196
		9.6	
1811			
8 April	2 June	7	ADM III/199
8 April	*18 June*	*71*	ADM III/199
20 July	27 July	7	ADM III/200
20 July	*26 August*	*37*¶	ADM III/200
		7	
1812			
19 May	28 May	9	ADM III/203
9 July	20 July	11	ADM III/203
27 July	29 July	2	ADM III/204
15 September	18 September	3	ADM III/204
26 October	2 October	6	ADM III/205
		6.2	
AVERAGE 1808–12		10.83	

* At this date 'tonnage ready' corresponds to the day the last transport needed was procured.

† Delivery was split into two separate deliveries, which left at different times with different convoys.

‡ Delivery travelled with two convoys, one on 1 May 1808 and one on 4 May 1808.

¶ In 1811, the each 'delivery' was planned to proceed to the Baltic on separate convoys. Partly this was to spread the risk of capture/destruction, but also to reduce the time perishable goods would be stored unused. Since deliveries were split into two, there was a deliberate delay in time between the order for provisions and the procurement of tonnage. Therefore, measuring the time between the original order and the final provision of transport tonnage is anomalously high, bearing no relation to the board's ability to procure tonnage. Therefore, italicised data has been left out of calculations of the overall average procurement averages.

APPENDIX 2. TIME TAKEN TO SECURE TONNAGE TO THE MEDITERRANEAN, 1800–2

VB order	Tonnage ready	Time taken	TNA reference
24 March 1800	2 May	39	ADM 111/154–5
10 February 1801	3 March	21	ADM 111/158
9 June 1801	6 July	27	ADM 111/158–9
16 September 1801	16 October	30	ADM 111/160–1
14 April 1802	12 May	28	ADM 111/163
AVERAGE 1800–2		29	

APPENDIX 3. TIME TAKEN TO LOAD VICTUALLING SHIPMENTS, 1808–10

Transports procured	Transports loaded and convoy arranged	Time taken	TNA reference
1808			
17 June	21 June	4	ADM 111/187, ADM 51/1824
19 July	28 July	9	ADM 111/188
20 September	29 September	9	ADM 111/188, ADM 110/58/283–4
7 October	14 October	7	ADM 110/58/328–9
		7.25	
1809			
25 May	15 June	20	ADM 111/192
10 June	4 July	24	ADM 111/192
7 September	12 September	5	ADM 111/193
12 September	18 September	6	ADM 111/193
23 November	29 November	6	ADM 111/193
		12.2	
1810			
1 May	11 May	10	ADM 111/195
4 May	21 May	17	ADM 111/195
25 July	7 August	13	ADM 111/196
		13.3	
1811–12[*]			
AVERAGE 1808–10		10.83	

[*] After 1810, the Victualling Board minutes become less revealing about the times in which transports were loaded. Indeed, with deliveries being planned months in advance from 1810, the time between transports being procured and their being loaded becomes less representative of their performance.

APPENDIX 4. TIME TAKEN TO DELIVER PROVISIONS TO VARIOUS AREAS OF THE BALTIC, 1808–9

VB order	Arrive at Gothen- burg/ Wingo Sound	No. days	Arrive Hanö/ Bornholm/ Karlskrona	No. days	Arrive Nargen Island, Gulf of Finland	No. days	TNA reference
1808							
7 June			25 July	49	6 Aug.	60	ADM 111/187, ADM 51/1825, ADM 52/3798
15 July			22 Aug.	36	6 Oct.	83	ADM 111/187, ADM 51/1825, ADM 52/3798
6 Sept. 23 Sept.			1 Dec.	69			ADM 1/7/461–2
1809							
20 May	23 June	34			21 July	62	ADM 111/191, ADM 51/1958, ADM 51/2345
20 May	12 July	53	10 Aug.	82	26 Aug.	98	ADM 111/191, ADM 51/2345, ADM 51/1979
16 Aug.	21 Oct.	66	10 Nov.	86			ADM 111/192, ADM 51/2976
6 Sept. 20 Nov.	9 Dec.	19					ADM 111/193, ADM 51/1996
AVERAGE		43		64.4		75·75	

APPENDIX 5. EFFICIENCY OF
VICTUALLING DELIVERIES, BREAD

* Covered by rations on board ships that left Deptford in April

April 1808 – March 1809

Month	No. men on station	No. rations needed (lbs)
April 1808	*	
May 1808	*	
June 1808	*	
July 1808	*	
August 1808	*	
September 1808	*	
October 1808	10,796	365,678
November 1808	10,144	304,320
December 1808	6,578	203,918
January 1809	6,336	196,416
February 1809	2,625	81,375
March 1809	3,596	111,476
Spanish Soldiers	9,897 (for 52 days)	514,644
TOTAL NEEDED		1,777,825

Delivery	No. bags	No. lbs delivered (112 lbs in a bag)
Shipment 1	5,500	616,000
Shipment 2	5,500	616,000
Shipment 3	5,500	616,000
Shipment 4	5,825	652,400
TOTAL DELIVERED		2,500,400

April 1809 – March 1810

Month	No. men	No. rations
April 1809	*	
May 1809	*	
June 1809	*	
July 1809	*	
August 1809	*	
September 1809	*	
October 1809	15,746	488,684
November 1809	15,390	461,700
December 1809	10,038	311,178
January 1810	5,827	180,637
February 1810	3,000	84,000
March 1810	3,000	93,000
TOTAL NEEDED		1,619,199

Delivery	No. bags	No. lbs
Shipment 1	6,000	672,000
Shipment 2	2,250	252,000
Shipment 3	2,500	280,000
Extra	270	30,240
Shipment 4	1,375	154,000
TOTAL SENT		1,388,240

April 1810 – March 1811

Month	No. men	No. rations
April 1810	*	
May 1810	*	
June 1810	*	
July 1810	*	
August 1810	*	
September 1810	*	
October 1810	15,900	492,900
November 1810	13,965	418,950
December 1810	9,897	310,000
January 1811	2,511	76,260
February 1811	2,511	70,000
March 1811	2,511	77,500
TOTAL NEEDED		1,445,610

Delivery	No. bags	No. lbs
Shipment 1	5,000	560,000
Shipment 2	8,000	896,000
Extra	1,563	175,056
TOTAL SENT		1,631,056

April 1811 – March 1812

Month	No. men	No. rations
April 1811	*	
May 1811	*	
June 1811	*	
July 1811	*	
August 1811	*	
September 1811	*	
October 1811	13,700	424,700
November 1811	13,500	405,000
December 1811	5,600	173,600
January 1812	5,600	174,282
February 1812	2,220	61,600
March 1812	2,220	68,200
TOTAL NEEDED		1,307,382

Delivery	No. bags	No. lbs
Shipment 1	5,500	616,000
Shipment 2	6,600	739,200
TOTAL SENT		1,355,200

April 1812 – March 1813

Month	No. men	No. rations
April	*	
May	*	
June	*	
July	*	
August	*	
September	*	
October	9,327	289,137
November	9,327	279,810
December	9,327	289,137
January	1,884	58,404
February	1,884	52,752
March	1,884	58,404
TOTAL NEEDED		1,027,644

Delivery	No. bags	No. lbs
Shipment 1	5,000	560,000
Shipment 2	500	56,000
Shipment 3	6,600	739,200
TOTAL SENT		1,355,200

APPENDIX 6. EFFICIENCY OF VICTUALLING DELIVERIES: SPIRITS

Because the spirit ration could be replaced by a wine ration at times, wine has been converted into the equivalent spirit ration. Men were given a pint of wine in place of a half pint of spirits per day.

* Covered by rations on board ships that left Deptford in April

April 1808 – March 1809

Month	No. men	No. rations (pints)
April 1808	*	
May 1808	*	
June 1808	*	
July 1808	*	
August 1808	*	
September 1808	*	
October 1808	11,796	182,838
November 1808	10,144	152,160
December 1808	6,578	101,959
January 1809	6,336	98,208
February 1809	2,625	40,688
March 1809	3,596	55,738
Spanish Soldiers	9,897 for 52 days	257,322
TOTAL NEEDED		888,912

Delivery	Gallons spirits	Pints spirits	Gallons wine	Equivalent to x pints of wine
Shipment 1	38,500	308,000		
Shipment 2	38,500	308,000		
Shipment 3	38,500	228,000	20,000	320,000
Shipment 4	20,387	163,096	40,775	652,400
TOTALS		1,007,096		486,200
TOTAL SENT				1,493,296

April 1809 – March 1809

Month	No. men	No. rations
April 1809	*	
May 1809	*	
June 1809	*	
July 1809	*	
August 1809	*	
September 1809	*	
October 1809	15,784	244,342
November 1809	15,390	230,850
December 1809	10,038	155,589
January 1810	5,827	90,318
February 1810	3,000	42,000
March 1810	3,000	46,500
TOTAL NEEDED		809,599

Delivery	Gallons spirits	Pints spirits	Gallons wine	Equivalent to x pints of spirits
Shipment 1	42,000	336,000		
Shipment 2			10,500	42,000
Extra	8,750	70,000	17,500	70,000
Shipment 3	945	7,560	1,890	7,560
Shipment 4	350	2,800	700	2,800
Totals		416,360		122,360
TOTAL SENT				538,720

April 1810 – March 1811

Month	No. men	No. rations
April 1810	*	
May 1810	*	
June 1810	*	
July 1810	*	
August 1810	*	
September 1810	*	
October 1810	15,958	246,450
November 1810	13,965	209,475
December 1810	9,897	155,000
January 1811	2,511	38,131
February 1811	2,511	3,511
March 1811	2,511	3,877
TOTAL NEEDED		722,805

Delivery	Gallons spirits	Pints spirits	Gallons wine	Equivalent to x pints of wine
Shipment 1	35,000	280,000	35,000	140,000
Shipment 2	39,666	317,328	39,666	158,664
		597,328		298,664
TOTAL SENT				895,992

April 1811 – March 1812

Month	No. men	No. rations
April 1811	*	
May 1811	*	
June 1811	*	
July 1811	*	
August 1811	*	
September 1811	*	
October 1811	13,700	212,350
November 1811	13,500	202,500
December 1811	5,622	86,800
January 1812	5,622	87,141
February 1812	2,220	30,800
March 1812	2,220	30,800
TOTAL NEEDED		653,691

Delivery	Gallons spirits	Pints spirits	Gallons wine	Equivalent to x pints of wine
Shipment 1	19,250	154,000	38,500	154,000
Shipment 2	32,666	261,328	32,666	136,164
		415,328		284,664
TOTAL SENT				699,992

April 1812 – March 1813

Month	No. men	No. rations
April 1812	*	
May 1812	*	
June 1812	*	
July 1812	*	
August 1812	*	
September 1812	*	
October 1812	9,327	144,589
November 1812	9,327	139,905
December 1812	9,327	144,568
January 1813	1,884	29,202
February 1813	1,884	16,376
March 1813	1,884	29,202
TOTAL NEEDED		513,822

Delivery	Gallons spirits	Pints spirits	Gallons wine	Equivalent to x pints of wine
Shipment 1	23,333	186,664	23,333	93,332
Shipment 2	14,000	112,000	28,000	112,000
Shipment 3	40,425	323,400	11,500	46,000
		622,064		251,332
TOTAL SENT				873,396

BIBLIOGRAPHY

Unpublished primary sources

National archives

ADM 1	Admiralty In-letters
ADM 1/4	Letters from the Commander-in-Chief, Baltic, 1801
ADM 1/5–12	Letters from Commander-in-Chief, Baltic, 1807–12
ADM 1/154/506	Letters from Flag Officers, Channel Fleet: 1813, nos. 374–571
ADM 1/3523	Letters from the Hydrographic Office to the Admiralty
ADM 1/3753–63	Letters from the Transport Board, 1807–12
ADM 2	Admiralty Out-letters
ADM 2/154–9	Admiralty Orders and Instructions, 1807–12.
ADM 2/525/546	Secretary's Letter: Public Officers and Flag Officers, 1759
ADM 7/791–5	Baltic Convoy Lists 1809–12
ADM 7/869:	Abstract of Salaries due to persons on the Victualling Establishment, 1805–182
ADM 8/69–100	List Book, showing the disposition of Ships, names of Officers 1792–1815
ADM 20/322–4	Treasury Ledgers, Naval and Victualling, 1808–9
ADM 51	Captains' Logs

ADM 51/1824	*Centaur*	ADM 51/2425	*Gluckstadt*
ADM 51/1958	*Curlew*	ADM 51/2564	*Mercurius*
ADM 51/1979	*Mercurius*	ADM 51/2567	*Manley*
ADM 51/1996	*Osprey*	ADM 51/2837	*Sheldrake*
ADM 51/2093	*Alonzo*	ADM 51/2934	*Victory*
ADM 51/2295	*Fantome*	ADM 51/2976	*Woodlark*
ADM 51/2300	*Drake*	ADM 51/3878	*Lancaster*
ADM 51/2345	*St George*	ADM 51/4062	*Hebe*
ADM 51/2396	*Fury*		

ADM 52	Masters' Logs
ADM 52/3798	*Superb*
ADM 52/3878	*Victory*
ADM 52/3741	*Centaur*
ADM 80/143:	Book of Orders and Letters of Captain (afterwards Admiral) Keats. 1808–9
ADM 80/145	Book of Orders and Letters of Captain (afterwards Admiral) Keats. 1808–9
ADM 97/88	Letters from the Physicians of the Fleet. 1809–17
ADM 101/83/3	Medical Journals, Office of the Director General of the Medical Department of the Navy and predecessors: Hospital ship *Alfred*. Includes an essay on yellow fever, covering dates 1797–8
ADM 102/241	Naval Hospitals' and Hospital Ships' Musters, *Gorgon* Hospital Ship, Baltic, 1808–11
ADM 108/150	Ship's Ledgers (transports) 1806–11
ADM 109/102–10	Victualling Board letters relating to Army Victualling. 1793–1816
ADM 110/58–64	Victualling Board Out-letters, 1808–12
ADM 111/19	Victualling Board Minutes 1723–5
ADM 111/159–61	Victualling Board Minutes 1799–1802
ADM 111/187–205	Victualling Board Minutes 1807–12
FO 22/58, 60–3	Foreign Office and predecessor: Political and Other Departments: General Correspondence before 1906, Denmark, 1808–12
FO 65/47, 71	Foreign Office and predecessor: Political and Other Departments: General Correspondence before 1906, Russian Empire, 1807–9
FO 73/47–50, 65	Foreign Office and predecessor: Political and Other Departments: General Correspondence before 1906, Sweden (later incorporating Norway), 1808–12
FO 90/68	Sweden: King's Letter Books 1799–1828
HD 3/6	John Ross, Memorandum for His Majesty, September 1834
WO/6/14	War Office to the Admiralty

Caird Library, National Maritime Museum

ADM B   Navy Board reports to the Admiralty
ADM BP   Navy Board out-letters to the Admiralty
ADM DP/21, 31 Victualling Board letters to the Admiralty, 1801–2, 1807–8.

Henley Papers Michael Henley and Son
HNL 13/17   Papers relating to shipment of coal in the *Ann*
HNL 13/20   Papers relating to cancelled order for coal for Anholt,
               August 1810, *Harry Morris*
HNL 13/22   Tenders to Transport Board for Coal Laden ships: *Mary*,
               Freedom, *Norfolk*, 1810; *Lord Rodney*, *Alice Henrietta*,
               London, *Zephyr*, 1812, *Anna*, *Alice*, *Trusty* and three other
               ships, 1813
HNL 13/23   Charterparties and papers relating to two shipments
               of coal for Victualling Board, June-November 1811
HNL 14/5   Papers relating to unsuccessful tenders of Henley Ships
               as Transports, and other correspondence with Transport
               Office, 1810–13
HNL 20/11   Papers endorsed as relating to Exchequer Bills bought
               and sold for William Dodds, master of Henley ships
               and ship-owner, 1806–10
HNL 34/30   Bill of lading and official papers relating to transport
               vge to Mediterranean, May 1800–2. Transport no.27
HNL 59/81   *Freedom's* vge, wage accts, etc, portage bill, receipts for
               dues, Apr-Dec. 1808

Papers of Lord Keith, George Keith Elphinstone
KEI/L/1–2   Letters to Lord Keith, 1799–1800
KEI/L/23–4   Letters Sent, Lord Keith 1799–1800

Papers of Charles Middleton
MID   Papers of Charles Middleton, 1st Baron Barham

Papers of Samuel Hood
MKH/110   Keats Letters to Hood, 1808
MKH/112   Orders from Saumarez to Hood, 1808–9
MKH/113   Keats Letters to Hood, 1808–9
MKH/114   Keats Letters to Hood, 1809

Whitworth Papers
WHW 1/6
YOR 7, 11, 16, 21   Letters to Charles Yorke, Lord of the Admiralty 1810–12

British Library

Add. 34934   Nepean Papers
Add. 37295   Liverpool Papers

Mulgrave Archive, Mulgrave Castle, Whitby

Box VII/MA 19–22: Letters to and from Lord Mulgrave, First Lord of the Admiralty 1807–10

Suffolk Record Office

HA 93/6/1/1–2500 Official Correspondence of Admiral Sir James Saumarez 1807–13
SA 3/1/2/1–7   Private Papers of the Saumarez Family, formerly at Shrubland Hall, Suffolk

New York Public Library

Constable-Pierrepoint Papers, Boxes 5, 9, 13, 32, 34

Kungliga Biblioteket, Stockholm

Ep.E.10.11, f. 109   Lars von Engeström Collection
Ep.E.10.11, f. 120
Ep.E.10.11. f. 123

Periodicals and parliamentary papers

An Account of the Number of Commercial Licenses Granted during the Last Ten Years. Parliamentary Papers, Miscellaneous, 1812.
Accounts relating to Navy and Victualling Contracts, and Pay of Shipwrights, 1790–1823. House of Commons Parliamentary Papers Online, 1823 (417). http://parlipapers.chadwyck.co.uk/fulltext/fulltext.do?area=hcpp&id=1823-008383&pagenum=1&resultNum=6&entries=7&queryId=../session/1340976289_9998&backto=FULLREC. Accessed January 2012.
Albion and Evening Advertiser
General Advertiser and Morning Intelligencer
Ninth, Tenth and Eleventh Report of the Commission for Revising and Digesting the Civil Affairs of His Majesty's Navy, VI. Parliamentary Papers, 1809.

Notifications, Orders and Instructions relating to Prize Subjects during the Present War, 1810 (London Gazette, 1806).

Papers Presented to the House of Commons Relating to the State and Condition of the Squadron Employed off Rochefort under the Command of Sir Richard J. Strachan, printed 15 March 1808, nos. 9–59. House of Commons Parliamentary Papers Online, 1808 (103). http://parlipapers.chadwyck.co.uk/fulltext/fulltext.do?area=hcpp&id=1808-001747&pagenum=1&resultNum=1&entries=1&source=config.cfg&queryId=../session/1340984783_22185&backto=RESULTS. Accessed January 2012.

Reports of the Commissioners Appointed by Parliament to Enquire into the Fees, Gratuities, Perquisites and Emoluments, which are, or have been lately received in the several public offices therein mentioned, VII, Fifth Report. House of Commons Parliamentary Papers, 1806.

Steel's Navy List 1809–1810

Published primary sources

Anon., *An Address to the People of England, upon the Subject of the Intended War with Russia* (London, 1791).

Anon., *Extracts from Publications Relating to the Culture and Management of Hemp, Published by the Order of the Trustees of the Linen and Hemp Manufactures of Ireland* (Dublin, 1808).

Anon., *An Inquiry into the State of Our Commercial Relations with the Northern Powers, with Reference to Our Trade with them under the Regulation of Licenses, the Advantage which the Enemy Derives from it, and its Effects on the Revenue, the Course of the Foreign Exchanges, the Price of Bullion, and the General Prosperity of the British Empire.* (London, 1811).

Anon., *Notifications, Orders and Instructions relating to Prize Subjects during the Present War* (1810).

Anon., *Report on the Manuscripts of J. B. Fortescue, Esq., Preserved at Dropmore*, V–VII (London, 1908).

Anon., *Treaty of Navigation and Commerce between His Britannick Majesty and the Emperor of Russia* (London, 1797).

Barham, Charles, *Letters and Papers of Charles, Lord Barham, 1758–1813*, ed. John K. Laughton, II, Navy Records Society 38 (London, 1909).

Baugh, Daniel A., *Naval Administration 1715–1750*, Navy Records Society 120 (London, 1977).

Boteler, Captain John Harvey, *Recollections of My Sea Life; From 1808 to 1830*, ed. David Bonner-Smith, Navy Records Society 65 (London, 1942).

Brough, Anthony, *A View of the Importance of the Trade between Britain and Russia* (London, 1789).

Colquhoun, P., 'A General View of the Whole Commerce and Shipping of the River Thames', in *A Treatise on the Commerce and Police of the Metropolis* (London, 1800).

Coxe, William, *Travels into Poland, Russia, Sweden, and Denmark, Interspersed with Historical Relations and Political Inquiries* (Dublin, 1794).

Crimmin, P. K., ed., 'The Supply of Timber for the Royal Navy, c.1803–1830', in *The Naval Miscellany*, VII, Navy Records Society 153 (London, 2008), pp. 191–234.

Eton, William, *General Observations regarding the Present State of the Russian Empire* (London, 1787).

Hunter, William, *A Short View of the Political Situation of the Northern Powers: Founded on Observations Made during a Tour through Russia, Sweden and Denmark in the Last Seven Months of the Year 1800 with Conjectures on the Probable Issue of the Approaching Contest* (London, 1801).

Kemp, Peter, 'Boscawen's Letters to his Wife, 1755–56', in Christopher Lloyd, ed., *The Naval Miscellany*, IV, Navy Records Society 92 (London, 1952).

Marsden, William, *A Brief Memoir of the Life and Writings of the Late William Marsden, Written by Himself* (London, 1838)

Martin, Thomas Byam, *Letters and Papers of Admiral of the Fleet Sir Thomas Byam Martin*, ed. Sir Richard Vesey Hamilton, II, Navy Records Society 12 (London, 1902)

Moore, John, *The Diary of Sir John Moore*, ed. J. F. Maurice, II (London, 1904).

Oddy, J. Jepson, *European Commerce: shewing new and secure channels of trade with the continent of Europe: detailing the produce, manufactures, and commerce of Russia, Prussia, Sweden, Denmark and Germany . . . with a general view of the trade, navigation, produce and manufactures of the United Kingdom of Great Britain and Ireland* (London, 1805).

Russell, Richard, *The Rope-Makers Guide or a Complete Key to the Art of Rope-Making* (London, 1804).

Ryan, A. N., ed., *The Saumarez Papers: Selections from the Baltic Correspondence of Vice-Admiral Sir James Saumarez 1808–1812*, Navy Records Society 110 (London, 1968).

Sandwich, John, *The Private Papers of John, Earl of Sandwich*, ed. G. R. T. Barnes and Lt Cdr J. H. Owen, III–IV, Navy Records Society 75 and 78 (London, 1936–8).

Spencer, George, *The Private Papers of George, 2nd Earl Spencer*, ed. H. Richmond, Navy Records Society vol. IV (London, 1924).

Steel, David, *Elements and Practice of Rigging and Seamanship,* I (London, 1794).

Sutherland, David, *A Tour up the Straits, from Gibraltar to Constantinople* (London, 1790).

Secondary sources

Albion, Robert Greenhalgh, *Forests and Seapower: The Timber Problem of the Royal Navy 1652–1862* (Hamden, CT, 1926).

Aldridge, David Denis, 'The Victualling of the British Naval Expeditions to the Baltic Sea between 1715 and 1727', *Scandinavian Economic History Review* 12/2 (1964), 1–25.

—— *Admiral Sir John Norris and the British Naval Expeditions to the Baltic Sea 1715–1727* (Lund, 2009).

Anderson, M. S., 'The Continental System and Russo-British Relations during the Napoleonic Wars', in K. Bourne and D. C. Watt, eds., *Studies in International History: Essays Presented to W. Norton Medlicott, Stevenson Professor of International History in the University of London* (London, 1967), pp. 68-80.

—— *Britain's Discovery of Russia 1553–1815* (London, 1958).

Anderson, R. C., *Naval Wars in the Baltic, 1522–1850* (London, 1969).

Andersson, Ingvar, *A History of Sweden,* trans. Carolyn Hannay (London, 1955).

Arthur, Brian, *How Britain Won the War of 1812: The Royal Navy's Blockades of the United States, 1812–1815* (Woodbridge, 2011).

Ash, Eric H., 'Expertise and the Early Modern State', *OSIRIS* 25/1 (2010), 1–24.

Aylmer, Gerald, 'From Office-Holding to Civil Service: The Genesis of Modern Bureaucracy', *Transactions of the Royal Historical Society*, 5th series, part 30 (1980), 91–108.

Baker, Norman, *Government and Contractors: British Treasury and War Supplies, 1775–83* (London, 1971).

Bamford, Paul Walden, *Forests and French Seapower 1660–1789* (Toronto, 1956).

Bartlett, C. J., *Castlereagh* (London, 1966).

Bateman, Victoria N., 'The Evolution of Markets in Early Modern Europe, 1350–1800: A Study of Wheat Prices', *Economic History Review* 64/2 (2011), 447–71.

Baugh, Daniel A., *British Naval Administration in the Age of Walpole* (Princeton, 1965).

Baugh, Daniel A., *Naval Administration 1715–1750*, Navy Records Society 120 (London, 1977).

—— 'Naval Power: What Gave the British Navy Superiority?', in Leandro Prados de la Escorura, ed., *Exceptionalism and Industrialisation: Britain and its European Rivals, 1688–1815* (Cambridge, 2004), pp. 235–60.

Binney, J. E. D., *British Public Finance and Administration 1774–1792* (Oxford, 1958).

Black, Jeremy, and P. Woodfine, eds., *The British Navy and the Use of Naval Power in the Eighteenth Century* (Leicester, 1988).

Blanning, T. C. W., *The French Revolutionary Wars 1787–1802* (London, 1996).

Bond, Gordon C., *The Grand Expedition: The British Invasion of Holland in 1809* (Athens, GA, 1970).

Bonney, Richard, ed., *The Rise of the Fiscal State in Europe, c. 1200–1815* (Oxford, 1999).

Bowen, H. V., *War and British Society, 1688–1815* (Cambridge, 1998).

—— and A. G. Enciso, *Mobilising Resources for War: Britain and Spain at Work during the Early Modern Period* (Pamplona, 2006).

Bowler, R. Arthur, *Logistics and the Failure of the British Army in America, 1775–1783* (Princeton, NJ, 1975).

Brackenbury, Mark, *Baltic Southwest Pilot* (London, 1983).

Brewer, John, *The Sinews of Power; War, Money and the English State 1688–1783* (New York, 1989).

Brown, Kevin, *Poxed and Scurvied: The Story of Sickness and Health at Sea* (Barnsley, 2011).

Bruijn, Jaap R., *The Dutch Navy of the Seventeenth and Eighteenth Centuries* (Columbia, 1993).

Buchet, Christian, *Marine, economie et société: un exemple d'interaction: l'avitaillement de la Royal Navy durant la guerre de sept ans* (Paris, 1999).

—— 'The Development of Victualling Board Bases in London, Portsmouth, Plymouth, Chatham and Dover, 1701–1763', *Transactions of the Naval Dockyards Society* 4 (2008), 53–68.

Chamberlain, Muriel, *'Pax Britannica'? British Foreign Policy 1789–1914* (London, 1988).

Christie, Ian R., *Wars and Revolutions: Britain, 1760–1815* (London, 1982).

Cole, Gareth, 'The Ordnance Board and the Royal Navy 1790–1815' (unpublished Ph.D. thesis, University of Exeter, 2008).

Collinge, J. M., *Navy Board Officials 1660–1832* (London, 1978).

Condon, Mary Ellen, 'The Administration of the Transport Service during the War against Revolutionary France, 1793–1802' (unpublished Ph.D. thesis, London University, 1968).

—— 'The Establishment of the Transport Board – A Subdivision of the Admiralty – 4 July 1794', *MM* 58 (1972), 69–84.

Connelly, Owen, *Napoleon's Satellite Kingdom's: Managing Conquered Peoples* (Malabar, FL, 1990).

Conway, Stephen, *War, State and Society in Mid-Eighteenth-Century Britain and Ireland* (Oxford, 2006).

Corbett, Julian S., *Some Principles of Maritime Strategy* (London, 1972).

—— 'Napoleon and the British Navy after Trafalgar', *Quarterly Review* 237 (1921), 238–55.

Coquelle, P., 'La mission d'Alquier à Stockholm', *Revue d'histoire diplomatique* 23 (1909), 196–239.

Crimmin, Patricia K., '"A Great Object with Us to Procure This Timber . . .": The Royal Navy's Search for Ship Timber in the Eastern Mediterranean and Southern Russia, 1803–15', *The International Journal of Maritime History* 4/2 (1992), 83–115.

Crosby, Alfred W., *America, Russia, Hemp and Napoleon: American Trade with Russia and the Baltic, 1783–1812* (Columbus, OH, 1965).

Crouzet, François, *L'économie britannique et le blocus continental 1806–1813*, I–II. (Paris, 1958).

—— 'Blockade and Economic Change in Europe, 1792–1815', *Journal of Economic History* 24/4 (December, 1964), 567–88.

Crowhurst, Patrick, *The Defence of British Trade 1689–1815* (London, 1977).

—— *The French War on Trade: Privateering 1793–1815* (Aldershot, 1989).

Currie, Ann, *Henley's of Wapping; A London Shipowning Family 1770–1830* (London, 1988).

Daunton, M. J., *Progress and Poverty: An Economic and Social History of Britain 1700–1850* (Oxford, 1995).

Davey, James, 'Within Hostile Shores: Victualling the Royal Navy in European Waters during the Napoleonic Wars', *The International Journal of Maritime History* 21/2 (December 2009), 241–60.

—— 'The Repatriation of Spanish Soldiers from Denmark, 1808: The British Government, Logistics and Maritime Supremacy', *The Journal of Military History* 74/4 (October 2010), 689–707.

—— 'Securing the Sinews of Seapower: British Intervention in the Baltic, 1780–1815', *International History Review* 33/2 (June, 2011), 161–84.

—— 'The Advancement of Nautical Knowledge: The Hydrographical Office, the Royal Navy and the Charting of the Baltic Sea, 1795–1815', *The Journal for Maritime Research* 13 (2011), 81-103.

—— 'Supplied by the Enemy: The Royal Navy and the British Consular Service in the Baltic, 1808–1812', *Historical Research* 85/228 (2012), 265–83.

Davis, Lance E., and Stanley L. Engerman, *Naval Blockades in Peace and War: An Economic History since 1750* (Cambridge, 2006).

Dixon, Peter, *Canning: Politician and Statesman* (London 1976).

Duffy, Michael, *Soldiers, Sugar and Seapower: The British Expeditions to the West Indies and the War against Revolutionary France* (Oxford, 1987).

—— 'The Establishment of the Western Squadron as the Linchpin of British Naval Strategy', in Michael Duffy, ed., *The Parameters of British Naval Power, 1650–1850* (Exeter, 1992), pp. 66–81.

——, Stephen Fisher, Basil Greenhill, David J. Starkey and Joyce Youings, eds., *The New Maritime History of Devon: From Early Times to the Late Eighteenth Century* (London, 1992).

Dull, Jonathan R., *The French Navy and the Seven Years War* (London, 2005).

Dwyer, Philip G., 'Prussia and the Armed Neutrality: The Invasion of Hanover in 1801', *The International History Review* 15/4 (November 1993), 661–87.

Ellemen, Bruce A., and S. C. M. Paine, eds., *Naval Blockades and Seapower: Strategies and Counter-Strategies 1805–2005* (London, 2006).

Esdaile, Charles, *The Wars of Napoleon* (London, 1995).

—— *Napoleon's Wars: An International History* (London, 2007).

Evans, Eric J., *The Forging of the Modern State: Early Industrial Britain 1783–1870* (London, 1996).

Feldbaek, Ole, 'The Anglo-Danish Wars 1801 and 1807–1814', *Revue internationale d'histoire militaire* (Commission internationale d'histoire militaire) 84 (2004), 100–15.

—— *Denmark and the Armed Neutrality 1800–1: Small-Power Policy in a World War* (Copenhagen, 1980).

—— *The Battle of Copenhagen 1801: Nelson and the Danes* (Barnsley, 2002).

—— 'Denmark and the Baltic 1720–1864', in Goran Rystad, Klaus R. Bohme and Wilhelm M. Carlgren, eds., *In Quest of Trade and Security: The Baltic in Power Politics, 1500–1990*, I, *1500–1890* (Lund, 1994), pp. 257–95.

Frost, Alan, *Botany Bay Mirages: Illusions of Australia's Convict Beginnings* (Melbourne, 1994).

Galpin, W. Freedman, *The Grain Supply of England during the Napoleonic War* (New York, 1977).

Gascoigne, John, *Science in the Service of Empire: Joseph Banks, the British State and the Uses of Science in the Age of Revolution* (Cambridge, 1998).

Gates, David, *The Napoleonic Wars 1803–15* (London, 1997).

Glete, Jan, *Navies and Nations: Warships, Navies and State Building in Europe and America, 1500–1860*, 2 vols. (Stockholm, 1993).

—— 'Navies and Power Struggle in Northern and Eastern Europe, 1721–1814', in Rob Hobson and Tom Kristansen, eds., *Navies in Northern Waters 1721–2000* (London, 2004), pp. 66–90.

Gradish, Stephen F., *The Manning of the British Navy during the Seven Years War* (London, 1980).

Graham, Gerald S., *The Politics of Naval Supremacy: Studies in British Maritime Ascendancy* (Cambridge, 1965).

—— *Swedish Naval Administration, 1521–1721: Resource Flows and Organisational Capabilities* (Leiden, 2010).

Hall, Christopher D., *British Strategy in the Napoleonic War 1803–15* (Manchester, 1992).

—— *Wellington's Navy: Sea Power and the Peninsular War, 1807–1814* (London, 2004).

Ham, V. R., 'Strategies of Coalition and Isolation. British War Policy and North-West Europe, 1803–1810' (unpublished Ph.D. thesis, University of Oxford, 1977).

Hamilton, Douglas, 'Private Enterprise and Public Service: Naval Contracting in the Caribbean, 1720–1750', *The Journal for Maritime Research* 6 (2004), 37–64.

—— *Scotland, the Caribbean and the Atlantic World, 1750–1820* (Manchester, 2005).

Hancock, David, *Citizens of the World: London Merchants and the Integration of the British Atlantic Community, 1735–1785* (Cambridge, 1997).

Hannay, David, *A Short History of the Royal Navy, 1217–1815* (London, 1909).

Harding, Richard, *Seapower and Naval Warfare 1650–1830* (London, 1999).

Harling, Philip, *The Waning of 'Old Corruption': The Politics of Economical Reform in Britain, 1779–1846* (Oxford, 1996).

—— and P. Mandler, 'From Fiscal-Military State to Laissez-Faire State, 1760–1850', *Journal of British Studies* 32 (1993), 44–70.

Hattendorf, John B., ed., *Doing Naval History: Essays towards Improvement* (Newport, RI, 1995).

——, R. J. B. Knight, A. W. H. Pearsall, N. A. M. Rodger and Geoffrey Till, eds., *British Naval Documents 1204–1960*, Navy Records Society 131 (London, 1993).

Herman, Arthur, *To Rule the Waves: How the British Navy Shaped the Modern World* (London, 2004).

Hill, Richard, *The Prizes of War: The Naval Prize System in the Napoleonic Wars 1793–1815* (London, 1998).

Hilton, Boyd, *The New Oxford History of England: A Mad Bad Dangerous People? England 1783–1846* (Oxford, 2006).

Hobson, Rolf, and Tom Kristansen, eds., *Navies in Northern Waters 1721–2000* (London, 2004).

Holmes, Geoffrey, *Augustan England: Professions, State and Society 1680–1730* (London, 1982).

Howard, Michael, *War in European History* (Oxford, 1976).

James, William, *The Naval History of Great Britain From the Declaration of War by France in 1793 to the Accession of George IV*, IV–V (London, 1902).

Kahan, Arcadius, *The Plow, the Hammer and the Knout: An Economic History of Eighteenth Century Russia* (Chicago, 1985).

Kaplan, Herbert, *Russian Overseas Commerce with Great Britain during the Reign of Catherine II* (Philadelphia, 1995).

Kennedy, Paul, *The Rise and Fall of British Naval Mastery* (London, 1976).

—— *Rise and Fall of the Great Powers: Economic Change and Military Conflict from 1500 to 2000* (New York, 1987).

Kirby, David, *The Baltic World 1772–1993: Europe's Northern Periphery in an Age of Change* (London, 1995).

—— and Merja-Liisa Hinkkanen, *The Baltic and the North Seas* (London, 2000).

Knight, R. J. B., 'The Royal Dockyards in England at the Time of the American War of Independence' (unpublished Ph.D. thesis, University of London, 1972).

—— 'New England Forests and British Seapower: Albion Revised', *The American Neptune* 46/4 (1986), 221–9.

—— *Shipbuilding Timber for the British Navy: Parliamentary Papers, 1729–1792* (New York, 1993).

—— 'Devil Bolts and Deception: Wartime Naval Shipbuilding in Private Shipyards, 1739–1815', *The Journal for Maritime Research* 5 (2003), 34–51.

—— *The Pursuit of Victory: The Life and Achievement of Horatio Nelson* (London, 2005).

—— 'Politics and Trust in Victualling the Navy, 1793–1815', *MM* 94/2 (May 2008), 133–49

—— and Martin Wilcox, *Sustaining the Fleet: War, the Navy and the Contractor State 1793–1815* (Woodbridge, 2010).

Lambert, Andrew, *The Crimean War: British Grand Strategy 1853–1856* (Manchester, 1990).

—— *Warfare in the Age of Sail* (London, 2000).

—— *Nelson: Britannia's God of War* (London, 2004).

—— 'The Crimean War Blockade 1854–6', in Bruce A. Elleman and S. C. M. Paine, eds., *Naval Blockades and Seapower: Strategies and Counterstrategies 1805–2005* (London, 2006).

Laughton, J. K., and R. V. Hamilton, eds., *Recollections of James Anthony Gardner*, Navy Records Society (London, 1906).

Le Fevre, Peter, and Richard Harding, eds., *British Admirals of the Napoleonic Wars: The Contemporaries of Nelson* (London, 2005).

Lievan, Dominic, *Russia against Napoleon: The Battle for Europe 1807–1814* (London, 2009).

Lloyd, Christopher, ed., *The Health of Seamen: Selections from the Works of Dr. James Lind, Gilbert Blane and Dr. Thomas Trotter*, Navy Records Society 107 (London, 1965).

—— and Jack L. S. Coulter, eds., *Medicine and the Royal Navy 1200–1900*, III, *1714–1815* (London, 1961).

Macdonald, Janet, *Feeding Nelson's Navy: The True Story of Food at Sea in the Georgian Era* (London, 2004).

—— 'The Victualling Board 1793–1815: A Study of Management Competence' (Ph.D. thesis, King's College, London, 2009).

—— *The British Navy's Victualling Board, 1793–1815: Management Competence and Incompetence* (Woodbridge, 2010).

Mackesy, Piers, *The War in the Mediterranean 1803–10* (Cambridge, MA, 1957).

—— *The War for America, 1775–1783* (London, 1964).

—— *Statesmen at War: the Strategy of Overthrow, 1798–1799* (London, 1974).

—— *British Victory in Egypt, 1801: The End of Napoleon's Conquest* (London, 1995).

Madariaga, Isabel de, *Britain, Russia and the Armed Neutrality of 1780: Sir James Harris' Mission to St Petersburg during the American Revolution* (London, 1961).

Mahan, Alfred Thayer, *The Influence of Sea Power upon History 1660–1783* (London, 1890).

Malone, J. J., 'The British Naval Stores and Forests Policy in New England 1691–1775' (unpublished Ph.D. thesis, University of London, 1956).

—— 'England and the Baltic Naval Stores Trade in the Seventeenth and Eighteenth Centuries', *MM* 58/4 (1972), 375–95.

Marshall, P. J., *The Oxford History of the British Empire: The Eighteenth Century* (Oxford, 1998).

Marzagelli, Silvia, 'Napoleon's Continental Blockade: An Effective Substitute to Naval Weakness?', in Bruce A. Elleman and S. C. M. Paine, eds., *Naval Blockades and Seapower: Strategies and Counter-strategies 1805–2005* (London, 2006), pp. 25–34.

Matthew, H. L. G., and Brian Harrison, eds., *Oxford Dictionary of National Biography*, XXI (Oxford, 2004).

McCranie, Kevin D., *Admiral Lord Keith and the Naval War against Napoleon* (Gainesville, FL, 2006).

Middleton, Richard, *The Bells of Victory: The Pitt-Newcastle Ministry and the Conduct of the Seven Years War, 1757–1762* (Cambridge, 1985).

Mitchell, B. R., and Phyllis Deane, *Abstract of British Historical Statistics* (Cambridge, 1962).

Morgan, John, 'War Feeding War? The Impact of Logistics on the Napoleonic Occupation of Catalonia', *Journal of Military History* 73 (January 2009), 83–116.

Morriss, Roger, *The Royal Dockyards during the Revolutionary and Napoleonic Wars* (Leicester, 1983).

—— *Naval Power and British Culture, 1760–1850* (Aldershot, 2004).

—— 'The Supply of Casks and Staves to the Royal Navy, 1770–1815', *MM* 93/1 (February 2007), 43–50.

—— 'Colonization, Conquest, and the Supply of Food and Transport: The Reorganization of Logistics Management, 1780–1795', *War in History* 13/3 (2007), 310–24.

—— *The Foundations of British Maritime Ascendency: Resources, Logistics and the State, 1755–1815* (Cambridge, 2011).

Muir, Rory, *Britain and the Defeat of Napoleon* (New Haven, CT, 1996).

Muller, Leos, *Consuls, Corsairs, and Commerce: The Swedish Consular Service and Long-Distance Shipping, 1720–1815* (Stockholm, 2004).

Munch-Petersen, Thomas, *Defying Napoleon: How Britain Bombarded Copenhagen and Seized the Danish Fleet* (Stroud, 2007).

Murray, John J., *George I, The Baltic and the Whig Split of 1717: A Study in Diplomacy and Propaganda* (London, 1969).

Niven, Alexander C., *Napoleon and Alexander I: A Study in Franco-Russian Relations, 1807-1812* (Lanham, ML, 1979), pp. 59–61.

O'Brien, Patrick K., *Power with Profit: The State and the Economy 1688–1815* (London, 1991).

—— 'The Political Economy of British Taxation, 1660–1815', *Economic History Review* 41/1 (1998), 1–32.

—— 'Merchants and Bankers as Patriots and Speculators? Foreign Commerce and Monetary Policy in Wartime, 1793–1815', in John J. McCusker and Kenneth Morgan, *The Early Modern Atlantic Economy* (Cambridge, 2000), pp. 250–77.

—— 'Fiscal Exceptionalism: Great Britain and its European Rivals from Civil War to Triumph at Trafalgar and Waterloo', in D. Winch and P. K. O'Brien, eds., *The Political Economy of British Historical Experience 1688–1914* (Oxford, 2002), pp. 245–65.

—— and Philip A. Hunt, 'England, 1485–1815', in Richard Bonney, ed., *The Rise of the Fiscal State in Europe c.1200–1815* (Oxford, 1999), pp. 53–100.

O'Gormon, Frank, *The Long Eighteenth Century: British Political and Social History 1688–1832* (London, 1977).

Packard, J. J., 'Sir Robert Seppings and the Timber Problem', *MM* 64/2 (1978), 145–56.

Padfield, Peter, *Maritime Power and the Struggle for Freedom: Naval Campaigns that Shaped the Modern World, 1788–1851* (London, 2003).

—— *Maritime Supremacy and the Opening of the Western Mind: Naval Campaigns that Shaped the Modern World 1788–1851* (London, 1999)

Pool, Bernard, 'Navy Contracts in the Last Years of the Navy Board, 1780–1832', *MM* 50/3 (1964), 161–76.

Porter, B. D., *War and the Rise of the State: The Military Foundations of Modern Politics* (New York, 1974).

Pritchard, James, *Louis XV's Navy: 1748–1762: A Study of Organization and Administration* (Montreal, 1987).

—— *Anatomy of a Naval Disaster: The 1746 French Expedition to North America* (Montreal, 1995).

Rackham, Oliver, *Ancient Woodland: Its History, Vegetation and Uses in England* (London, 1980).

Rodger, N. A. M., 'The Victualling of the British Navy during the Seven Years War', *Bulletin du Centre d'histoire des espaces atlantiques* (1985), 37–54.

—— *The Wooden World* (London, 1986).

—— 'Sea Power and Empire, 1688–1793', in P. J. Marshall, ed., *Oxford History of the British Empire: The Eighteenth Century* (Oxford, 1998), pp. 169–83.

—— 'Weather, Geography and Naval Power in the Age of Sail', *Journal of Strategic Studies* 22/2 (1999), 178–200.

—— *The Command of the Ocean: A Naval History of Britain, 1649–1815* (London, 2004).

—— 'The Idea of Naval Strategy in Britain in the Eighteenth and Nineteenth Centuries', in Geoffrey Till, ed., *The Development of British Naval Thinking: Essays in Memory of Bryan Ranft* (Abingdon, 2006), pp. 19–33.

Rönnbäck, Klas, 'Balancing the Baltic Trade: Colonial Commodities in the Trade on the Baltic, 1773–1856', *Scandinavian Economic History Review* 58/3 (November 2010), 188–202.

Rose, J. H., 'Napoleon and English Commerce', *English Historical Review* 8/32 (October 1893), 704–25.

Ross, John, *Memoirs and Correspondence of Admiral Lord de Saumarez, from Original Papers in the Possession of the Family*, 2 vols. (London, 1838).

Rothenburg, Gunther Erich, *The Art of Warfare in the Age of Napoleon* (Bloomington, IN, 1981).

Ruppenthal, Roland, 'Denmark and the Continental System', *Journal of Modern History* 15 (March 1943), 7–23.

Ryan, Anthony N., 'The Navy at Copenhagen in 1807', *MM* 39 (1953), 201–10.

—— 'The Defence of British Trade in the Baltic, 1807–13', *English Historical Review* 74 (1959), 443–66.

—— 'Trade with the Enemy in the Scandinavian and Baltic Ports during the Napoleonic War: For and Against', *Transactions of the Royal Historical Society*, Fifth Series, 12 (1962), 123–40.

—— 'The Melancholy Fate of the Baltic Ships in 1811', *MM* 50/2 (May 1964), 123–34.

—— *The Saumarez Papers*, Navy Records Society 110 (London, 1968).

—— 'An Ambassador Afloat: Vice-Admiral Saumarez and the Swedish Court, 1808–1812', in J. Black and P. Woodfire, eds., *The British Navy and the Use of Naval Power in the Eighteenth Century* (Leicester, 1988), pp. 237-58.

Salmon, Patrick, and Tony Barrow, eds., *Britain and the Baltic* (Sunderland, 2003).

Scott, H. M., *The Emergence of the Eastern Powers, 1756–1775* (Cambridge, 2001).

Simms, Brendan, '"An Odd Question Enough". Charles James Fox, the Crown and British Policy during the Hanoverian Crisis of 1806', *The Historical Journal* 38/3 (September 1995), 567–96.

Sparrow, Elizabeth, *British Agents in France 1792–1815* (Woodbridge, 1999).

Spencer, Frank, 'Lord Sandwich, Russian Masts, and American Independence', *MM* 44/2 (May 1958), 116–27.

Steer, Michael, 'The Blockade of Brest and the Victualling of the Western Squadron, 1793–1805', *MM* 76 (1990), 307–16.

Stone, Lawrence, ed., *An Imperial State at War: Britain from 1689–1815* (London, 1994).

Syrett, David, *Shipping and the American War, 1775–83: A Study of British Transport Organization* (London, 1970).

—— *The Royal Navy in European Waters during the American Revolutionary War* (London, 1998).

—— *Shipping and Military Power in the Seven Years War: The Sails of Victory* (Exeter, 2008).

Tallis, John, *London Street Views 1838–40* (London, 2002).

Vale, Brian, 'The Conquest of Scurvy in the Royal Navy 1793–1800: A Challenge to Current Orthodoxy', *MM* 94 (2008), 160–75.

Van Creveld, Martin, *Supplying War: Logistics from Wallenstein to Patton* (Cambridge, 1977).

Ville, Simon, 'The Deployment of English Merchant Shipping: Michael and Joseph Henley of Wapping, Ship Owners, 1775–1830', *Journal of Transport History* 5 (1984), 16–33.

—— *English Shipowning during the Industrial Revolution: Michael Henley and Son, London Shipowners, 1770–1830* (Manchester, 1987).

Voelcker, Tim, 'From Post-Captain to Diplomat: The Transformation of Admiral Sir James Saumarez in the Napoleonic Wars' (unpublished Ph.D. thesis, University of Exeter, 2007).

—— *Saumarez vs Napoleon: The Baltic 1807–1812* (Woodbridge, 2008).

Ward, W. R., 'Some Eighteenth Century Civil Servants: The English Revenue Commissioners, 1754–98', *English Historical Review* 70 (1955), 25–54.

Watson, J. Steven, *The Oxford History of England: The Reign of George III, 1760–1815* (Oxford, 1960).

Wells, Roger, *Wretched Faces: Famine in Wartime England, 1793–1801* (Gloucester, 1988).

Wilkinson, Clive, *The British Navy and the State in the Eighteenth Century* (Woodbridge, 2004).

Williams, M. J., 'The Naval Administration of the Fourth Earl of Sandwich 1771–82' (unpublished Ph.D. thesis, University of Oxford, 1962).

INDEX